ON CRICKET

James Lawton by Harold Riley

ON CRICKET

JAMES LAWTON

FOREWORD BY
MIKE ATHERTON
EDITED BY
IVAN PONTING

dewi lewis media

ON CRICKET
by James Lawton

This edition first published in the UK in 2008 by
Dewi Lewis Media Ltd
8, Broomfield Road
Heaton Moor
Stockport SK4 4ND
www.dewilewismedia.com

The chapter texts by James Lawton first appeared in *The Independent*

Press cuttings: Pages 13-15, *Daily Express;* Page 16, *News of the World;*
Page 17, *Mail on Sunday*

> Edited by
Ivan Ponting

> Design and Artwork Production
Dewi Lewis Media Ltd

> Print and binding
Biddles Ltd, Kings Lynn

ISBN: 978-1-905928-04-0

10   9   8   7   6   5   4   3   2   1

CONTENTS

Contents

FOREWORD　　　MIKE ATHERTON

The arrival of that species known as the "chief sports writer", is always an occasion of much rejoicing amongst us more narrow-minded, specialist and humble reporters. Not out of any deference, you understand, but simply for the reason that the Test match at hand must be taking place in one of the nicer parts of the cricketing world – Sydney, say, or Barbados, perhaps. The "chiefs" have the pick of the crop and would never be seen in bleak outposts like Multan or Faisalabad.

As it happens, I believe that newspaper readers are enjoying a golden time with regards to the chief sports writers of what used to be called Fleet Street. Simon Barnes, Martin Samuel, Richard Williams, Paul Hayward, Oliver Holt, Jim Holden and, of course, Jim Lawton are all bright and able; they all have something different to offer and, more often than not, they are a terrific read. That Jim was crowned top of the pops at the *What the Papers Say* awards this year is a fine testament to his enduring qualities.

Some of those qualities stood out when last I worked alongside Jim during the Ashes series of 2006. Often, during the memorable Adelaide Test match, we agreed to meet for dinner with Simon Barnes of *The Times*. Jim was always the last to arrive. That could be taken to mean that he's a slow worker; more realistically it suggested that this is a man who cares deeply about his work even, dare I say it, after all these years. His enthusiasm for sport remains undimmed (he's still out there at events when many of his generation might have settled for the armchair and a windy column) as does his professionalism and craftsmanship.

During dinner, talk would inevitably turn to sports writing and writers. I remember Jim saying how important it was for a sports writer to take a position and how important it was for him to be right more often than wrong. Both lines of thought were probably in response to my quizzing him about the outspoken position he took on England's chances at the last football World Cup. He'd have looked damned foolish, I said, if England had triumphed. It was a lesson learned and an approach that informed my equally damning predictions of England's likely performance at the forthcoming cricket World Cup.

Taking a strong and courageous position is what Jim's most famous brush with cricket, or more accurately a cricketer, was about. And what a monument to try to slay: Viv Richards in his own Antiguan backyard! It is a claim to fame that not many sports writers can boast – that the captain of an international team delayed his entry on to the stage so that he could get something off his chest because of something you've written. But, then, good sports writing is not a popularity contest.

Clichéd, perhaps, but the mind's eye image of a sports writer is of the well-travelled, hard-living, non-conformist showing considerable grace under the tightest of deadlines. A latter-day, poor man's Hemingway, perhaps (although I dare say that Hemingway might have felt compelled to tone down some of Jim's more flowery adjectives). Now, with the internet and satellite television revolution upon us, the days of that romantic vision of the trade might be numbered. Not quite the last of the Mohicans, Jim, I'm sure, gives thanks that the majority of his career pre-dated those twin developments.

Latterly, at *The Independent*, it seems to me that he has enjoyed almost a second coming as a sports writer. Writing for that newspaper carries considerable weight and clout, and Jim's work there is required reading for those who are interested in sport and sports writing. And even though we may occasionally sneer when the "chiefs" ride into town – "after all, what do they really know?" – they always seem to find, drawn from that well of accumulated wisdom from all sports, a greater truth.

It is always a pleasure to see Jim at the cricket these days, just as it is always a pleasure to read his take on things. A pleasure you can now have all over again by browsing this collection.

Mike Atherton of *The Times*
June 2008

INTRODUCTION

As an accredited noncombatant, a sports writer should know his place and his role. It is to observe and not ever to attempt to intrude into the action. However, it is probably natural enough to experience a frisson of pride when reporting that of all the great sportsmen I have seen and known in the glory of their talent there are quite a number with whom I am still able to share, say, a glass of wine and memories of how it was when their extraordinary deeds were the richest coinage of a privileged professional life.

This is especially so in the case of Sir Vivian Richards. Indeed, if you had told me on a sultry morning in Antigua in the spring of 1989 that one day I would be able to claim him for a friend rather than a bitter adversary, I would have been as astounded as Fidel Castro had he ever received a gold-embossed invitation to a gala night at the White House.

Certainly the circumstances were less than promising. He towered above me in the cramped little press box that stood on stilts and seemed too fragile to support the scale of his wrath. It was anger that was as refined as it was spectacular and it was directed entirely towards me. His vice-captain, Desmond Haynes, had led the West Indians out into the field against England. Viv entered the press box with what could only be described as the belligerence of the finest-bred fighting bull of Andalucia, and his first words will probably stay in my bones as long as I live. "Where is James Lawton?"

The reasons for his extreme ire unfold over the page, but at the distance of nearly 20 years my explanation remains pretty much as it no doubt was on that morning when I found myself an heir to the once anonymous man who shot Liberty Valance. I had attempted to interview the great man as he appeared, in his rage at the dying of the light of his great talent, to be close to something of a public nervous breakdown. And then I reported to my newspaper the extraordinary collision in which he told me that I was playing a very dangerous game, that I was on his island, in his empire, and that, frankly, he couldn't guarantee my safety. At the time his friend Sir Ian Botham said that he should have finished the job on the spot, a position from which, I'm relieved to report, he has subsequently withdrawn.

Ironically enough, a week earlier in Barbados I had written of Richards the great warrior magnificently defying the decline of his awesome power as arguably the greatest batsman the world had ever seen. He scored 70 runs of stupendous application, once hitting Devon Malcolm for an epically mis-timed six. But then that mattered little when his agent faxed him the front page of the *Daily Express* and he carried his injured pride, two steps at a time, up into the press box.

In that opportunistic way of newspapers, the *Express* wrote an editorial saying that I deserved a medal for standing up to the man who had for so long browbeaten English cricket. I was happy to settle for something not less but infinitely more – rapprochement with one of the greatest sportsmen who ever lived.

It happened down the years in various places across the world, but most enjoyably over a glass of rum on a cruise around his beloved island. As the sun set the toast was to his enduring glory – and, naturally, my health.

James Lawton
June 2008

Daily Express

SATURDAY APRIL 14 1990 — WEATHER: RAIN — 25p

RICHARDS: Shouted

West Indies skipper
Richards threatens
to 'whack' our man

LAWTON: Offer

CAPTAIN VIV BLOWS HIS TOP

From **JAMES LAWTON** in Antigua

WEST INDIAN skipper Viv Richards threatened me with physical violence in an astonishing outburst yesterday.

He shouted: "You write anything bad about me and I'll come and whack you."

Then he added: "A lot of crap is being written about me and it is time someone was sorted out. I'll start with you.

"I'll do it," he swore at me in the presence of a witness, a fellow-journalist.

The uncharacteristic outburst came when I approached him shortly before he joined the West Indian team meeting at their beach hotel.

I invited him to give his version of an incident in which he was alleged to have given the V-sign to departing England captain Allan Lamb during Thursday's play in the final Test in Antigua.

Richards, 38, uttered a stream of obscenities, then asked: "What gesture..? It's none of your business...It's nobody's business. Why don't you ask players like Daffy (English all-rounder Phil DeFreitas) about his gestures?"

He then issued another physical threat before entering the hotel conference room.

A few minutes later Richards emerged from the meeting and shouted fresh threats to me.

He also repeated: "It's nobody's business what gestures I make. I'm playing cricket out there.

"If I hear you have written anything bad about this, I'll come and find you and I will whack you."

Opportunity

On several occasions I pointed out the television pictures had highlighted his "gesture" and I was merely offering him the opportunity to explain his view of the incident.

He shook his head angrily and said, with several oaths: "I don't have to explain myself to anybody."

Earlier West Indian Cricket Board officials, including chairman Jackie Hendriks and manager Clive Lloyd, had played down on-field

Page 38 Column 1

James Lawton

REPORTS ON THE WEST INDIES CAPTAIN'S LATEST OUTBURST

King Viv's fallen from grace

VIV Richards, the great bold batsman, may still be the king of cricket. But as a man in charge of his emotions, who is aware of what is expected of a Test captain, I'm afraid he has become the king with no clothes.

Over the last week or so his behaviour has touched bewildering depths of stridence and intimidation.

Yesterday's bizarre eruption—reported on Page One—came when I invited him to explain his whirling run across the field and V-sign gesture after England skipper Allan Lamb was dismissed.

Angered

But the V-sign was just one small example of his constant over-reactions to situations on and off the field in the last few days.

Before this there was abundant evidence that the 38-year-old master batsman was building into an irrational fury as he fought to carry the Test series against the surprisingly combative England team.

'He has returned like a man possessed'

Furious at the first Test defeat in Jamaica, angered at reports that he was seriously ill and perhaps suffering from cancer, Richards returned to the action in Barbados like a man possessed.

On the first day of the fourth Test he walked down the wicket to share punching gestures with his batting partner, Carlisle Best.

Then two days later he triggered the great umpire controversy when he sprinted towards official Lloyd Barker, clicking his fingers in the most elaborately furious appeal perhaps ever seen in Test cricket.

Yesterday West Indies manager, Clive Lloyd, sought to defend his volatile captain.

Said Lloyd: "Viv is a winner and like all great competitors he does get very involved. I can't speak of the latest gestures, but I know Viv isn't really a vulgar man—he just gets so involved in the game.

"No great harm is meant by any of this."

But the fact is Richards has been stretching the concepts of "competition" to unlikely levels.

Here on the first day's play he even involved himself in the orchestrating of the band when the West Indian bouncer attack reached a mid-afternoon climax.

"I don't have to answer to anyone," he snarled at me yesterday.

In Antigua and most of these islands this is unquestionably true. He is the king of all he surveys, a miracle-worker on that most important of all places in the Caribbean, the cricket field.

This is perhaps not so true in Trinidad, where his comments about West Indian success flowing from the ascendancy of players of African descent caused deep insult.

But Richards is still—in the words of his manager—"the most important man in the West Indies."

Richards, by his mere presence at the batting crease, can still spread excitement around a cricket ground more quickly than any man alive.

In Barbados his assault on England's chief fast bowling threat, Devon Malcolm, was both brilliant cricket and high theatre.

Malcolm bowled a stream of short-pitched deliveries.

Richards smote him for two sixes and a four—and Malcolm was condemned to a miserable match, so disappointing that some believe he has to prove here in the next day or two that his Test career has not been broken.

Richards in that mood is a cricketing god or, as I wrote at the time, the Black Caesar.

More recently he seems like a man consumed with resentment, indeed a man whose very psychological equilibrium might be called into question.

There is no satisfaction in writing these words.

Viv Richards can still, with the last of his talents, be one of the great glories of cricket.

But for the moment—it has to be said—his glory is covered in a cloud of wrath.

No king, certainly, has sat more uneasily on his throne.

Viv Richards lets rip again

MASTER BLASTER!

Whoever gets in my way now had better watch out

■ FLASHPOINT — Viv Richards reacts

VIV RICHARDS was top again in Antigua y...

Master Blaster Richards exp... sensational row in the Press box of leading the West Indie againstEngland for the second day of the stormy Fifth Test.

Windies manager Clive Lloyd didn't know where his captain was as Desmond Haynes took the field in charge.

Richards was still in his ordinary clothes as he launched his second tirade in two days against sports writer James Lawton.

From DAVID NORRIE

PROTAGONISTS ... Viv Richards (left) confronts sportswriter James Lawton (right) at the final Test

RICHARDS VENDETTA

Furious Viv stays off field to continue row

THE row between Viv Richards and sections of the touring media boiled over into the press box yesterday.

Richards, astonishingly, ignored his responsibility as West Indies captain in order to pursue his argument with a newspaper journalist.

Richards has been deeply offended that a private incident with James Lawton of the Daily Express concerning his gestures to the crowd on Thursday made front page headlines.

And instead of leading his team out ▒tart of the second day's play, an ▒ Richards left captaincy to Des ▒ while he chose to take the

By PETER HAYTER

matter further. He said :'I'm in a very angry mood right now. Anyone who gets in my way should be careful.

'I'm really boiling. No-one knows how much I have been hurt and how badly I feel about the things that are constantly written. I am incredibly angry and I went up to the press box to let certain people know that.'

Richards was still in the middle of his verbal explosion in the press box when Haynes took the players out on the field and subsitute fielder Brian Lara took the skipper's place.

Players looked around in dismay as West Indies bowled the first eight balls of the day while Richards revealed his personal agony. Only team manager

ENGLAND LOST WITHOUT ILLINGWORTH WORK ETHIC

Published: 7 June 2000

It's maybe just as well quite a large section of the populace has been a bit preoccupied with the thought processes of Kevin Keegan. Otherwise the tumbrels might have been rolling down to Trent Bridge. Or, more relevantly, Lord's.

Certainly the hour of revolution cannot be delayed too much longer. Not unless English cricket is happy to sink into the unchallenged status of having the world's worst team, a possibility made far from unthinkable on the last day of a Test match in which the cricketers of Zimbabwe put away the fear of burning farms at home and concentrated on the ash-pile of another travesty of a professional performance by England.

Who or what is to blame for this one? Andrew Caddick bowled about eight miles an hour slower than he did at Lord's, apparently, and conditions were less favourable, but then what can you expect of a "nerd"? That description of Caddick by the former coach David Lloyd might have been dismissed as a random piece of autobiographical cruelty, but for some of us it did speak of a professional culture where a morsel of controversy, and maybe a few extra sales, was worth more than on-going trust between men still involved, one way or another, in the support of an embattled game.

But then perhaps we should cut to the real issue. It is a lack of leadership which at times like this beggars the mind all over again. The chronic problem is that there are no means for leadership to express itself. You cannot have leadership by committee, selection or otherwise. You cannot solve problems when responsibility is shifted as effortlessly as a stolen purse by Neapolitan street urchins.

Ray Illingworth tried to change this a few years ago. He pushed his remit as chairman of the selectors to the limits but mostly met with frustration – and sneers. He was dismissed as a curmudgeon, an egotist and worse. What he was was a man of hard professional values who knew that something was fundamentally wrong with the organisation of the England team. Yesterday he was saying: "I see the 'contracted' England players are being sent back to their counties. That's right. Someone like Caddick needs work, needs to get in a groove – and so does Darren Gough, though he's a more difficult case because of his injury record. One thing is certain. They never invented a system of nets which properly substituted for playing the game.

"When I was chairman I knew what had to be done. I felt I knew the players we had to go with, but you couldn't have selectors tearing around the country and then ignoring their reports. That would have come down to bad manners apart from anything else.

"The point is, one man should be in control, should pick the players, crucially the captain, and then he should stand or fall by his decisions. That's how Bobby Simpson rebuilt Australia. It's pretty basic really. You have to give players a good run, obviously, really give them the chance to inflict the talent you suspect they have. But there are limits. When I was chairman I asked Graeme Hick where he wanted to bat. He said he liked to go in at No 3 because then he could help control the shape of the game. Then when things went a bit wrong, he wanted to bat at No 5. Where does patience end and indulgence start? It's a tricky one. Look at Mark Ramprakash, a talented cricketer, no doubt, but only one hundred in 39 Tests. That's not good enough, is it? Sooner or later you have to decide whether a player, for all his talent, is missing something vital."

Illingworth's tragedy, and maybe the English game's, was that his elevation came too late in his professional life. A gulf of generations had occurred and nowhere more critically than in his relationship with Mike Atherton, a cricketer he admired and defended vigorously through the "dirt-in-the-pocket" affair. Illingworth, for some shrill observers, was too easily presented as yesterday's man. But then it was some yesterday. He won the Ashes in Australia without turning his pacemen into assassins. He led tough with a set of implacably defended principles. The most basic was the requirement of a professional cricketer capped by his country to play out his guts. That, at least, would have held as good at Trent Bridge this week as back on some distant, steaming day at the Gabba.

LARA FULFILS PROPHECY OF A MARXIST MYSTIC

Published: 09 August 2000

According to Brian Lara, or at least his ghost writer, the weight of Caribbean history was heavy on his shoulders when he went to the wicket at Old Trafford and delivered that glorious shellburst of an innings.

"Maybe," he wrote, "this is the time for us to draw some motivation from the history books. There is no doubt in my mind, and several renowned Caribbean thinkers like C L R James have written at length on the subject, that the history of how the West Indies came to be has provided a massive inspiration for our cricketers through the years." Rarely since the eve of Agincourt has a man of action made such a swift transition from patriotic sentiment to thrillingly executed, valiant performance.

Here, where we yearn so desperately for a quickening of the blood when our national teams take to the field, we can only weep for all the times that the likes of Glenn Hoddle and Kevin Keegan gave their arid tactical pep talks when they could have been recalling the Charge of the Light Brigade, or, perhaps more appropriately after the Portugal result, the defence of Rorke's Drift.

However, sometimes there is a piece of sporting action which drives a huge hole into the most practised of cynicism and if Lara's summoning of old battles, and ancient hurts, seemed to be stretching it a bit, it is still true that at the crease he lacked only a warrior's breastplate. Lara, as he has done from time to time before, played with an exquisite passion, a self-possession and a single-mindedness that validated all those fears that his absence, as once seemed so likely, would have heavily impoverished this English summer. Whatever happens in the remaining Tests, we have been touched by the greatest of talent, and this is somehow only accentuated by the fact that on this occasion it was not without flaw.

Indeed, at times it was more than anything a sheer triumph of will. This, you would have to believe, would have most pleased the man whose name Lara invoked before one of his most important innings. C L R James, the author of the classic *Beyond the Boundary*, who asked what anyone knew of cricket who only cricket knew, was the Marxist mystic who saw in the game a beauty which soared beyond its painful association with the colonialists who heaped so much oppression on his people.

He revered above all others Learie Constantine, W G Grace and Frank Worrell, but he refused to be locked into the past. He died before the rise of his fellow Trinidadian Lara, a circumstance which, given his idealistic streak, no doubt deprived him of joy and despair in roughly equal measure. But James was sure there would be other great players, and perhaps one above all in the way of a Grace or a Bradman; what he couldn't know was the amount of distraction and pressure they would find in a world changing beyond his, or any contemporary's, power to grasp.

Wrote James: "Some young romantic will extend the boundaries of cricket with a classic perfection. He will hit against the break so hard the poor bowlers will wish he would go back to hitting with it. He will drive overhead and push through any number of short legs, as W G Grace used to do, and a whole race of bowlers will go underground for 15 years. We will extol his eyesight, his wristwork, and his audacity. He may come from Pudsey or South Sydney, Nawanager or Bridgetown, and he will be doing what W G did, so reshaping the medium that it can give new satisfaction to new people."

For a little while, around six years ago, we thought that the messiah had come from Cantaro, a sprawling little township a few miles along the highway from Port of Spain. But then James's projection of a heroic new cricket empire, centred on one young man's genius, said as much about the innocence of the world the writer inhabited as the one his saviour of the game would inherit.

I flew to Trinidad with Lara, along with what seemed like roughly half of Fleet Street, after he scored his record-breaking 501 against Durham. He was bemused by his entourage, and readily reached a compromise that in return for a few days of freedom on his favourite beaches he would devote the best part of a day to public relations. He led a convoy to his mother's home in Cantaro, a spotless little house dominated by a sewing machine in the parlour. His mother spoke of her pride in her son's achievements – though she pointed out a little testily that it did not stretch to that of Curtly Ambrose's mother, who was known to run into the street ringing a bell whenever her son claimed a wicket – and how as a boy he had smote little green oranges with the bat made by one of his brothers. You had to wonder then how well the new life of Brian Lara would survive in all the glare.

By chance, Viv Richards had been on the same flight from London, which had put down in Antigua, by schedule rather than the King's command. At one point of the journey, Lara slept, cradled by his great hero, who declared: "It makes me so proud that this boy has become a man so quickly. This boy who I kept back a bit when I was captain of the West Indies because I knew he was so special and I wanted him to grow in his own space, his own era. He has set himself the greatest standards any cricketer has achieved. I'm a religious man and when people told me cricket was dying, I said: 'Man, a Moses will come to deliver us.' Well, Moses has come and his name is Brian Lara."

It wasn't quite so and the more you thought about it, the more improbable it seemed; Lara had moved from one world to another, and it was no longer one which permitted the kind of parting of the waves which had been routine work for Grace and Bradman and Sobers. Lara talked bravely of his challenge, though. He said: "I'm telling myself that these are just scores I've put up (the 501 against Durham, the 375 against England in Antigua which broke the watching Sobers' record and prompted Lara to kiss the ground); I have big scores, but I know that in the past players were not great at around the age of 25. When it's all over, I just want everyone to say when they look back at my time that I was consistent towards my cricket."

They have rarely said that since that great eruption in 1994. One flew from Trinidad to Los Angeles for the onset of the American World Cup of football, and within hours of arriving witnessed the murderous drama of O J Simpson, when a great nation appeared to be going collectively mad. C L R James spent quite a bit of time in America, but he would have been as mystified by the Simpson circus trial as the complications that came into the life of a young compatriot who was blessed with a sublime ability to hit a cricket ball. But no doubt he would have been thrilled by what happened at Old Trafford last Sunday afternoon. He would have reached out hungrily for the remnant of a dream. Like the rest of us.

ENGLISH DIGNITY A VICTORY FOR THE GAME

Published: 05 September 2000

If England buried the West Indies at the Oval yesterday, if they ended 31 years of servitude beneath the lash of Roberts and Marshall, Garner and Holding, Ambrose and Walsh, they at least had the grace to extend full military honours.

Indeed, there was an understanding of the nature of their opponents, and the extent of their achievements which made this victory so sweet, that shone brilliantly amid the crassness of so much of modern cricket and modern sport.

The sword was wielded magnificently by, among others, Darren Gough, who ended the faint but still breathing possibility that Brian Lara might just commune with the gods again and deny England a moment in cricket history, but it was not accompanied by even a hint of that shoddy triumphalism which these days so often passes for sporting celebration.

Here in the afternoon sunshine was a game finding the best of itself. A game demeaned so heavily in recent years by gamesmanship and, unthinkably, even corruption, no doubt, but also a game which for five days in Kennington re-learned something magical about its capacity to both charm and fascinate.

Courtney Walsh said he was moved by the guard of honour formed by English players when he and Curtly Ambrose went out to bat in the hopeless cause, and who could not have been similarly touched? This was the antithesis of the worst of the sledging that has grown beyond healthy proportion in recent years. It spoke of dignity and a proper respect. It was good for the kids to see. It was good for everybody to see. It was an exhortation to better days and a reminder of what sport played at the highest level is supposed to represent.

So much for the sentiment. The Oval was also about certain hard realities. It revealed more starkly than ever the disturbing erosion of West Indies cricket and provoked fresh worries that the impact of the American TV sports culture on the Caribbean has detached the game, at least to some degree, from the emotional heart of the region's life.

The big question could not have been more poignantly posed as first Ambrose, then Walsh, walked with their bats on to the sunlit field. Who injects ice into the veins of the West Indies' opponents now that the Kings have taken their last hurrahs? With respect to the improvement of young Nixon McLean, it seemed very much like the end of something that had been so hard and relentless it might have been a harsh and unchangeable fact of nature imposed on a whole generation of battered, demoralised English batsmen.

It meant, surely, that there was a certain sadness in the celebration. Of course England deserved their long-awaited glory – it had been achieved fairly and squarely and with a consistent resolution that had to be deemed the most fanciful ambition before the appointment of the tough pro from abroad, Duncan Fletcher, as coach.

But the concern was not to do with the validity of England's triumph or the intelligent leadership of Nasser Hussain, produced from the depths of a personal crisis in form. It was that the resurrection of England had at least been assisted by a slippage in something we had assumed would always be with us. For decades West Indian cricketers played their game with a ferocity and a genius which briefly marked the football of Hungary, a small nation inflamed by their wonderful ability to strip all opponents down to size. Now, you had to at least wonder, is cricket passing by the Caribbean Kings of Cricket as football did the Magnificent Magyars?

Perhaps the prognosis is a little bleak. The emotion showed by Lara when he ran out the brilliant young Ramnaresh Sarwan to cut short a diadem of a partnership, spoke of someone deeply affected by his new circumstances. The volcanic talent is still in place, we saw that clearly in his breathtaking emergence from a period of playing himself in, and who knows, the experience of the last few months may just re-activate his will. It is a thought, anyway, that might just comfort a West Indian heart.

The heart of Mike Atherton was clearly without need of any more sustenance. If England's sense of achievement permitted any precise measurement it was maybe in the expression on Atherton's face as he looked down on an Oval *en fête*. No one's spirit has been more impaled by the failures of England through the nineties. And no one, as captain or player, has soldiered on quite so doggedly. He once said that if the captaincy of England ultimately imperilled his pleasure in playing the game he would have to give it up, and he did so in the Caribbean dusk in Antigua two and a half years ago. He said he would continue to support the cause of England as long he was selected – and his back held.

Four years earlier, in Trinidad, he had suffered one of Ambrose's most searing firestorms – losing his wicket first ball as his team, set a modest total for victory, crumbled to 46 – just two better than England's worst ever score. Ambrose took 6 for 24 in ten overs. He was immense, unplayable in his fury. But later Atherton said: "This is a terrible day for English cricket, we just lost a series in the third Test match of a five-match series, and we felt we had an excellent chance. What can I say? Only that we will all have to work very hard to turn this situation around."

Atherton was an obdurate character as captain, quirky and perhaps a little arrogant. But when he was around there was a sense of a major player and a man of significance. That aura didn't leave him with the chains of office, and it has never been more apparent than in this summer of renewal for English cricket. Nothing was more appropriate than his central role in the final victory. So yesterday was a supreme experience in his sporting life.

It was also a fine day for cricket and the idea that if you bring enough resolution to a task the chances are you will get there in the end.

COWDREY A TRUE GREAT IN ANY ERA

Published: 06 December 2000

The worst thing anyone in cricket ever said about Colin Cowdrey came more as a sigh of regret than an insult.

"A magnificent bat," of course said an old pro. "Pity he's a bit of an old sheep in sheep's clothing." The remark needs some considerable explanation before setting it against a mountain of runs, many of them so effortlessly compiled it was said that sometimes he had reached his 50 before everyone in the ground realised he was at the crease.

Cowdrey, always a true amateur in a fast-changing world, always diffident to a fault, simply never grasped quite how good he was.

The point seems to be rendered absurd by the briefest examination of Cowdrey's Test career. He was the fourth highest-scoring England batsman of all time; he scored 22 mostly technically flawless centuries in 114 Tests; and his 7,264 runs came at an average of 44.06. Some who bowled against him said that if he had a better eye, that if it picked up the line and the pace of a ball any quicker, it could have served as a one-off radar system.

Former England skipper Ray Illingworth, for whom Cowdrey played in the Ashes-winning team of 1971 in Australia, agrees that for all that dazzling record, in some ways Cowdrey indeed only scraped the surface of his talent. "He was a marvel at the batting crease," said Illingworth, "but sometimes when you bowled against him you used to think: 'Crikey, it's a good job he's not really going for it'.

"You could bowl against Peter May on a good wicket and know for sure that unless you got lucky you were going to get absolutely murdered. They both came from the same kind of background, but if May was clinical he could be savage if he was on top. It wasn't the same with Colin. He could provide a perfect lesson in the art of batsmanship, but you always had a sense that there was a lot more he hadn't shown you."

Certainly Cowdrey and Illingworth looked at the game from opposite poles. Illy was the ultimate pro; Cowdrey the definitive amateur. Cowdrey's first instinct was to walk. Illingworth's wasn't.

"It's true that we came from different worlds," said Illingworth. "Back when we started off, amateurs still had their own dressing room. That situation helped, I think, to make Cowdrey a bit of a loner. He was always amiable, but somehow he was also always a little separate from the rest of the lads. It was just the way he was."

But then no one, not even the hardest-boiled pro, doubted that there was also more than a touch of iron in the mild-mannered, generously contoured figure who, with such prescience, had been provided with the initials MCC.

Yesterday Ian Botham, who inhabited not so much a different pole as a separate planet when he took over as a cornerstone figure of English cricket, said that the great batsman could, like Don Bradman and Garry Sobers, have shuffled naturally into any age of the game.

Jeff Thomson, the Australian paceman who with his partner Dennis Lillee terrified a whole generation of English batsmen, was quick to recall Cowdrey's warrior status. "He was a great cricketer and a great bloke," said Thomson, who with Lillee launched a ferocious attack on Cowdrey when he returned to Test cricket in 1974 at the age of 42. "He was the only one," recalled Thomson, "who really tried to get in behind the ball."

Perhaps nowhere was the contradiction of Cowdrey the consummate cricketer and Cowdrey the man of faltering conviction more pronounced than in Port of Spain in Trinidad in 1968. Then, Cowdrey won his most famous victory as a Test captain when the West Indian skipper Sobers shocked his countrymen by offering England a victory target – and the chance to win the series – that they, and most of the English dressing room, considered suicidally generous.

Sobers invited England to score 215 runs in two-and-three-quarter hours, eminently achievable even on a wicket that was beginning to take a little spin. "Garry took some terrible criticism," recalls Illingworth, "but when you think about it, it wasn't such an outrageous decision. Garry had sussed out Colin pretty well. He knew Cowdrey would sniff out the possibility of an ambush and Sobers had a picture of England batting out the last hour or so with fielders ringed around the bat. In fact, Colin was far from sure about going for it. He consulted about eight people in the dressing room, including Ken Barrington and Tom Graveney. They said: 'We've just got to go for it'. But the captain wasn't sure. In the end he compromised. He said they would give it a go for a couple of wickets."

John Edrich gave England a confident start with a brisk 74 and Cowdrey and Geoff Boycott were at the wicket when victory came with three minutes and eight balls to spare. But there was no question about it being Cowdrey's triumph. In the first innings, after Seymour Nurse and Rohan Kanhai's partnership of 274 had carried the West Indians to 526 for 7 declared, Cowdrey responded with a beautifully etched 148.

A wolf may not have lurked in the whites of Lord Cowdrey of Tonbridge. But one of the greatest of cricketers did. Mere ferocity would not have made his talent any finer.

SRI LANKA SERIES EXTINGUISHES ALL OF GAME'S VALUES

Published: 13 March 2001

Nasser Hussain and his victorious team-mates will probably feel betrayed, but there is an overwhelming instinct to push away the Bollinger. And ask if it is surely not time to end the masquerade of a Test series in Sri Lanka, to tell all participants that they have already done quite enough damage to what we now laughingly refer to as the good name of the game.

The questions that need to be asked are really quite basic. Has any element of this pitiful travesty of a sporting contest shown the capacity for redemption? Has anyone stepped up to display an iota of self-examination? The answers to both questions are bleakly negative. It is an affair which has lost point and conscience and, if any kind of decent value system was at work, the urge to stop it now would surely be irresistible.

But, of course, we lurch on to the denouement in Colombo, to the concluding evidence that the old game can hardly ever have been so ill-served.

Until reading the comments of the England captain, Hussain, one might have thought that bringing an early end to the incompetence of the umpires and the philosophical squalor of the players of both sides might have been a touch extreme. Couldn't someone draw a line, someone of weight like Mike Atherton, saying that enough was enough; that there was something here at stake beyond the destructive momentum of tit for tat? If Atherton could get his finger out of the chest of Kumar Sangakkara, he might be the one to say that maybe everyone had to take a step back.

But then you read that a meeting to soften the naked hostility of the team ends in a slanging match, that invitations to a celebration party for Muttiah Muralitharan's 300th Test wicket are torn up and tossed into a rubbish bin and you know that the potential for grace is batting around zero.

Hussain makes nonsense of the idea of anything like a fresh start when he brushes aside behaviour which would have been disgraceful had it come from a bunch of indulged and malevolent schoolboys as "disappointing", and then says: "If you take that to one side, and have it as a game of cricket played on a good pitch against a competitive side, it gave us great satisfaction and there was no bad taste left in the mouth."

Someone should market the Hussain mouthwash. Plainly it has astonishing powers.

It can apparently wash away the taste of what until this last year or so might have been deemed the ultimate crime of cricketers, which is to say a headless, heartless extinguishing of just about all that made the game worth the candle. Perhaps with so much corruption in the air, with a former senior policeman scurrying across the world collecting data on charges of match-fixing, with two former Test captains already found guilty of the crime, it is tempting to see the loutish reaction to pathetic umpiring as something of a misdemeanour. But it is a view which should be dismissed with some contempt.

The moral texture of the game, heaven knows, has been fraying for long enough. But we have reached pretty near bottom in Sri Lanka. We have seen sport as a long and elaborate squabble. We have seen the end of even a semblance of respect.

Of course the case for umpires receiving much wider technological assistance had long been made before this latest bout of catastrophic officiating, and we certainly shouldn't linger too long over the bleatings of Dickie Bird on behalf of the "authority" of officials. The important thing is not the prestige of the man in the white coat, but the avoidance of decisions which make the game a joke. The good news is that as a result of the Sri Lanka series, these matters are now under "urgent review". But who is reviewing the vertiginous decline in the behaviour of Test cricketers?

Hussain has done much to redeem England as a competitive force, but what is he doing for the future of the game, and ultimately the team, when he so lightly dismisses the effect of their contribution to such a wretched collapse in standards of self-control? He said it was "disappointing" and pushed on with a discussion of the merits of the win.

Does he really think that the nation is warmed by victory in such circumstances? The available, crushing evidence suggests that he does, along with one of the "heroes" of Kandy, Craig White. Said White: "We know what is coming in Colombo, but this was a tremendous test of character."

Indeed, we know what is on the cards in Colombo. It is, all the off-field evidence suggests, rather more of the same. It is anti-cricket, anti-sport. No one wants a bloodless game. No one wants meek submission to an outrageous lack of justice. We want fire with dignity. What is wanted is sportsmen at work; tough, hard pros, by all means, but also men who understand that what they are doing requires something that takes them a little beyond the basic measurements of win and loss. In Sri Lanka no such men have announced themselves. Until they do, Test cricket is relegated to the status of a tawdry joke.

WASIM'S VIGOUR OVERRIDES THE NAGGING DOUBTS

Published: 04 June 2001

In still another superbly achieved crescendo of this extraordinary match, Wasim Akram bowled with an intensity and a warrior swagger which explained every nuance of how it was that he came to Old Trafford for the final time with 409 wickets from 100 Tests behind him. Earlier, he had batted with similar fury and panache, hitting 36 runs off 41 balls as Pakistan made another push to steer a wonderful game of cricket beyond England.

But it was his duel with his former Lancashire team-mate Mike Atherton, as cussed and obdurate as ever, which made the blood race, that most reminded you of all the glory – and sadness – of modern cricket.

Who, after all, represents more comprehensively than the big man from Lahore the splendour and the doubts which now surround the game?

On his 35th birthday, on his penultimate day of competitive cricket on this old ground which he has filled with the pyrotechnics of his talent and his nature for so many years, it was as though he was consciously reaching down to make a statement about both himself and his game. Branded by the Qayyum Report, pronounced unfit to captain his country by a compatriot High Court judge, Wasim has talked of legal appeal, of a reinstatement of his reputation. In the murky waters left by the judicial drowning of South Africa's former captain Hansie Cronje, that is a task which, given the current climate, could involve an interminable journey through smoke and mirrors. In the meantime, Wasim, as he announced so extravagantly in the Old Trafford gloaming, still has a little time to play.

He did it with such relish, with such an edge of commitment, that the very idea that he should carry this burden of suspicion was made to seem bizarre. But if it is Wasim's cross, it is also cricket's. Certainly weekend reports – fuelled by Pakistani batting collapses in the first Test match at Lord's – that cricket's roving ombudsman, Sir Paul Condon, had warned players of fresh match-fixing attempts did nothing to lift the shadows which are now as implicit in cricket as they are at a running track when an athlete breaks the pattern of his form. It is a game – as England's stand-in captain here, Alec Stewart, can attest – which no longer has citizens above suspicion. Indeed there is now a bureaucracy of watchfulness, one which so far has proved only that while it can ask a thousand questions it is quite incapable of providing a single answer.

So cricket and a man like Wasim operate fitfully, as a watery sun has flitted here between the dark clouds. For some time, at least, nothing can be quite taken at face value. Wasim overthrows for the four which brings up the century of Michael Vaughan, a happenstance of the game, no doubt, but then a little later he throws down the wicket of Graham Thorpe with a volley which might have been fired from a high-powered rifle. A matter for speculation? Only in the poisoned waters of modern cricket, perhaps, and if Pakistan were less than resolute at Lord's, what about the implosion of England's first innings after the departure of Thorpe and Vaughan?

Set against such fevered introspection, the match which today carries the potential for more epic performance, and, who knows, an historic victory for England, has indeed been a marvel of extravagant expression. Even much of the sledging has been of a superior, almost wry quality. Pakistan's captain, Waqar Younis, demanded a smile from Atherton after a failed attempt at creasing his skull. Atherton duly obliged.

Such grace made a bad memory of the acrimony that disfigured the recent series in Sri Lanka, though maybe Andrew Caddick and the Pakistani wicketkeeper Rashid Latif, who had their knuckles lightly rapped by the match referee for their squabbling on Saturday, would say that the Old Trafford square hasn't always resembled a meeting room of the chapel sisterhood. What it has been, at least the evidence of one's eyes insist, has been an arena of superbly pitched sporting conflict.

Nothing was better than the last phase of yesterday, when Atherton and his opening partner, Marcus Trescothick, so purposefully raised the unlikely possibility of an English victory after Pakistan had methodically set a target of 370 runs.

Trescothick survived the assault of Waqar with particular force, hooking a six which brought a disbelieving shake of the head from the bowler. Atherton was purely, doggedly Atherton. His duel with Wasim quickly acquired a classic dimension, something to create an echo of his marathon scrap with Allan Donald in Johannesburg a few years ago. Atherton didn't flinch, and it may well prove at the very least a useful sparring session for the coming trial against his nemesis, Australia's master of pace Glenn McGrath. The sustained precision of McGrath is no doubt beyond Wasim now, but here he could have done no more to remind the game of an old fire.

Wasim has said: "It hurts me when people talk about me being involved in things like gambling and match-fixing. My performance speaks for itself. I have always given 100 per cent to every team I have played with."

Old Trafford gave him a thunderous benefit of the doubt when his brilliant little red-blooded cameo of an innings was over yesterday. The old ground, man, woman and child, rose to him. No one could have done more to make a crowd want to believe.

TECHNOLOGY ESSENTIAL TO ELIMINATE ERRORS

Published: 05 June 2001

Test cricket as a superior form of sport, something which makes the one-day version look like a cheap hustle in the park, has rarely been so gloriously validated as it has at Old Trafford these last few days.

Pakistan deserved the victory because it was they who produced most from a richer, deeper seam of quality that over the five days filled up the ground and in the end made it not so much a jaded, architecturally disastrous relic but a vibrant, flag-bedecked battleground. England had their heroes in Thorpe and Vaughan, Trescothick and Atherton, but old fissures resurfaced and we can be sure all of them will have been noted by the watching Australians. Pakistan, for one reason or another, had too many big and committed players to permit the English renaissance to stretch into a fifth straight series win. Inzamam-ul-Haq, Waqar Younis, Wasim Akram and Saqlain Mushtaq, humiliated at home in Karachi, swept aside at Lord's, produced both fire and stunning quality.

Most of all it was an unforgettable victory for cricket in the Test form. It was an assault on the spirit that first day when Inzamam performed so imperiously before the wind-scoured, thinly peopled terraces, the inevitable result, you had to believe, of all those years of one-day circus, of trundling bowlers and hit-and-miss batsmen of the instant gratification game.

In such circumstances, of course, there has to be one set of losers. Unfortunately in this superb Test match there were two: England and the two umpires. The umpires, inevitably when surrounded by such a volume of shot and shell, made critical errors, and not the least of them – as anyone who was watching on television was relentlessly reminded – was the freedom of Saqlain and Akram to bowl a stream of uncalled no-balls. It was perhaps an over-generous compensation for the fact that the hugely admired David Shepherd had earlier made a big and errant contribution to the shape of the last day. The amiable "Shep" insisted to Saqlain that when Yousuf Youhana swooped for a catch at short leg the ball had come off the pad and not the glove of Marcus Trescothick. Television told us instantly that Shepherd was wrong. The ball had come off the glove, as the Pakistanis insisted.

Television men who bombard us with a battery of computerised graphics which take all mystery and speculation away from the flight of the ball were also quick to tell us that such decisions level out. It is no longer good enough. Ray Julian, the retiring county umpire who is regularly awarded the official of the year trophy by the Professional Cricketers' Association, would dispute the argument, as would the watching institution Dickie Bird. Julian says: "I do worry that the day will come when the umpires do nothing more than call no-balls and wides. These days you're more busy when you are the third umpire. The technology has been great for some of the armchair fans, but I'm not convinced that the genuine cricket lover wants it too much."

Why on earth not? W G Grace was only partly right when he barked at the umpire who had given him out that the ground was filled with spectators who had come to see a great batsman and not a great umpire. The highest aspiration of an umpire is, of course, impossible. It is to get every decision right. As a servant of the game, it might be reasonable to assume his acceptance that time – and technology – has cut a great swathe through his God-like standing. Bird, as we all know, has become vastly wealthy on the sales of his memoirs, and heaven knows he enriched the game with his quirky, endearing personality.

But then perhaps never so clearly before have we seen the limitations of the human eye and judgement of the sporting action as we did at Old Trafford yesterday. With no doubt impeccable honesty, David Shepherd made a decision which might just have denied a winning team its just deserts. Such margins of error cannot be preserved. Test cricket, a spectacle so magnificently revived, deserves better. It is operating in a new world, and it must get to the pace of it.

WAUGH TRIUMPHS IN PSYCHOLOGICAL WAR

Published: 16 June 2001

No gang of gunfighters ever took over a town as hard-eyed and authoritatively as Steve Waugh's marauders did Old Trafford this week.

If the field was an eerily floodlit Main Street, littered with English dead, the committee room where Waugh later coolly analysed the effect of the night's work had the demeanour of an extremely solemn wake. The usually indefatigable Dickie Bird, whose optimistic view of the world often suggests it could only be threatened by an elephant gun, caught the mood well enough when he held up his arms and asked: "For heavens sake, what are we going to do?" So much for the prospect of the most evenly fought Ashes series in a decade and a half. One cricket-orientated bookmaker guessed at the starting odds: Australia 2-1 on, England 5-1 against.

After the latest thrashing of England in the triangular NatWest Series, the odds looked like a gift lacking only wrapping paper and pretty ribbons. For some time Australia have been recognised as the world's best cricket team. But no analysis of the achievements of the reigning world champions, no browsing of the form lines that will be carried into the opening Test at Edgbaston next month, can begin to match the impact of their physical presence.

Waugh embodies their style and their aura. The Australian captain is about as equivocal as Ned Kelly on the rampage, but shows no disposition to crow. He simply celebrates the latest compelling evidence of his team's rage to win.

He refused to trash England's feeble batsmanship and he was almost uncomprehending when someone asked if, in view of their searing progress towards next Saturday's Lord's final of the one-day series, he might have a little difficulty in motivating his players. "If anyone needs motivating at this level, in this team," said Waugh finally, "I reckon they'd be better off playing marbles." Waugh's vowels were as hard as granite, and so was the look in his eyes.

Most striking of all was Waugh's lack of coyness about the psychological impact of Thursday night's performance, especially that of the beautifully balanced assault of the pacemen Jason Gillespie and Glenn McGrath. Of course, he said, you could not forget that England were without such pillars as Mike Atherton, Graham Thorpe and the captain, Nasser Hussain. Nor could you so easily relate performance in one-day and Test cricket. But maybe there was some long-term value to be drawn from the extent of Australian mastery.

"I think you could say," said Waugh, "we won a few battles tonight. The way Gillespie bowled Vaughan was maybe particularly significant."

Gillespie, with the pace phenomenon Brett Lee breathing fire at his shoulder, bowled Vaughan, such a resolute force in the second Test against Pakistan, first ball. It was not so much a dismissal as an evisceration. It was Vaughan's second successive duck. He walked back to the pavilion in a daze. Two weeks ago he was being hailed as the cornerstone of English batting. Now he looked more of a candidate for therapy. He was scarcely alone.

Gillespie and McGrath bowled with a passion and a proficiency which seemed to dwarf the demands of the occasion, but then it was really a question of grasping what the issue really was. It was not the prize of another one-day tournament bauble. It was the destruction of another team's psyche, and long before the result had been settled in the surreal night that objective had been dramatically achieved. At one point Waugh had three slips, two gullies and a short leg. If he had had a howitzer, no doubt he would have employed that too.

Seeing such raw aggression in a one-day game was rather like encountering Billy the Kid at a tea-dance. But it wasn't the violent intent of the Aussies that lingered so strongly in the mind. It was the sense of supremely accomplished professional sportsmen who have come to realise that ruling the world has to be a performance all of a piece. It is something you cannot put down and then pick up when the time is deemed right.

What Australia did so tellingly on Thursday night was decide that it was time to turn the screws on England, to back them into a corner filled with doubts. If Vaughan was the most recognisable victim, identifying others was not so difficult. Andrew Caddick and Darren Gough bowled well, but their relative success came in stark isolation. They were supported by a demoralised Dominic Cork. After McGrath and Gillespie, Waugh sent in an exuberant Shane Warne. The accumulation of Australian accomplishment was at this point stunning.

So, too, was the quality of their leadership. Waugh turned the game with his beautifully crafted 64. When the heart-stirring Ricky Ponting left after a few sumptuous shots, Matthew Hayden and Adam Gilchrist having also gone cheaply, Waugh carried his burden with an easy, feathery touch. At 36, he knows that his innings is drawing to a close, but not before he has defined his legacy. It is one which stretches beyond the boundary markers, and at Old

Trafford this week we saw it in all its unbridled force. When he arrived here a few weeks ago, he explained his philosophy with an emphasis that was indeed reflected at every point in the latest defeat of England.

"'No regrets' and 'never satisfied' are the two things I've always believed and tried to instil into the team," he said. "I believe in giving players responsibility; if they need motivating, they just don't belong in the team. I'm not interested in a side that relies on a couple of stars to win. What happens if they fail or they are injured? My job is to get all 11 to take responsibility and get everyone playing to the best of their ability and playing together. I want guys who I could rely on in the trenches, who know what's expected and don't need shouting at."

In another dressing room such words might carry more than a hint of the platitude, but on Waugh's lips, at this time, they are more an explanation than so much wishful thinking. Waugh raised some cynical eyebrows when he had his men stop off in Gallipoli and consider for a little while the sacrifices of another Australian generation. He certainly broke the hard-drinking, hard-swearing mould when he involved himself in a Calcutta charity for young, abandoned girls afflicted with leprosy, a decision he reached while reading an appeal notice pushed under his hotel door. At the time he was agonising over a defeat which he considered highly avoidable. "I guess such things give you a little perspective," he says.

But then they scarcely lessen the requirement to win. After admonishing his brother, Mark, and Warne for their "foolishness" in passing on information to an Indian bookmaker, he swore that he could just not imagine an Australian throwing a game. He said he would cut the face of such a pariah out of any team photograph.

You could see him doing it, coldly, deliberately. Such an edge pervaded everything Australia did in the damp Manchester night. Waugh's men played with an unshakeable rhythm. Their talent invaded every corner of the old ground. But their will was the thing. It simply crushed the life out of England. Dickie Bird wondered, despairingly, about what could be done. In the silence that followed you could have heard a dingo bark in Rochdale.

DO NOT FEAR THE PAKISTAN PHENOMENON

Published: 21 June 2001

Most of Tuesday is spent at Trent Bridge compiling an identikit of the Pakistan cricket fan who, in the course of a couple of weeks, has become sport's Public Enemy No 1. It is arduous but not distasteful work, and the resulting deafness is almost certainly temporary. That is another reason for deciding not to put his picture on the most wanted list.

Let's call him Raz. He is in his early twenties, plainly works out in the gym and is a bit of a peacock, with plenty of personal jewellery. When his budget stretches he likes to wear, along with green-and-yellow Pakistan robes and face – and hair – paint, Emporio Armani T-shirts and designer jeans. He is essentially amiable and well mannered, proffering a ready apology when you jump at the whistle he blows so shrilly a few inches from your ear and the banner he has carelessly jabbed in your ribs.

Unlike the culturally homogeneous football thug, his head does not appear to harbour a hundred demons and he seems infinitely more likely to nod and smile than smash you over the head with a beer, or in his case, a Coke bottle. There is a link or two, however. His attention span, even when one of his heroes, that prince of pacemen Waqar Younis, is in full pomp, is generally just a few seconds. This is the key to Raz. He is, despite all of his exaggerated enthusiasm, not really a cricket fan.

This is not to say that what happens on the field is irrelevant to him. He adores the explosion of communal passion which comes when a rival wicket falls or when somebody like Yousuf Youhana drills the ball past cover point, and when a war drum is produced at the height of Waqar's brilliant performance in the victory over Australia, he eagerly joins a hand-clapping procession around the boundary fence. But then, just as quickly, he is on his mobile phone, demanding to know: "Where the bloody hell are you, Waz? I feel like an ice-cream."

One of his number gives you the low-down on Raz: "He means no harm. He is just a boy wanting to have a little fun – and maybe smoke a little weed."

Spending a little time with Raz and his companions is certainly a surreal experience. Even when a firecracker goes over the fence and lands perilously close to Australia's young fast bowling star Brett Lee, thus provoking the team captain, Steve Waugh, into his promise to march the team off the field if he feels their safety is endangered, you could still distil all the latent menace in the ground and have scarcely enough to create an unruly bonfire party.

"Hey, man," Raz tells a steward who for several hours has worn an expression of such immutable good nature you wonder if he hasn't invested a little in some face-painting of his own, "we've paid good money for our tickets, ten, 15 quid, what's wrong with a few high spirits?" It is an argument which plays better, at least on the surface, with the steward than it does later with the aggrieved Waugh.

The Australia captain, who a few years ago was threatened with decapitation when a flying bottle narrowly missed him when he rushed from the Kensington Oval in Barbados during a rather more serious riot, is susceptible to none of Raz's arguments. Such people, he says, are "idiots difficult to control". But they must be hammered by the kind of fines which have been legislated back home in Australia. "That works," Waugh says, "and it has to be installed here. We've had problems for some time. They must be resolved. Certainly as captain I don't have any problem at all with insisting on absolute safety for my players. If a similar situation comes up at Lord's in the final on Saturday I won't have any problem doing the same as I did here tonight."

Mercifully, most of cricket, and the new Sports Minister, Richard Caborn, who has poked his head above the parapet briefly here after the revelation that in a head-to-head sporting knowledge contest with Raz there is no guarantee he would win, has recoiled at the idea of the England and Wales Cricket Board chairman, Lord MacLaurin, that "snarling dogs" might be the answer. That, and possibly the importation of a few squads of lathi-wielding policemen from the subcontinent, is a bold idea roughly 50 years out of date. Most of the game accepts, it seems, that it has to do better.

Nottinghamshire County Cricket Club's chief executive, Dave Collier, is, not without some justification, pleased with the handling of the security crisis. He agrees that but for the rogue firecracker, and the walk-off it promoted, it would have been a near-optimum performance. The pitch invasion at the end was relatively low-key and, as Collier points out, signs in English and Urdu had indicated that spectators were free to go on to the field once it had been vacated by the players. At the potentially troublesome Ratcliffe Road end, where security is most concentrated, the invasion only happens when police and stewards put down the plastic fencing and clear a way.

An obvious dilemma for cricket is that if the majority of Raz's companions have come to Trent Bridge without the foggiest idea of the great Inzamam-ul-Haq's batting average, they have filled the ground and created an extraordinary level of excitement. It is bogus excitement, according to one immaculately suited enthusiast who has travelled from Pakistan for the cricket. "It has little to do with the game," he snaps. "These people have not grown up with the game. It is not really part of their culture, like it is back home. It is something they have picked for the excitement of it – and maybe some identity."

It is a forcefully expressed identity, heaven knows. Those who can't run to Raz's Armani gear, wear shirts and robes which bear such legends as "100 per cent Paki" and "Proud to be Pakistani" and many carry life-size cardboard cut-outs of heroes like Waqar and Inzi and Wasim Akram. One of Raz's pals marches interminably along the boundary carrying a huge sign which proclaims: "Saqlain is the Spin Doctor, Warne is the Patient." Another shouts: "Waqar will win this Waugh."

During the game there has been a steady stream of the worshipful to a room assigned for "prayers". There are many families whose youngsters are daubed in green and yellow. In all the tumult there have been just two unpleasant incidents witnessed at the Ratcliffe end, excluding the firecracker apparently aimed at Lee. In the press at the boundary fence at the end, a stout Pakistani fan is exchanging insults with a police officer and one of the policeman's colleagues picks up a missile which has landed, weightily, in the outfield. But there is no arrest.

What English cricket plainly has in the Pakistani community is a passing and vexatious phenomenon which needs careful but unofficious handling. From his perspective, Waugh, a superb cricketer and a deeply impressive leader of men, naturally sees Raz as an idiot. He is a nuisance, an unwelcome distraction from the serious business of playing world-class cricket. But he also helps to fill a ground with life and, most of the time, considerable humanity. His patronage, in the long run, is probably worth encouraging – and shaping.

A brilliant start would be to get him to watch the cricket.

WHEN WE WERE KINGS

Published: 29 June 2001

Long before the comedy series *Men Behaving Badly* was made, Ian Botham was indulging in a spate of laddishness that would have challenged the imagination of any TV scriptwriter.

He was, ultimately, The Lad. His nickname, Beefy, was perfect. By his own admission, his devoted and long-suffering wife, Kath, had the responsibility of two "children" – him and his equally strapping, boisterous son, Liam, who would grow up to be a rugby star.

But there was greatness, too, in the big lummox from Lincolnshire. It came in an expansion of the spirit that would later express itself in painful walks that took him the length of the country, and across the Alps in the footsteps of Hannibal, in the cause of fighting leukaemia. Botham was a Test cricketer confounded by the limitations of his role. He had an appetite for the epic that appeared to be insatiable. Until, that is, a few days in Yorkshire 20 years ago when Botham dominated a cricket match that was like no other in the history of the game. It was a Test match against the oldest enemy, Australia – an enemy he waylaid with the sheer force of his nature.

The anniversary of Headingley 1981 – which falls next month, when, coincidentally, Australia's cricketers are once again in England playing for the Ashes – is about many things, and probably about none more than the sheer implausibility of what happened under the glowering sky of Leeds. It is about the fact that, thanks to Botham, England overturned odds of 500-1 posted in the Ladbrokes tent at the ground on the third day of the five-day match, at a point when it seemed they had been utterly outplayed; a statement of probabilities so comic in its dismissal of England that two of the Australian players, Dennis Lillee and Rodney Marsh, took modest flutters against the chance that their world would shift on its axis and they would fail to secure a victory.

But Headingley is also about the gripping of a nation, an outbreak of communal joy that was most notably generated on a sports field in this country when England won the World Cup by beating Germany at Wembley in 1966. But the drama of that was contained; it was all of a piece. The plotline of Headingley stretched over two days. Its unfolding, in those days before Teletext and e-mail and mobile phones and rolling news, crept up on the nation, and then enveloped it. Radios were tuned, and girls in the typing-pool exchanged snippets of information. Car horns began to toot. On the last day, callers who got through to the switchboard at Headingley and were told the score, and the fast-burgeoning prospect of English victory, got up from their desks, announcing: "We're coming down."

The bleak old ground – half-empty when the match was drifting towards the seemingly foregone conclusion of an Australian victory – began to swell again with spectators. English tourists on the holiday belt of southern Europe sought out bars with televisions receiving the BBC. Mrs Thatcher's theory about there being no such thing as society was being hammered as fiercely as the Australian bowling. It was alive and well and toasting Botham in raki and Pernod.

Headingley had other heroes apart from Botham. Most notably, there was Bob Willis, long, slim pace bowler of Warwickshire, as quiet and introspective as Botham was extravagant. Willis was 32, and his Test career was thought to be over; but here, magically, it was revived, as the Australians crashed to undreamt-of defeat. Graham Dilley, a young, blond, tearaway fast bowler from Kent, who confessed to a murderous hangover on the morning of the Sunday rest day – Botham had staged a party in his Lincolnshire village on the Saturday night – made a vital contribution to the action. Chris Old, a native son of Yorkshire, struck some telling blows, and another Yorkshireman, Geoff Boycott, put in a classic display of defensive batsmanship.

But at the heart of the phenomenon there was always Botham, spilling over with life and combat and, if not optimism, a total resolution to make some kind of mark, some act of defiance that would be registered against the scale of Australia's anticipated victory.

Botham is no longer a lad; indeed, there is a hint of urbanity as he moves around the cricket grounds of England as a leading television commentator, well suited to and secure in his role as both an icon of the game and an intimate of the great names of world cricket. In recent broadcasts, his partnership with his old West Indian rival Michael Holding has been particularly effective.

He has created a certain distance from those hell-raising days when his face, often blurred by excessive celebration, was as likely to be seen on the front page of *The Sun* as the sports pages. But he knows he will never be separated from Headingley, from the unprecedented and unsurpassable violence of his innings of 149 not out, a piece of sporting endeavour whose fame will surely never die.

His first reaction is to laugh when you mention Headingley, a little as though it were an old joke. But his eyes do not laugh. "No one," he says, "will ever let me forget Headingley, especially the Australians. Whenever I see Allan Border (one of the Australian victims, who would later become one of Test cricket's most distinguished captains), he tells me that it was just a slog. I tell him he's dead right. That's exactly what it was, a slog. But it was some slog, and there will never be a day when I'm not happy that I was able to make it.

"It was good for me and my family – and I like to think it was good for the country. If people want to remember me by that – though I like to think I did a few other things – obviously I'm not going to complain. In life you get into scrapes and you have bonuses. As bonuses go, Headingley wasn't bad."

There is some reason to believe that it was more than that. At the time, some saw Botham as the mere shell of a cricketer; and, as he went into the Headingley match, there was no doubt whatsoever that, for all his celebrity, he was far from guaranteed his place in the team.

In the previous Test, at Lord's, he had been dismissed for a pair of ducks – a disaster that deprived him of the England captaincy.

Vitally, though, for both his career and the history of English cricket, Botham made the team, under the revived captaincy of the brilliant tactician and psychologist Mike Brearley. Admirers hoped that he would stir, and maybe revivify, the embers of his huge natural talent. Instead, he made a great convulsion.

For the first three and a half days, the match ground toward an Australian victory – for a 2-0 series lead. It seemed so inevitable, that their emotional skipper, Kim Hughes, said that he could "taste the Ashes". Botham, who came in to bat in England's second innings at 2.15pm on Monday 20 July, felt he could really do no more than play out the string as vigorously as possible. If he was lucky, he would crash a few shots over the boundary.

He had, at least, had the consolation of reinstating the impact of his bowling, claiming six wickets in the Australians' first innings; good figures but hardly decisive, in that Australia, buoyed up by a dour century from the opener John Dyson, had compiled 401-9 declared – a total that Hughes extravagantly claimed was "worth a thousand" on the treacherous, uneven Headingley wicket.

That statement seemed less of an exaggeration, though, when England, despite a flailing half-century by Botham, dwindled far short of the 202 required to avoid the follow-on and were required to bat again, 235 behind. England were 133-6 when Dilley, wearing a borrowed blue helmet, walked out at 3.04pm that Monday afternoon to join Botham, who had at that point scored 22 relatively slow runs. It was a hopeless position.

Dilley – a bowler rather than a batsman – recalls that when he was greeted by the great hero at the wicket, their brief discussion did not include any mention of the vaguest possibility of victory. Dilley later told Rob Steen and Alistair McLellan, authors of the new book *500-1: the Miracle of Headingley '81* (BBC Books): "Beefy asked me if I had already checked out of the hotel yet. I hadn't, because I thought it would be the wrong thing to do. He just looked at me and said: 'I have, but I forgot to pay the extras bill. I hope I don't have to go back'."

Dilley asked Botham what he should do. "Play shots," he said. "The game's gone. Just enjoy it." Dilley did. He carved away at the Australian attack, which featured the great Lillee, an extremely quick Geoff Lawson, and Terry Alderman, who briefly but brilliantly exploited British bowling conditions. As Botham beamed his pleasure, Dilley roared past his 50 and was beginning to think in terms of a century, before the fantasy was abruptly ended when Alderman clean bowled him.

Botham, meanwhile, his hotel extras suddenly a small and no doubt negotiable problem, marched on. His century came off 87 balls in two hours and 35 minutes. His second 50 took just 30 balls and 40 minutes. The 64 runs he had contributed to the century after the tea interval included 14 fours, a six and just two singles. It was the mayhem of a blacksmith. One of Australia's shell-shocked fieldsmen, Graeme Yallop, said: "I had never seen anything like it, and I never expect to again. It was an educated slog. Some of the shots were unbelievable."

Botham recalls: "Dilley and I played some idiotic shots, but they succeeded. He laughed and so did I. We felt like men in a play, following a script someone else had written. Everything had a dreamy feeling about it, particularly as it happened so quickly."

When the England innings was over, with Botham undefeated and unbowed, there was still no reason to believe that the hero had provided more than a surreal passage in an otherwise formal Australian victory. England had scored 356 – 149 from Botham and 56 from Dilley. The Australians had to score only 130 to win, and they progressed comfortably enough until the shrewd Brearley gave the ageing Willis one last chance to re-state his credentials as a front-rank Test bowler. Brearley set Willis, who had been toiling uphill from the Rugby Stand end, for an assault from the Kirkstall Lane end.

Suddenly, Willis had the wind billowing in his white shirt, and his deliveries had zip and craft. The Australians, drained by earlier dramas, became convinced that the fates now entertained the idea of only one result, and promptly collapsed. Willis took eight wickets and his unforgettable place beside Ian Botham.

The next day's headlines spoke of "the new Jerusalem" and hailed a "golden age" for England. A summer that had until then been dominated by the news of Irish hunger strikers and riots in Brixton and in Birmingham, but most of all by the wedding plans of Prince Charles and Lady Diana Spencer, suddenly had another, and more lasting, talking point.

Now, as another all-conquering Australian team threatens to dominate another English summer – the first Ashes Test starts at Edgbaston, Birmingham, next week – we can only hope that another Ian Botham will rally to the English banner. Sadly, though, that is a frail fancy. Botham and the game with which he will always be associated are, you have to suspect, beyond reproduction.

Four months after victory at Leeds, Botham and Dilley had some hard evidence that this might indeed be so. They came together once again as England struggled at 50-6, chasing an Indian total of 241, in Bombay.

Dilley recalls: "Both (Botham) asked me: 'Do you remember Headingley?' I said: 'Yeah, of course I do.' 'Come on,' he said, 'let's do it again.' Two balls later, my off stump was cartwheeling out of the ground."

"Headings", Botham was saying the other day, "could only come once in anyone's lifetime. Pity, really."

THOSE WHO THINK AUSTRALIAN, PLAY AUSTRALIAN

Published: 31 July 2001

After Mark Ramprakash made what seemed like his breakthrough century for England in the West Indies a few years ago, he stood in the shower for some time, letting the water wash over him in a strange and deeply personal purging of all the years of frustration. Later, you had to be impressed with the ferocity of his ambition to build on that achievement which had been so elusive.

Strange, then, that Ramprakash should in the last few days have been such a forceful voice against the appointment of Rodney Marsh as head of the new England cricket academy. If ever there was a cricketer open to the value of new ideas, a new approach, one that might just unlock the imprisoned talent of a player as gifted but tortured as himself, you would have thought Ramps would have been the man. But, no, Ramprakash thought the job should have gone to an Englishman; Gatting or Gooch, he didn't seem to mind, but an Englishman for sure.

It makes such a forlorn statement about so much of the thinking in English cricket. It seems to say that somehow we will muddle through, and that to give the reins to such a rumbustious Aussie as Marsh is a kind of defeat. It is, in fact, quite the opposite. It is to signal terminal weariness of defeat. It is to admit that we are roundly stumped.

Some may say that we are in danger of giving too much reverence to the Australian way of doing things in sport, that the last of our resolve is draining away and that we cannot re-make it with a job-lot of Australian coaches. Of course we cannot. But we can be wise enough to recognise long-standing deficiencies. We can say that in so many areas of sport we have simply lost our way, and that if the Australians have found a superior way, only pig-headed chauvinism prevents us from taking some advantage.

Certainly that was the approach of the British swimming authorities when they appointed their Australian performance director, Bill Sweetenham. At the Olympics last year our swimmers were almost as futile as the Irish team at Montreal in 1976, which provoked Peter Byrne of the *Irish Times* to write: "Good news from the Olympic pool – none of our swimmers drowned." Last week, Britain picked up seven medals at the World Championships in Japan, and Sweetenham's reaction was significant. "We're not on track yet," he declared. "We still need a massive change of attitude from the governing bodies."

That is the style English cricket has bought into with the signing of the formidable, reformed hell-raiser Marsh. Like the swimming guru, he is not a man to make a banquet out of a cheese biscuit. He demands performance levels below which there is simply no future. Shane Warne learned that on his conversion from beach bummery. Marsh's other proven knack is in recognising high talent and then drawing it out.

It is here that the differences between Australia and England in an Ashes series which has already become a travesty of competitive values has been so painful. While an Australian Test player of the competence of Justin Langer is obliged to give way to Damien Martyn, a batsman in the hottest of form, England's chairman of selectors, David Graveney, talks about the value of the untried Nottinghamshire batsman Usman Afzaal as a "street fighter". One of the keys to street fighting is knowing what you are up against. In the first Test at Edgbaston, Afzaal, rather embarrassingly, squared up to Warne and promptly had his wickets mown down. As Steve Waugh deploys his troops, Graveney plays a game of chance and speculation.

Wherever you look in the English game you are confronted by waste. It was poignant over the weekend to hear the view of some experts that Phil Tufnell had bowled himself back into contention, only to listen to Graveney explaining why Robert Croft, a splendid pro but with Test figures of bewildering feebleness, had again got the nod. It is wearisome to hear so often that Tufnell remains the best slow bowler in the country, but that his nature betrayed any chance of a sustained impact. Inevitably, you think of the bolshie young beach boy Warne. What might Marsh have made of Tufnell?

Or John Crawley? The Lancashire captain, who has a Test average of 37-plus and is still two months short of his 30th birthday, scored nearly 200 runs in the Roses match over the weekend. He batted with depth and composure, and it was easy to remember him performing with much promise at the Sydney Cricket Ground against well-stacked odds a few years ago. What went wrong? The usual things, not least the absence of someone to shake into him an awareness of what he had to win – and lose. Someone like Rodney Marsh.

TUDOR'S TALENT IS FINALLY PUT TO USE

Published: 03 August 2001

Something wondrous and intoxicating happened at Trent Bridge just after 5pm. An extremely tall young cricketer jumped almost his own height in pure exhilaration. He was an Englishman, and Englishmen are not expected to do such things while engaged in Test matches against Australia. They are supposed to slope about the field, occasionally sighing hugely, and generally catching the mood of a holding cell on Death Row.

With a couple of honourable exceptions, England did this almost to perfection right up until the moment the 23-year-old Alex Tudor sent back the Australian opener Matthew Hayden, a man about whom his captain, Steve Waugh, had warned ominously on the eve of this third Test: "He looks as if he's full of big runs."

Tudor ensured that he wasn't with a beautifully pitched delivery which sent Hayden back for a mere 33, an initiative which seemed to send an electric charge coursing through the entire England team, most notably his senior paceman team-mate Darren Gough. "The Dazzler" was lit up sufficiently to promptly remove Ricky Ponting, Waugh's other nomination for a stack of runs, and Michael Slater, the Aussie opener who set the tone for the series by clubbing Gough for four fours in his first over of the first Test at Edgbaston.

For a little while at least, Australia's relentless mastery of this English summer was no longer a grinding reality and Tudor threw himself into the chore of breaking the crisis management of captain Waugh and his brother, Mark.

Most astonishing of all, Tudor seemed to be enjoying himself, though this wasn't quite the Himalayan challenge it might have appeared. Three years ago young Tudor whipped out both of them in a stunning arrival in Test cricket at Perth. But then what? An undefeated 99 against New Zealand – Tudor can also bat – and a stream of failed fitness tests.

Indeed, his presence in this Test match came only after a drama straight from the script of *Casualty*. No one, least of all Tudor it seemed, was sure about his ability to last out a five-day Test, a fact somewhat anticipated by various members of the coaching staff at his county, Surrey, earlier in the week, when no one was prepared to make a definitive assessment. So he came into the action yesterday about as gingerly as a novice nun ordering a lemonade in a dockside bar. He was, though, as anyone could see quickly enough, well worth the trouble.

He was also a walking case file for the head of the new English Cricket Board academy, the Australian Rod Marsh. Marsh, a huge influence on the career of the enduringly brilliant Glenn McGrath – 5 for 49 yesterday as England crumbled to 185 once the resistance of Marcus Trescothick and Alec Stewart had burned out – is the kind of guru-troubleshooter who surely would have confronted the Tudor dilemma long before it became another doleful symbol of waste in English cricket.

Tudor is plainly a thoroughbred and his physical make-up, rather like that of Liverpool's prodigious young England footballer Steven Gerrard, may in any circumstances have worked against his instant development as a major Test figure. But at what point is a young professional sportsman of great talent confronted with the imperatives of his career? How deeply has English cricket investigated the reasons why Tudor's career has been so retarded? The knock on him has been that his talent has always run ahead of his resolve. Why? It is a matter of confidence, of nurturing. Would the crack of a whip prove more beneficial? Does he need a course of physical strengthening? Has he a clear idea of such options and potential rewards?

They were questions which cried out for some answers as Alex Tudor leaped skywards at that point at which the Ashes series finally took on some kind of genuine competitive life in the late afternoon yesterday. When Gough became a fighting cock again and Andrew Caddick, catching the uplift, forced Steve Waugh into a fending shot which Mike Atherton, tormented from the second ball of the day when he was erroneously given out, gathered in with absolute conviction.

Tudor struck again when Atherton's safe hands this time accounted for the other Waugh, and when Caddick had Damien Martyn caught by Stewart, England were on blazing levels of self-belief which could only have been a fantasy 24 hours earlier. As Atherton, who inherited the captaincy again rather as a beleaguered infantryman might draw the short straw, said before the game: "What looks like the smallest thing at the time, can change a Test match and a whole series."

When Alex Tudor passed a fitness test yesterday morning no one could have reasonably said it had quite that power foretold by the captain. But it did. It was the mightiest of sporting catalysts. It did, after all, persuade all of England, however briefly, that Steve Waugh's Australians could indeed be beaten.

CRICKET AT MERCY OF
A RICH MISTRESS

Published: 04 August 2001

Losing one potential match-winner without legal reason can be an unavoidable accident; losing two, as this briefly beautifully poised Third Test did yesterday when Marcus Trescothick fell to a no-ball delivered by Shane Warne, is undoubtedly careless.

But the bigger problem is that such mishaps, which tend to be received with an official shrug even when they are as potentially calamitous to one of the sides as Thursday's second-ball dismissal of the England captain Michael Atherton, are accumulating so quickly now that the entire game is in danger of being submerged in ridicule.

Such a possibility was only intensified last night when Atherton, batting with magnificent defiance, was eventually ruled by umpire Srinivas Venkataraghavan to have snicked a ball from Warne into the gloves of wicketkeeper Adam Gilchrist. The omnipotent television snickometer said Venkat had got it wrong. It was not as though the spinmaster was in need of any help, as he proved with the ravaging impact of claiming four English wickets for 11 runs in 36 balls.

Cricket's plight is that of a man of modest means consumed by the wiles of a rich and demanding mistress. Television funds the game but is not exactly sparing in its demands. Before both Atherton, twice, and Trescothick had returned to the pavilion the truth, revealed in relentless technological detail, was out for the most casual television viewer. Both men should have been going nowhere but further into the heart of the battle.

Sixteen years ago, when the Ashes-swaying dismissal of the Australian batsman Wayne Phillips created a firestorm of controversy which still has embers today, the issue was relatively straightforward. Did the ball touch the ground on its way from Phillips' bat to David Gower's hands via the body of Allan Lamb? David Constant, who was, ironically enough, the third umpire yesterday required to rule on Trescothick's fate, decided that it did not. Nor did it yesterday, Constant could see clearly, when the batsman's shot bounced up off the shin of square leg Matthew Hayden and was gathered up by the alert Gilchrist.

In cricket's old world there would not have been a ghost of a problem beyond the ill luck of Trescothick, who had again taken the fight to the Australians in an opening stand of 53 with his captain and fellow victim Atherton. The trouble was that television, at first tentatively, then conclusively, showed that the ball which dismissed Trescothick was a no-ball. Constant, though, would have had no power to intervene had the television evidence been as blindingly emphatic as it was on several occasions when Pakistan swept England to a confidence-eroding defeat in the second Test at Old Trafford earlier this summer.

What it means is that cricket is locked into a problem that will never be solved piecemeal. It cannot divorce itself from the demands of television and its *Hawk-Eye* technology, its insatiable desire for fresh gimmickry, so the drive must be for compatibility, for some logical resolution of the lunacy of providing the world and its dog with an instant explanation of the game's most intricate and vital moments while the umpires in the middle – and in the stands – are obliged to operate with at least half a blindfold.

Against the drama that continued to unfold here between the showers yesterday the debate may seem arid, but it is vital to the irrigation of any game, and the stakes are of course multiplied dramatically here as England fight to win back their pride against their oldest and most formidable enemy. Atherton is, as so often down the years, the cornerstone of England's batting and for him to go second ball when he was, as the first glance of the re-run told us, plainly not out, was a shocking scar on the balance of the game. His fate last night only compounded the injury he expressed with mute insolence on another forlorn return to the pavilion.

Would England have made a fight on that first day, done better than the paltry 185, if Atherton had had the chance to dig in? Before the age of television's all-seeing eye, the issue would not have come into such clear and disruptive focus. Now, it is a recrimination waiting to happen.

In the taut gloaming last night Atherton faced one of the great challenges of his career after Mark Butcher quickly followed Trescothick to the pavilion. For television it was just about perfection as Atherton's nemesis Glenn McGrath, England's destroyer on the first day, wheeled in, technically flawless and sending off, inevitably, waves of menace, and at the other end Mark Ramprakash, so desperate to re-invent himself as an authentic Test batsman, squared up to a Brett Lee made cocky by the superb dismissal of Butcher.

Here was sporting conflict of a very high level indeed, and wonderful for the camera. Once McGrath came close to cutting Ramprakash in two, and the lingering close-ups of the batsman seemed almost an intrusion into a private ordeal.

Fine for television, and fine for cricket, up to a point which needs to be resolved. If you take the best of a game you are surely obliged to help tidy up the rest, and at the moment the game and its mistress surely need to sit down and discuss the rest of their lives. The burden is on the game, and that it is a heavy one was proved all over again when Lee was called for a no-ball the moment he appeared to have lured Ramprakash into a snick into the gloves of Gilchrist. Almost instantly, TV showed that umpire John Hampshire had been right. Soon enough, however, Ramprakash had destroyed himself with a rash charge down the wicket at Warne, a disaster compounded within minutes by a similar rush of blood to Alec Stewart's head.

Back in the pavilion, though, Ramprakash and Stewart had one comfort which Atherton and Trescothick might have envied. They had at least died legally, and by their own hands.

NEVER MIND THE ASHES, WHERE IS ENGLAND'S FIRE?

Published: 06 August 2001

That Andrew Caddick gave up the Ashes with a no-ball, after a brief but mesmerisingly beautiful exhibition of flawless batting from Damien Martyn and Mark Waugh, was a parable not from the cricket bible *Wisden* but the real thing. Judgement had come down written on large stones, all of which had been used to batter the head of English cricket.

England, as currently constituted, had no place in the temple of the game represented by the historic rivalry and were duly thrown out.

Their challenge to a superbly gifted, and spirited, Australian team was always a fiction and the concern now must not be the scale of defeat, which has been as profound as anyone could have predicted even as Steve Waugh's tourists were dismantling England's confidence limb by limb in a catastrophically hapless one-day campaign, but the meaning of it.

What it means is that we no longer have an authentic rivalry with our oldest cricket enemy. We have an open-ended source of rebuke, a recurring statement of inferiority – it stretches over seven series of English futility now – that will never be silenced by the ramshackled, crisis-hopping parody of a system which is geared not for the radical transformation required but the preservation of individual roles within the game.

In a sporting culture more attuned to the realities of world-class competition David Graveney, the chairman of selectors, would have already been asked to submit his resignation. Not because Graveney is personally responsible for the decline of England's position in competition with Australia – that is a much longer story – but simply because his selection policy this summer has been little more than a series of speculative lunges crowned by the farcical confusion which accompanied the choosing of the latest team on the eve of the potentially decisive third Test.

Usman Afzaal was brought in as "street-fighter" for the Tests because the Australians in the one-day games had "worked out" Owais Shah, a player previously nominated for his talent and his competitive character – some talent, some character if it was judged too fragile to survive fleeting individual failure in a huge collective disaster. What was the depth of that original assessment, and the calculation that Afzaal would deal with the pressures of the first Test of an Ashes series? At Edgbaston he resembled a plucky, hyperactive rabbit caught in the headlights. Dominic Cork and Craig White were asked to deliver again that which had plainly gone missing.

After Saturday's debacle, during which White was not asked to bowl, an Australian journalist could only shake his head when he was told by England coach Duncan Fletcher that Robert Croft had been chosen on the strength of his consistent record against Australia rather than the match-winning break-out of Phil Tufnell in what now seems like another lifetime, and his potential batting contribution. Here, Croft scored three runs and bowled three overs, and though he claimed the currently devalued wicket of Ricky Ponting his mere presence at this point was still another strain on logic.

But these are the details of what amounts to a collapse of a way of sporting life. Judged on a wider sweep, the problem of English cricket remains pretty much that of football until the Football Association had the nerve to admit it needed outside help and appointed the sophisticated, consummate professional Sven-Goran Eriksson. Cricket, to be fair, has edged in that direction with the appointment of the Australian Rod Marsh as head of the new academy, the need for which was dramatically confirmed here when, at last, some of Alex Tudor's vast potential was drawn out. English football, like English cricket now, was always too ready to draw a veil over the direst of failure. Almost unbelievably, when you consider the workaday reactions of the rest of the sporting world, Glenn Hoddle and Kevin Keegan were allowed to continue as national coaches even after the most grotesque of failures in, respectively, the World Cup and the European Championship.

Such official reactions would have drawn only outright mirth in places like Italy – and, most pertinently for English cricket, in Australia.

Within an hour of this latest crushing defeat, the talk in the Nottingham pavilion was of the need for new faces. But which faces, and what kind of preparation for their arrival in the big-time? What psychology will be applied? What real grooming has gone on?

Michael Atherton, who long after it must have seemed like an old if still vivid nightmare, was asked to carry the burden of the captaincy again, was almost coy on Saturday afternoon when asked if this latest and most devastating of Ashes defeats had made another, and perhaps conclusive statement, about the failure of English cricket to properly compete with Australia, had indeed illuminated not a decline in playing standards but the collapse of an entire sporting culture. "It's a deep question," he said guardedly, "and I have expressed myself on this before."

When he did, suggesting that county cricket was the relic of another age, he was, of course, pursued by a backwoods lynch mob, who called him an ingrate snarling at the hand which had fed him. He was as right then as he would be today, despite the cosmetic approach of turning the county competition into two divisions. Is it just a coincidence that the main title contenders, Yorkshire and Somerset, are both hugely buoyed by Australians, Yorkshire by the prodigious batting of Darren Lehmann and Somerset by the captaincy of Jamie Cox?

There is another truth, though, and it was plainly evident at Nottingham this last weekend. The difference between England and Australia this summer has not been just about competitive standards in the respective domestic cricket, and an imbalance of talent, but the sheer spirit and intensity of the winners.

England's coach Fletcher forlornly confirmed the point when asked to name the most striking attribute of his team's conquerors. Australia, he said, were a fine team, possibly the greatest he had ever seen, full of talent and experience and success, but the thing that struck him most was their enthusiasm, their togetherness, their absolute refusal to become jaded by the glut of their triumphs. He noted the mood of their arrival at the grounds, early and in a buzz of anticipation for the coming action. It was, he suggested, the light tread of pure winners.

Also of a team who like and respect each other. Shane Warne had earlier given an impressive example of this with his insistence that, while he had taken the wickets, Jason Gillespie had done quite as much to undermine England with the relentless hostility and control of his bowling. Vice-captain Adam Gilchrist, who with the injury shadow over the magisterial Waugh may have to take control of the drive for a historic whitewash on English soil, expanded the sense of unity when he announced his relief that there was no Ashes presentation while his captain was having scans in the local hospital. "That would have been terrible, he has been such a leader, such a captain," said Gilchrist. "As it is, I expect to give him a hug and a beer when he comes back – and before he bores us to tears by putting on a John Williamson CD."

Williamson is an Australian folk singer, a Willie Nelson with attitude, much loved by Waugh. Williamson is inflicted on the Australian players relentlessly, and for some of them the anthem *True Blue* is the torment of their lives. But, of course, they endure it. If the music is good enough for the captain, it is surely good enough for the troops. A former England coach, David Lloyd, once thought the refrain of *Jerusalem* would work the same magic in his dressing room. Maybe one day it will. In another life – and a new, and workable system of English cricket.

THE DOG OF WAR WHO
SAVAGED ENGLAND WIMPS

Published: 17 August 2001

W G Grace would surely have approved Ricky Ponting's emphatic refusal to walk when Mark Ramprakash claimed a brilliant grass-level catch, an appeal which inevitably failed when it was taken to the arbitration of the big television eye in the sky.

The great doctor's unwavering conviction was that cricket fans came to watch him bat rather than umpires umpire and no amount of technological development, including the landing of a man on the moon, would have been likely to disrupt his belief. Here at Headingley yesterday you could be equally certain that only the most doggedly committed England supporter would have traded the wicket of Ponting, before he had scored, for what flowed from his early crisis.

What it was was batsmanship of the cricketing gods. Three times he pulled for sixes so easily he might have been a librarian picking a book from a shelf, dusting it down, and returning it to its place in one swift and practised movement. The victims, Andrew Caddick, Alan Mullally, and Alex Tudor, wore the glazed expressions of men pushed to the limits of their resolve. England's bowlers, and notably the moody Caddick, had had some reason to believe that they might just retrieve something of pride from the embers of this Ashes series when Michael Slater and Matthew Hayden were both back in the pavilion with a mere 42 runs on the board. Caddick claimed both wickets and there was a growing conviction in his stride. But Ponting's survival represented still another trapdoor through which England were about to plunge.

Ponting, the 26-year-old Tasmanian nicknamed "Punter" for his passion for greyhound racing, sprang it with a touch and authority which up until now had been strangely missing from the high summer of Australian achievement.

While the Waugh brothers, Adam Gilchrist and the re-emerging Damien Martyn variously applied the broadsword and the rapier, Ponting – whose three sixes were augmented by 11 fours in his eighth Test century – remained strangely mute. The Tasmanian devil was behaving mostly like a pussycat. But it couldn't go on, the captain, Steve Waugh, insisted before the third Test at Nottingham. "Ricky," said Waugh, "has missed out so far in the Tests but I expect it to end here. I think he is about to make big runs."

The captain spoke prematurely, but the beauty of Ponting's knock yesterday made it the most trivial of miscalculations. Class of this purity can be suppressed only for so long.

Ponting was, in fact, going over old, memorable ground. His first century came here four years ago, and in even less promising circumstances. Australia were sagging at 50 for 4 when he set about the England attack in 1997. Yesterday it wasn't so much an assault as an undermining, an easy exertion of the most complete dominance of bat over ball. England's resolve to rescue pride was again turned to rubble. Sometimes the inclination is to weep for England, so thoroughly have they been mastered these last few months. But then the tendency of life – and cricket – is to reward those who do most to harness their talent and rarely has there been such a mis-match as the one that has proceeded through this summer.

Yesterday, right from the start, after a three-and-a-quarter-hour rain delay, there was little relief from England's ordeal. Mullally allowed a Slater shot from the first delivery of the match to roll through his fingers for a four. Darren Gough's expression might have been the death mask of a martyr.

Mullally then proceeded to drop Slater. It was the worst of *déjà vu*, but when Ponting, with the obdurate support of Mark Waugh, took hold of the game, such mishaps became the merest trifles. For England the depressing truth was confirmed on a tide of beautiful batsmanship. If two, three, even four Australian batsmen fail, one is bound to come off and utterly reshape the game in their side's favour. It has happened in each Test; the Waughs, Gilchrist, Martyn, briefly but crucially in Nottingham, have all stood in the face of English hope and turned it promptly to dust.

Ponting owns 27 greyhounds and maybe it was a visit to a local track earlier this week which unlocked the force of his exuberant talent. He had a fine time among the animals he so admires for their sleek and beautifully delivered power and certainly there was much of the greyhound about his own performance. He was a dog of war with fantastic springs in his heels. Of all his work yesterday, nothing was better than the drive through extra cover which brought up his 50. It was all balance and fluency and the ball didn't so much race to the boundary as glide.

For England there is no doubt the painful reflection that maybe Ramprakash did make a superb catch, and that, if it had stood, the bowlers would not have been put so elegantly to the sword and there would indeed have been a stirring of resistance to the idea that Australia can now beat England at any time and in any circumstances. Realists among them though will surely assign such thoughts to the realm of fancy. The fact is that if Ponting had gone, his place would have been taken by Martyn, and then a new boy called Simon Katich, who would have been followed by Gilchrist, who has generally proved himself a cyclone dressed in white.

Ponting just happened to come good yesterday. For the Australians, it was simply a rather breathtaking law of averages.

FIGHTER WHO SAVED THE ENGLISH SUMMER

Published: 21 August 2001

If we are very lucky it could just be that Mark Butcher produced more than a gem of an innings at Headingley yesterday, something to be remembered beyond an outstanding example of the English genius for winning great cricket battles when the war is already over.

The most satisfying aspect of Butcher's masterful performance in a victory which, however we choose to shape it, could never be more in itself than a waft of consolation, is that it grew out of the will of a proven fighter, a man who has this summer provided the most obdurate opposition to the Australian march to the Ashes. That he has not been an integral part of the English set-up since he showed genuine steel under the fire of Curtly Ambrose and Courtney Walsh in the West Indies three and a half years ago is maybe just another story of missed opportunity in the matter of first recruiting and then absorbing cricketers who have the depth of character and talent that goes into making a proper Test career.

Butcher, given even the vagaries of selection policy and an almost total failure to understand the Australian stock-in-trade of recognising the real players and then investing a little time and a little faith, should not lack for a feeling of permanence now. Nor should the man who made such a resolute alliance with him yesterday, the returning captain, Nasser Hussain. The latter may have fragile fingers but there is nothing wrong with his spine.

It is something the Australians recognised at the dawn of the contest, with Mark Waugh, who once shared the Essex dressing room with him, saying before the first Test: "I'm not writing off England for various reasons, including the fact that Nasser Hussain hates to lose as much as anyone I've ever known in the game."

As interesting, even thrilling, as anything that happened yesterday was the Australian reaction to Butcher's magnificent innings. When his century came, the Aussies were unabashed in their admiration, with the big battler Matthew Hayden leading the posse to shake his hand. It was almost as if they were nearly as pleased as the crowd to find themselves in an authentic test of wills.

One certainty is that the fifth Test at the Oval, while still an academic matter in the strictest sense, will carry more than a hint of intrigue. Will Steve Waugh win his extraordinary battle for fitness? Will Adam Gilchrist, the stand-in captain who has been such a scourge of England all summer, recover his composure after granting England what some will describe as the most generous declaration since Sir Garfield Sobers was charged with handing victory to the late Colin Cowdrey?

Will such as Glenn McGrath, Jason Gillespie, Brett Lee and Shane Warne, all victims of Butcher's supreme day in the sun, come steaming in pursuit of revenge? As Steve Waugh said at the weekend: "There's been a lot of talk about us getting a whitewash, making history, but these are by-products of playing the best cricket you can. What you want most of all is to be involved in great Test cricket and as a team I think we have done a lot to put the interest back in this top level of the game. I hated all the bribery stuff, how the name of the game was being dragged down, and the best antidote to that is providing the highest form of cricket you can. We have to give people reason to have faith in the game again."

That was surely the achievement at Headingley, though not in the way Waugh would have ordained. What happened, clearly enough, was that Gilchrist decided he was dealing with a broken force, a side incapable of defying his attack for more than three sessions at the end of a Test match. It was a declaration that spoke of both great confidence and a desire to make a cricket spectacle. An American sceptic once said that football was as inherently thrilling as kissing your sister. The modern Australian cricketer has put dwindling, deadlocked Test matches in pretty much the same category.

Yesterday Mark Butcher gave him massive help. At Lord's, in the second Test match, Butcher put down two catches and was punished with body language from the victim, Darren Gough, which would not have gone amiss on a pantomime stage. Yesterday Butcher was utterly beyond reproach. He gave us great theatre and the beautiful drama of a man realising all his strength and all his talent.

Excessive celebration of victory in a dead rubber is naturally avoided by all serious sporting nations, and English cricket will do well to eschew such seriously flawed triumphalism. But nor should it stint its admiration for Butcher, the man who fought his way to a perfect expression of talent which, for one reason or another, less than two months ago seemed destined to fade into obscurity. His chance came when Graham Thorpe was injured – and let

Butcher into the Surrey one-day side. From that unpromising ground, the hero of Headingley saved his career. And, who knows, the battered spirit of English cricket.

ATHERTON WALKS AWAY WITH HIS BAT HELD HIGH

Published: 29 August 2001

Michael Atherton always thought the wheel would turn. He said it in places like Port of Spain and Sydney, Harare and Auckland and by a fishing stream in his Lancashire roots, but of course it never did and now that he is gone officially from the field there is a hole in the fabric of our sporting life as big as the Oval gasholder.

It is not so easy to say quite what was once filled by this vacuum. Character, oodles of it, of course. A deep love of battle, no doubt. But also something much more complex and elusive. A quirky way of thinking, perhaps, an obduracy, an ambition to defy any odds which you could taste in any corner of a ground and which made his defeats, of which there was never a great shortage, go to both his heart and your own. He didn't walk with the tide or the times. He didn't issue soundbites.

Atherton may have been a loner, and as such not ideally suited to the demands of captaining a modern sports team, but there was something in him which touched anyone who has ever been in an unpromising fight, and he never lost the affection of his team-mates who on Monday night gathered for a farewell dinner. Once, around the nadir of his reign as England captain, he slapped a rubbish bin with his bat on his way back to the pavilion. A man sparing of words had spoken a thousand.

Atherton, almost from the start, was tetchy, stubborn, dismissive. Not only did he refuse to suffer fools, from time to time he flayed them, not least the Pakistani journalist who claimed that his love life had perished the moment he was dismissed as a buffoon by this haughty sahib of English cricket. After surviving the crisis which threatened to overwhelm him at the dawn of his captaincy, the ball-tampering incident at Lord's, Atherton scored a brilliant 99 at Headingley before telling a press conference ready to re-sanctify him that maybe his innings had quietened "the gutter press".

The following morning, after glancing at the papers, he wore a rueful smile but his eyes still reminded you of steel.

If for him the captaincy of England was a ball and chain, it could also be a glory. If you worked at it long and hard enough, if you ignored the pain in your back and the one elsewhere which came when you picked up your morning newspaper and noted that the comedian Jimmy Tarbuck was among those calling for your head. But, of course, the wheel never turned, not a full revolution, and it was maybe Atherton's awareness this summer that it would not happen for him, at least not against the most oppressive of his opponents, Australia, that finally pushed him into retirement.

Some may say that the dust of failure accompanied Atherton's last strides from the arena of Test cricket, that he failed as a captain and that even his fabled fighting character, and the fourth highest total of runs amassed by an English batsman, 7,728, yielded a batting average of just 38 runs, two short of the generally agreed threshold of front-rank Test performers. But sometimes it is impossible, even offensive, to measure a man's footprints with a list of numbers which tell you nothing of either his meaning or his circumstances.

Sometimes those circumstances weighed him down almost to the point of despair. Certainly his game and a fine technique suffered, never more so than in the early winter of 1997 in New Zealand after a nightmarish tour of Zimbabwe, when England had been pilloried not only for sub-standard performance but what was perceived as a terrible arrogance. Over lunch in Auckland, Atherton speculated on what odds the London bookmakers would put against his scoring a century in the coming Test. He said that he felt good for one, he had been going back to basics, giving himself some time in the nets to straighten out a stance that had been undermined by the barrage from men like Curtly Ambrose, Courtney Walsh, Glenn McGrath and Allan Donald.

For a few days he had put aside the cares of captaincy and worked with the bat. The odds were 14 to 1. He batted beautifully at Eden Park for 86 before falling to a freak catch. It seemed, for an anguished moment, that whatever he did he would be thwarted. But then he batted superbly for a century in Christchurch, one of 19 in his Test career.

The essence of Atherton was in his battles against Donald in Johannesburg and Trent Bridge, when the great South African grimaced and yelled and Atherton stood his guard so resolutely he might have been forming a square at Waterloo.

His moment of final decision as England captain came in the dusk in Antigua in 1998, when his highest hopes of winning in the Caribbean, after a stirring victory in Trinidad, had been swept away by a renascent Ambrose and Walsh. He had offered his resignation at the end of the previous summer, only to be talked out of it by Lord's and, perhaps more persuasively, his father.

Atherton walks away with his bat held high

Before the Antigua Test, which England needed to win to tie the series, he walked on the beach and thought more carefully than ever before about his future.

He had said several times that when the weight of office threatened his basic pleasure in playing the game he would quit, and this was perhaps the time. "When this Test is over a lot of questions are going to be asked by others, and by me," he said, "and I will not skip over them. This is my 52nd Test and of course things haven't gone as well as I'd hoped. When I came into the job there was a model out there for me. It was the Australian captain Allan Border. He took over in very difficult circumstances but slowly the wheel turned for him.

"Well, it hasn't really turned for me and I have to accept that. I like to think we are a better team now, more committed, and I think it's true we've had some pretty rough luck out here. But all that has to be pushed aside in five days time, when I know I have to make a decision. You don't make long-term decisions when you're in the trenches fighting for your life."

Tributes to Atherton varied in their generosity yesterday. Among the kinder, unsurprisingly enough, was Ian Botham, who spoke of Atherton's competitive character and courage under the burden of constant back pain. Steve Waugh talked of his commitment, his talent, his willingness to fight, which, when you put it all together, "gave you everything you would want in a Test cricketer." Bob Willis said there was a certain naïvety to Atherton's captaincy, but allowed that his bowling resources had always been slender.

In a wry moment of reflection, Atherton once said that he had finally worked out the trick of being a great captain. It was to have a great side. For him it was never an option. So it meant he had to fight down all the years. Just because the wheel refused to turn, it didn't mean that he had to bend.

A TEST ENGLISH CRICKET MUST NOT BACK AWAY FROM

Published: 24 October 2001

Travelling to the subcontinent as a cricketer has never been a stroll on the shady side of the street. Indeed, eight years ago half the England team were brought to their knees, if not their haunches, by a serving of curried prawns.

Ian Botham famously declared that he wouldn't wish the overall experience on his mother-in-law, and the distinguished correspondent Dickie Rutnagur once concluded a running match report from the subcontinent with the cheery declaration: "That will have to do for now, old boy, the pavilion appears to be on fire."

All that was, of course, before the world became a potential tinder box, but if there are plainly genuine concerns to be expressed about the security of the England team in India, it is still to be fervently hoped that the majority of the selected squad agree to take part in the forthcoming tour.

Yesterday those concerns were discussed in a meeting between the players, Indian security advisers and the Foreign Office. Assurances were duly given, and the players now have a few days in which to make their decisions on whether or not to travel. The question surely carries us beyond the boundaries of sport and its relevance to the life of the real world.

That was a legitimate debating point when the authorities in America and Europe cancelled some of the sporting programme in the first shock waves of the terrorist atrocities.

Then, arguments that it was wrong to bring a pause to the routines of life and that to postpone big football matches out of respect for the still uncounted dead was somehow to surrender to terrorism seemed irrational if not puerile.

But that was six weeks ago. England's cricketers are now being asked to make the adjustment of priorities and nerve, that were in reality required of the whole world long before the smoke cleared in Lower Manhattan.

The quandary can be spelled out easily enough. Do the English cricketers do what half the hugely rewarded Chelsea football team did last week when they refused to travel to a match in Tel Aviv? Do they say that the world has simply become too dangerous a place for a professional to operate anywhere but in his own backyard? Surely not.

The invitation here is not to foolhardiness. It is to make a calculated decision about the risks involved in a tightly monitored, highly secured cricket tour. If the concerns of young family men prove too great, and they pull out, they can be respected for their personal priorities. But it cannot be said that they have done a whole lot for the value of sport as any kind of metaphor for the great challenges in life.

They will have opted for the illusion of life without danger, for displaying their skills only in arenas hermetically sealed against the tempestuous forces of life that, terrorist outrages or not, will always be more visible in a place such as India than in the county ground at Worcester.

For those players still locked in private debate there might be some perspective to be found in the experiences of the great England batsman Bill Edrich, who, in the course of one day and night, flew a bomber mission, scored a century for Norfolk and, it was strongly rumoured, successfully wooed a local barmaid.

His friend and rival, Australia's Keith Miller, always said that playing a match, at Lord's or any similarly hostile tribal setting, always seemed a relatively mild test of the intestines once he had crash-landed his Mosquito during the Second World War.

Today, the more anxious cricketers will be told that the world has changed. But really, by so much?

INDIA SECURE VICTORY FOR THE SPIRIT OF TEST CRICKET

Published: 27 August 2002

It's true the Indian cricketers are a noisy lot. They appeal too often and too stridently, and this no doubt has much to do with the nature of their captain, Sourav Ganguly. In any field of driven sportsmen, he can never be far from the front rank of the starting grid.

But then it is surely right that sometimes we should say to hell with tranquillity and the comfort zones of well-heeled success. If there is a touch of madness in Ganguly, if his ear-splitting cries of triumph can have the effect of breaking glass, his passion for winning has surely invigorated this English summer.

Which patriotic Englishman could, if he still had within him the embers of a love of sport as it should be played, as it should carry us away from the day-to-day realities of our lives, suppress a surge of pleasure when the Indians levelled the series at Headingley yesterday? If he exists, he is surely to be avoided when the talk turns to what is most important about the games we play.

Nasser Hussain, who rose for a while so majestically above the trough of mediocrity which gripped his team after such crushing work at Lord's in the opening battle, will probably not appreciate the point, but the Indians won not only for their own fervent following but for anyone with an enduring taste for the wonderful ebb and flow of Test cricket.

Its inherent superiority over all other forms of the game was once again comprehensively restated as Anil Kumble winkled out the last English resistance and his team-mates fielded and caught with a passion and a dexterity that must have satisfied even the remorseless Ganguly.

There were a score of cameos to linger in the mind as the Indians pushed to create the stirring prospect of a decisive final Test at the Oval, and none was more moving than the sight of the Prince of Indian cricket, Sachin Tendulkar, who had so recently played such a god-like innings, holding the boyish head of 17-year-old Parthiv Patel in his hands and explaining why it was so important that he pushed aside the pain which had reduced him to a hobble and made it through to the moment of triumph in India's biggest ever win on foreign soil.

Patel is the little drummer boy of the Indian team. He may have had a bit of a nightmare behind the sticks, but he never lacked for psychological nourishment from his senior team-mates. It is the kind of thing you don't see a lot of in modern sport. You see a lot of posing and self-interest and professional contentment, but the Indians have brought another spirit.

Their unabashed joy at their moment of victory at Lord's when they won the final of the one-day tournament was unforgettable – so, too, were the zig-zagging celebrations when Ashley Giles was run out and a famous victory was suddenly within touching distance yesterday. Hussain kept a stiff upper lip in defeat, and spoke well and graciously. It was worth noting that his innings, during which at times he looked a very major cricketer indeed, had been such a big help in defining the extent to which the Indians craved the win which they had begun to fashion from the opening shots five days earlier.

Rahul Dravid's award of man of the match for his magnificently conceived century was apparently a unanimous decision, which told us, among other things, that there had been at least one point in the commentary box when Michael Atherton and Dermot Reeve found it possible to agree.

Their dispute over whether or not Hussain had attempted to play a shot while surviving an lbw appeal was wonderfully knockabout and encouraged the wild belief that it might eventually be accompanied by thuds and groans. Such a possibility was reduced yesterday when the combative Reeve was joined by the urbane Mark Nicholas, whose rhetorical style, while not mealy mouthed, is less inclined to produce instant mayhem.

This, however, is not a complaint. *Channel Four's* coverage, guided with his usual brilliance by Richie Benaud, remains a model for intelligent and entertaining sports broadcasting. Indeed, it might only be enhanced by the recruitment of Geoff Boycott, who will no doubt sail beyond, as he does all other inconveniences, the troublesome effect of the nodules discovered at the back of his throat. Boycott v Atherton, in anything like their more trenchant moods, would be a treat for any cricket fan.

In the meantime, however, Ganguly v Hussain will do very nicely. Above all, they are fighters who care deeply about what they are doing, and they have lifted the summer quite gloriously.

BOTHAM THE MAN TO REVIVE ENGLAND'S FIGHTING QUALITIES

Published: 12 November 2002

Enough, already of the self-flagellation, Nasser. Of course, inserting the Aussies at the Gabba did rather expel you from the Erwin Rommel school of tactical thinkers, but then he did have the Afrika Corps. What you have is the demoralised residue of decades of ego-ridden waste and muddled thinking.

So you looked around at team-mates who have the culture of defeat in their bones, you saw they were gulping before Glenn McGrath or Shane Warne had sent down their first deliveries, and you flinched. It wasn't your finest moment but nor was it a catch-all for the reasons why England are as far away as ever from inflicting a flea bite on the tough professional hide of Australia.

Several Ashes series ago, before Steve Waugh took his team on to an entirely superior level of operation, but some time after the beating of England had become synonymous in the Australian mind with kicking a crippled dog, the tough No 3 batsman David Boon was asked to explain the ease with which he so regularly finished on the winning side. "Well, a little consistency helps, mate. Playing England over the years is like running into a cast of thousands," said Boon. "It seems to us that the Poms just don't know how to go about building a winning team. The key is knowing who your best players are and then putting a little trust in them."

It also helps if you don't saddle those best players with the obligation to perform in something as arcane and ultimately irrelevant as the County Championship. However many times it is remodelled, it is a home mostly for time-serving trundlers for whom simulating the demands of an average Australian state match is not so much a tough call as a journey into fantasy.

England's coach Duncan Fletcher has, understandably enough, been quick to contradict his captain's assertion that one reason he asked one of the most formidable batting line-ups in the history of the game to go to the crease was that his own troops were pop-eyed with apprehension.

On this one, we have to take our choice, but looking at the traditionally flawless Gabba strip would not at the best of times have encouraged too much English optimism. With men like Matthew Hayden, Damien Martin and Adam

Gilchrist in such god-like nick, it was surely the equivalent of being asked to shove your head into the mouth of a cannon. Hussain's call may have been generally disastrous but it did, according to the priorities of English cricket, have one huge benefit. It provided a clear-cut excuse behind which a multitude of frailties could hide. It also placed the captain of England squarely, and this was the best bit, in his classic role as ready-made scapegoat.

Apologists for an England who disintegrate at the first sight of a green cricket cap say that there has been some improvement since Hussain and Fletcher came together, and no doubt this is true – to a limited extent. There is a degree of Test match parity now with India, Pakistan and South Africa and if you look hard enough you might just pick out the beginnings of consistency in selection. But the heart of the team, when exposed to the highest levels of competition, remains alarmingly brittle. Against Australia, England do not lose. They are separated from their intestines. Ian Botham's verdict was as caustic and robust as ever. "They were like startled rabbits," he declared of his countrymen, and if anyone was entitled to say that, it was surely the hero of Headingley.

What English cricket needs more than anything is hard professional leadership. It needs someone to stand up and take the flak rather than shuffle it towards another corner. The England captain will always be a target, of course; he goes on the field and shapes the action as much as he can and if he can be linked, as Hussain so clearly was in Brisbane, with a crucial tactical miscalculation, there is scarcely any limit on the critical retribution. It is at that point that the vortex into which so many of Hussain's predecessors have been drawn begins to take hold.

England need somebody to do the job which Ray Illingworth, the Ashes-winning captain, defined when he was still young enough to do it properly. It is someone who picks the team, including the captain, and makes all the important decisions off the field. It is someone who is big enough, respected enough, to say: "It is my judgement and I'll keep using it until you take away the job." Botham fancies his chances and such an appointment would surely represent a rallying point, especially when the now eviscerating challenge of Australia comes around.

Who is the spokesman and figurehead of English cricket in the current maelstrom Down Under? It is David Graveney, the chairman of selectors, a knowledgeable cricket man who organised the professional players' union and got himself into the great bureaucratic archipelago of the game. He never played Test cricket, which puts him, you would have thought, at some disadvantage when he rules over a committee formed by his captain, his coach and his fellow-selector, Geoff Miller, who did play Test cricket, including eight times against Australia. Committees do not bring leadership. They had one running the England football team before the arrival of Sir Alf Ramsey, with inevitably feeble results.

Committee talk certainly will not get England out of their current plight. It will take a new way of thinking, a new aggression and for that you need someone like Allan Border, who did such a superb job in helping to rebuild the Australian image of what a Test team should be. You go for a Border on the principle that if you can't beat them you had better get one of them to join you. Or you break the crumbling mould and take a flyer on "Beefy" Botham, who as a very young man once chased Ian Chappell out of a Melbourne bar.

Maybe Botham would have to do it from memory, but it appears that he still has one – and a vital one, too. It is of a time when an England captain could never have admitted to looking into the eyes of his players and seeing fear.

FAREWELL TO WAUGH: A BAD LOSER AND A GREAT WINNER

Published: 07 January 2003

Ian Botham, who was perhaps even more disorientated than the rest of us by the imminence of an England victory, asked a strange rhetorical question in the early hours of yesterday morning. Why on earth, he wondered, was Jason Gillespie batting in a lost-cause fifth Test of a long-dead series with his injured arm bandaged and padded against the hazards of a crumbling pitch and Andrew Caddick's late surge of competitiveness? Even at such an hour, it was maybe not the most taxing of inquiries.

Gillespie, Beefy must have briefly forgotten, is Australian. So, despite his wound, he carried his bat for three runs which were only meaningless if you did not believe the difference between winners and losers is not a passing mood but a lifetime habit.

Andy Bichel also had an injured arm. He scored 49. When Matthew Hayden was stopped from any further contribution by an extremely dubious lbw decision, he put out the glass in the dressing room window. The captain, Steve Waugh, despite scoring a brilliant century two days earlier, one that put him on Sir Don Bradman's mark of 29 centuries in probably his last Test match, completed the final strides of his return from the wicket at a sprint. No one had seen him do that before – but then maybe it was the end, and, if it was, who but he could know quite what tensions had been released?

But then the ball had trickled behind him and removed a bail. The cause of the pain written all over Waugh's normally inscrutable face was, we could be sure, that a random piece of misfortune had denied him the chance to make one last stand for all the principles he had brought to an extraordinary career.

To all of this you might add – and be right to do so – that the Aussies are the world's worst losers. Of course they are. That's why they win so relentlessly.

If Waugh does call it quits later this week – and the expression of his wife as she stood up to join what could very well be his Last Hurrah at the Sydney Cricket Ground suggested he might – he will leave a sweeping legacy for every cricketer who makes a private vow to be great. We were reminded of the force of Waugh's remarkable will in the dog days of another Ashes series two summers ago, when the captain flogged himself for fitness after being carried off with a serious knee injury in the Test at Trent Bridge which had brought the Australians another series win.

A fine century by Mark Butcher at Headingley brought England one of their now traditional consolation victories over the Australians, and in between the rehabilitation work – which, against all odds, saw Waugh return for the final Test at the Oval and wince his way to an innings of 157 not out, underpinning an Australian win by an innings and 25 runs – he watched the play at Leeds with mounting horror.

He was asked why it was so important for him to play at the Oval – the series had been won, Australia were demonstrably superior. "If you start to think like that," he said, "you might as well pack it in. You don't get so long to play this game and you have to take every opportunity you have. I'm captain of Australia and it's my job to be finishing the series at the Oval. So that's why I'm working so hard right now. Some time my responsibility will be over, but until it is I know what I have to do."

No doubt that was the imperative which took Gillespie into Caddick's firing line, and why one of England's chief pleasures at finally winning on a tour which dragged at their spirits so cruelly was surely that they had beaten a team who still plainly cared so much.

For English observers outside of the imbecilic Barmy Army, there were some other sharp points of encouragement after the horrors of the winter. One was the majestic development of Michael Vaughan. Another was the refusal of the bowlers Matthew Hoggard and Steve Harmison to be destroyed by their ordeal of fire. Most significant, perhaps, was the captain Nasser Hussain's insistence that everyone should return to the "bottom line" of another 4-1 defence and understand what that meant.

"It's blatantly obvious," he said, "that Test cricket is now being played in completely different conditions to what we play our county cricket in at home." A lesser competitor would have been reduced to gibberish. But Hussain maintained his nerve and his batting and those who have long railed against the evasions and the complacency of the English game have surely recruited a biting witness for the prosecution case.

Losing to Steve Waugh's Australians was never going to be a matter of shame, but failing to learn the most important of lessons would have been a different matter. There could be no better teacher than the man who raced up the steps at the SCG, cursing not a piece of bad luck but the end of the battle.

SUNSET FALLS ON CRICKET'S GOOD NAME

Published: 08 February 2003

As the eighth World Cup of cricket opens ceremonially against the spectacular backcloth of Table Mountain and Atlantic rollers today, the prospect is of beauty – and an uncommonly ugly beast of a tournament.

Predictably, England's players were last night taken to the 11th hour of their "moral crisis" over whether or not to travel to Robert Mugabe's political rat-hole for their scheduled opening game with Zimbabwe. The expected rejection of the appeal to Justice Albie Sachs that the game be played elsewhere brought another impasse that seemed unlikely to be resolved before the tournament is officially launched.

It is a situation that, after months of wrangling between the International Cricket Council, Downing Street and Lord's, makes a final, searing statement about the vacuum of leadership that has been evident at all levels of the affair.

Right to the bitter and incoherent end the absence of heroes, and still more glaringly, statesmen, confirmed the idea of a World Cup with the overriding priority of protecting television interests and the bottom-line profit margins – a bleak conclusion that scarcely needed the underpinning of abandoned principle implicit in the decision of the team of principal hosts South Africa to dedicate their efforts to the late Hansie Cronje.

Cronje, the favoured son of a leading South African cricket official, sold out his game in the most craven fashion. But then short of taking "dirty" money, it is hard to know how the administrators could have served cricket more poorly in the build-up to a tournament that in the past has been a glorious shop window for all that is most thrilling in the game.

Maybe there will be some echoes of past splendour as 14 teams stretch across 54 matches to the final showdown in Johannesburg on 23 March.

Perhaps Brian Lara will rekindle his native genius to the point of producing something to rival the spellbinding, World Cup-winning centuries of his compatriots Clive Lloyd and Viv Richards in 1975 and 1979.

Sachin Tendulkar might eclipse the 175 of Kapil Dev against Zimbabwe that shattered the calm of Tunbridge Wells in 1983. Steve Waugh's successor, Ricky Ponting, no doubt has the potential to match his predecessor's tournament-saving 120 at Headingley in 1999, when Waugh, after being dropped by a carelessly celebrating Herschelle Gibbs, told the South African: "You've just dropped the World Cup, mate".

The same charge could be levelled at the organisers of the World Cup of 2003, the tournament that announces a strict pecking order of imperatives.

At the top of the list: grabbing every rand and rupee, pound and dollar that might be on the table. At the bottom: bringing into the light and facing all the issues that for so long have deeply complicated any open-hearted welcome for the start of the action.

Even without the appalling fog over Zimbabwe, the thinking behind this World Cup would be disturbing enough. That it will run 12 days longer than the World Cup of football in Japan and South Korea, which at times seemed to impinge upon eternity, is concern enough. But then you consider the treadmill that has been endured by the England players in Australia these last few months, and it is almost enough to explain their hopelessly late engagement in the moral and practical issues involved in the demand that they play a single game in Mugabe's Zimbabwe.

The "greening" of cricket, we have long known, has been eating away at the buoyancy of the game's greatest performers, but now surely we see in this tournament something of an ultimate gulag of the spirit. Reports that Lara has regained some of his appetite are encouraging, but we know the ravages of burn-out that have so frequently afflicted the batsman, who with Tendulkar seemed so capable of ushering in a new and utterly authentic golden era.

Now the glow given off by Lara is more that of a firefly than a steady-burning star, and if in the past he has created many of his own problems, who can say that some of them were not made inevitable by the pressures on a modern international cricketer – demands that are grotesquely underlined by the route march of the body and the spirit that comes under starter's orders in Cape Town today,

However draining it will be, though, there is the reasonable hope that the kind of vibrant brilliance which suffused Sourav Ganguly's Indians at Lord's last summer will surface with redeeming force. The history of the competition is, after all, laced with exceptional deeds. Aravinda de Silva's unbeaten 107 carried Sri Lanka to an astonishing victory over Australia in 1996 – after a semi-final triumph in Eden Gardens that provoked riots all over India. Three and a half years ago at Lord's, Shane Warne was mesmerising as the Pakistanis subsided under his spell. Who knows, Michael Vaughan, the shining warrior of

England's hellish tour of Australia, may light more influential fires of inspiration in the next few weeks?

Sadly, though, there are areas of this World Cup beyond redemption's touch.

Nothing is capable of flattening out the memory of the administrative palsy that brought on the fever of conscience that came so late and dubiously to the England dressing room. Or the gut-wrenching hypocrisy of Downing Street, when, after failing to lift a practical finger against the atrocious regime of Mugabe and the suffering it was imposing on people of all classes and colours, heaped the full burden of foreign policy on the shoulders of a bunch of cricketers.

However we judge the vacillations of Nasser Hussain and his men, the lack of example and care they received from in and out of the game make them as much victims as culprits. Now they are obliged to simply play their game. However much weariness they may feel in their minds and their bones, it will surely be something of a relief.

THE GOVERNMENT, NOT THE PLAYERS, ARE ZIMBABWE VILLAINS

Published: 11 February 2003

The drama in Cape Town, which at the weekend obliged my colleague Angus Fraser to paint a picture of a sports team in the throes of a collective nervous breakdown, was all played out, at least in moral terms, some time ago – certainly before yesterday's announcement by the England and Wales Cricket Board that Robert Mugabe's Harare was not a proper place for representatives of a nation which likes to think of itself as civilised to play a game of cricket.

Unfortunately, the boundaries of even these catholic sports pages are not expansive enough to deal with quite all the issues of truth and leadership and morality raised by this utterly gut-wrenching affair. However, there is a duty to dismiss some of the more superficial judgements.

The most oppressive – and essentially unfair – is that Nasser Hussain and his players are the chief culprits, and that this is so even if their waverings were yesterday cast in an even paler light by the magnificently brave gesture of Zimbabwe's Andy Flower and Henry Olonga when they walked on to the field with black armbands and a stirring unity of purpose.

A white player and a black player made a joint statement in which they railed, shoulder to shoulder, against the iniquities of life in their homeland. They shielded younger players from any responsibility. They stood together not as sportsmen but whole, brave men.

It was surely a brilliant example for anyone caught in an issue of morality and conscience, and it dramatically underlined the reality that England's players have not exactly walked in the footsteps of Sir Thomas More or the Maid of Orleans while leaving so late any engagement of the question of whether or not they should give even marginal aid to Mugabe's loathsome regime.

It's also true that their vacillations last winter over whether or not to tour India – provoked, apparently, by the conclusion that the terrorist outrage in New York had made the world a more dangerous place – is a memory that insists on lingering and, rightly or wrongly, conditioning some responses to their indecision in the luxury hotel in the shadow of Table Mountain.

But, please, let's draw up a proper list of villains. The players are nowhere near the top.

Yes, Hussain was initially perhaps a little too eager to return to the poisonous chalice of Zimbabwe, but the validity of his first responses, while less than Solomonesque, have stood up to the long weeks of controversy pretty well.

He said it was "faintly ridiculous" for the Government to load up the imperatives of conscience on the players and management of England while their own policy on the Zimbabwe issue was not so much insipid as non-existent. Businessmen flew into Harare without the merest sigh from Downing Street.

Faintly ridiculous? It was a lot more than that. It was fundamentally dishonest, a piece of political opportunism that became all the more alarming when you put it into the context of the build-up to the war against Iraq.

The England and Wales Cricket Board have been like putty in the hands of the Government. How easy it has been to cast them as mere money grubbers, but here again it has been hard to sympathise with their desperate pursuit of a compromise which would preserve their financial rewards from contracts already signed with the International Cricket Council and also head off the gathering threat of boycotts by Zimbabwe and South Africa, scheduled tourists of England.

If the game in this country had not been so persistently bedevilled by poor leadership, if the grinding futility of county cricket had been properly addressed, if there was any real sense of the dynamism that has marked the inexorable supremacy of the Australian game, the Doomsday implications of walking away from what we considered improper demands by the World Cup organisers would not be quite so apparent.

The overriding sense of all this is that the agonies of English cricketers in Cape Town – so graphically portrayed by their former team-mate Fraser, who suddenly felt a huge and poignant divide – could have been lessened sharply, if not wholly avoided, by something that smacked of genuine leadership. It is the single most pressing need in English cricket.

No one could say that they have the inside track on any perfect solution. The Government's role has simply been disgraceful, and, in response, English cricket could scarcely have displayed a more disunited front.

No one has gained, except perhaps those hard-pressed souls who are fighting, and risking their lives, to free their country from a tyrant, without a scrap of help from the old mother country. They have at least received the oxygen of being constantly on the front pages of newspapers which, in the rage of the Government's desire to bomb Baghdad, might otherwise have been drawn away from the horrors besieging our former colony.

That the cricketers of England have been reluctant to carry the burden of British foreign policy in southern Africa should not really be a matter of national disgust. More reasonably, we should mourn the state of a world that puts that simple requirement to play the game so low down on their list of current priorities – and thank God for Andy Flower and Henry Olonga's reminder that, in the end, there is a way to play a boy's game with the bearing of a man.

BOYCOTT KEEPS HIS FINGER ON
THE PULSE OF ENGLISH CRICKET

Published: 12 August 2003

Geoff Boycott is in brilliant, pulverising form. His criticism of English cricket has gone to the bone. He has savaged its lack of proper leadership, the self-absorption of experienced players who should be helping their younger colleagues rather than gazing at their own navels, its all-round ineptitude – and a total failure to act for the common good of the game.

One theory is that Boycott is in a mood of such thanksgiving after his bruising but successful battle with throat cancer that he is offering himself up as cricket's saviour.

This idea, however, is not being countenanced, for the moment at least, too strongly in his native county. The overwhelming reaction to news that Freddie Trueman had invited his former team-mate to lunch – over which they could discuss some plan of resurrection for the game that made them – has been greeted with a degree of cynicism. "That's all very well, tha knows," said one insider, "but which of the buggers will pay?"

I suppose even those of us who have long treasured Boycott's rough but wonderfully acute capacity to get to the heart of a cricket matter – and who still believe that the speed with which he was jettisoned by broadcasting organisations and the establishment was a scandal greater than anything that emerged clearly in a French courtroom five years ago – have to be honest. Altruism has not always flowed strongly through his veins.

Indeed, one veteran cricket man was yesterday insisting that there was nothing apocryphal about the story which is supposed to sum up the Boycott approach in his own playing days.

You know the damning tale? It happened in the 1970 Ashes tour when John Gleeson, the Australian spinner, was tying down the English batting. Gleeson wasn't devastating England in the fashion of Shane Warne. He wasn't unleashing the kind of "flipper" which distorts the dreams of Mike Gatting. But England just couldn't get him away. Gleeson had been a problem from the start of the Test series, but then Basil D'Oliveira came to join Boycott at the wicket at Melbourne and both batsmen began to play him with a degree of assurance. While they were doing a little horticulture in the middle of the pitch, D'Oliveira couldn't contain himself. He said: "Geoff, I've worked him out". Boycott is alleged to have replied: "I can see that – but don't tell the others".

No, perhaps this doesn't sit too well with the thrust of Boycott's latest epistle to the lost tribe of English cricket, in which one of his most trenchant criticisms is that the young Lancashire fast bowler James Anderson, a star in Australia and the World Cup, went utterly without guidance while bowling "rubbish" in the two Tests against South Africa. Did he expect an "old sweat" at Lord's to offer something that he failed to produce in Melbourne all those years ago – a sense of team, a belief that hard lessons won, and of great benefit to your own batting average and future career prospects, should be ungrudgingly passed on?

Charitably, you could say that Boycott was young then and too deeply embedded in that Yorkshire imperative that if "thy do owt for nowt, do it for thissen". An exaggerated reflection of attitudes in the Yorkshire dressing room back in the sixties and seventies? Maybe, maybe not. It is true, though, that as the team contemplated the next stage of their travels around the counties, there was, during an evening's drinking, a spirited debate about car pool expenses and those who were not paying their way. The dispute was not about payments for petrol, but oil.

One current Yorkshire theory is that Boycott, after an enforced spell of introspection, is hungry to express himself again not so much in commentary, where his views have been bitingly relevant but largely ignored for so long, but in the politics of cricket. There is a feeling that the potential partnership of Boycott and Trueman, who was conspicuously praised for his hard work and professionalism when Boycott discussed Anderson's problems and the downgrading of county cricket by the Duncan Fletcher-Nasser Hussain regime at the weekend, could lead to a bid for the Yorkshire presidency.

Yorkshire today, England tomorrow? No doubt it would cause mayhem in the Long Room, but at this point in the sad decline of English cricket who would care about that?

Boycott's voice, blessedly restored, is the outstanding one in any discussion on the plight of his game. It carries authentic rage and is informed by the certainties which come with outstanding success. So he told D'Oliveira to keep his trap shut. The point is that, thankfully, he has managed to grow older – and, whatever they are saying in Yorkshire, very much wiser.

HUSSAIN CLEARS DEBT WITH GUTS AND APPLICATION

Published: 15 August 2003

At one minute past five here at Trent Bridge yesterday Nasser Hussain stopped the clock on the worst days of his cricket life. He scored his 13th Test century, but that is a statistic. The story was that he found again the best of himself.

He was no longer caught in a tumult of angst. He was a great batsman doing a mighty turn for his team.

Of course, in the broad sweep of his career, Hussain didn't owe anybody anything when he walked to the wicket and he flinched only momentarily when he was introduced as Ed Smith, the latest long shot up from the Shires.

Everyone knew who he was, however, and, to the huge benefit of England's imperilled cause, this included Hussain himself. He looked like a man who had finally emerged from that tunnel of self-absorption and personal crisis which had heaped damage on his reputation and brought English Test cricket a sense, it seemed, of almost climactic futility.

This certainly was the short-term debt Hussain knew he had to redeem as Graeme Smith's potentially rampant South Africans crowded around the bat after the cheap dismissal of Hussain's embattled successor, Michael Vaughan, and Marcus Trescothick.

Hussain stood firm – and a former England captain said a little later: "It seems to me Nasser has got his head straight. He's put away old baggage and he's a batsman again." This was announced quite imperiously with his first scoring stroke. It was a beautifully carved boundary through the covers off Makhaya Ntini, the ten-wicket destroyer of England earlier in the series.

Ntini's shoulders slumped and when you look back on the day it was one of the pivotal moments. Mark Butcher led the response to the early setbacks, but it was Hussain who always seemed to be in ultimate charge of the resistance. This became a reality after tea when he launched himself into a series of sumptuous off-drives.

Though this third Test match is still delicately poised on a wicket expected to be an ambush site by mid-afternoon tomorrow, Hussain serviced his debt with both guts and application that impressively restored his credit rating as a Test cricketer of the first rank.

Forgiveness for the petulant mindset which led to his shockingly abrupt decision to resign after England were outplayed in the first drawn Test at Edgbaston – and a surly, emotional hangover that made the English dressing room a place of grinding tension during the thrashing administered by the cyclonic Smith and his team at Lord's – is unlikely to be instantaneous. Hussain's defection as captain left a rawness unlikely to be healed entirely by one day's brilliant work, and some will say that Vaughan's disastrous early departure – in terms at least of his own immediate confidence and authority – was another by-product of the sudden pressure brought by Hussain's ditching of his responsibilities as captain.

His achievement was still vast, however, yesterday. It was no less than to remind the nation that here indeed, when you got right down to it, was a player passionate about the need for English cricket to compete properly at the highest level. And as he applied himself so thoroughly to the task, you were reminded of the meaning of most of his captaincy – a relentless pursuit of higher competitive standards.

So, he was briefly consumed by his disappointments, his sense of an unravelling of a grand ambition. He lost touch with his own trumpeted declaration that success could come only through the commitment of a team rather than the whimsy of an individual.

But there was nothing whimsical about Hussain when he reannounced himself yesterday. There were certainly some anxious moments: on 97, he played an alarming shot through his legs, and before he reached his century another run came from an overthrow which threatened the wicket of his partner, Smith.

But Hussain's nerve held brilliantly and, as the shadows came to Trent Bridge, England plainly were back in the series which had threatened to pass them by.

For England there are still huge problems of policy, of gathering together the strength of a national game which has never seemed in more disarray. Butcher was Butcher, defiant and possibly maintaining an encouraging record of never having scored a century for a losing England team. Hussain had cleared away the fog and batted in a way that might have spread doubts in a South African team that some hard critics believe had been immensely flattered by the astonishing form of Smith and their crushing victory at Lord's.

But none of this is reason to believe that crisis still does not lurk at every corner of English cricket's immediate future.

These, however, were considerations which could be reasonably put on one side at one minute past five: when Hussain did more than complete a superb century. He had again found a point to play the game that has dominated his life.

VAUGHAN'S RABBLE SHOW VALIDITY OF ILLINGWORTH'S FEARS

Published: 26 August 2003

Ray Illingworth, who is considered by some reasonable judges to have been the most astute Test captain England ever had, must some days feel he is now operating in his own private dust bowl. The erosion of his reputation has been relentless over recent years.

Mike Atherton put the boot in on the pages of his acclaimed autobiography when he reviewed their always taut relationship during Illingworth's spell as chairman of selectors.

More recently, Illingworth has been lashed bitterly for his suggestion that the new England captain – Michael Vaughan, like him a Yorkshire player – is no doubt a wonderful batsman, but might not be a natural leader of men. This assessment, one critic claimed, finally cemented Illy's reputation as a "mumbling boor". That's as mebbee, as they would say in Yorkshire, but it could happen that the miserable old bugger might just be right.

Vaughan's defenders will no doubt argue that he faced a fiendishly difficult task after his predecessor, Nasser Hussain, walked out on the job so petulantly. They will also say that he deserves time to bed down into an assignment of terrible pressure. But I'm afraid they can keep on saying these things on the hour of every day until the final Test match at the Oval without dislodging for a single second a conviction which simply cannot go away. It is that England at Headingley were a leaderless rabble of quite shaming proportion.

No one is better able to analyse, both morally and technically, the debris left by the appalling débâcle than my colleague Angus Fraser, for whom the wretchedness of the English bowling must have represented a shocking betrayal of everything he stood for as a Test player of great accomplishment and pride. But then it is also true that there were aspects of the performance which had to be dismaying for an Englishman with only the most rudimentary knowledge of the game.

In terms of body language alone, comparisons between Vaughan's team, and that of the 22-year-old Graeme Smith, were gut-wrenching. Yesterday, when the last rites of a Test match England at several points held by the throat were completed so massively in South Africa's favour, Vaughan, three Tests into the job, looked a broken man. He talked of bouncing back at the Oval as England had done at Trent Bridge, but even as he did so you could see in his eyes that he was discussing not just a leap of faith but also of practicality.

In one sense, Vaughan could only be seen as a victim. He inherited chaos, and now he has to make something of competitive attitudes which for five days had been utterly exposed as insubstantial. Illingworth's point that he might not have the force of personality to pull off such a huge challenge was perhaps, on reflection, not the aside of an irredeemable curmudgeon but a genuine insight of someone who indeed knew what he was talking about.

Before the remarkably driven Smith was appointed he was interrogated thoroughly by the South African selectors. He was asked what he was prepared to sacrifice in order to succeed in the job. Laconically, he said, "My youth". Smith impressed the selectors with the force of his nature and his understanding of the problems he might encounter. He also said he didn't see the folk hero Lance Klusener as part of his plans. He didn't think he would fit into the dressing room he had in mind.

We do not know quite how closely England selectors examined the captaincy credentials of Michael Vaughan. Did he relish working with a coach and a former captain, Hussain, who hitherto had been virtually joined at the hip? Did he endorse the rubber stamping of veteran Alec Stewart's Last Hurrah march to the climax of his Test career at his home Oval? If he was going to carry the can after Hussain's defection, would he be in charge of all its contents? Could he be sure that he would be given the means to drive out a culture of fear which was so depressingly confirmed by the decision to restore the 40-year-old Stewart to the team after the young Chris Read had made such impressive progress in the one-day series?

These last few days no cricketing soul has appeared to be more tortured than Vaughan's. Before the Trent Bridge Test, he said that his style would not change. He would stay relaxed and smiling.

By the end of the Headingley match he seemed about as relaxed and happy as an inhabitant of Death Row. Conviction has drained from his batting. Perhaps the most damning indictment of England's performance came from the great South African batsman Barry Richards. Appalled, like most observers, by England's decision to accept the invitation to leave the field for bad light when Mark Butcher and Marcus Trescothick had the South African bowlers on the ropes, Richards said that it seemed to him that England didn't even know when they were on top, and could there ever be anything more indicative of a team without direction and positive leadership?

It is to Trescothick's credit than he shouldered the blame for that terrible miscalculation, but when he did so you were bound to note that before the emergence of Vaughan as a world-class batsman it was the former who was being groomed for the England captaincy. That he wasn't the man for the job was revealed by one flash of illumination in the Headingley gloom. Vaughan may yet overcome the shakiest of starts, but to do so he will need the kind of support, on and off the field, which has been so brilliantly exploited by Graeme Smith.

In the meantime, we perhaps might give more of an ear to someone as unfashionable and crotchety – and deeply knowledgeable – as Ray Illingworth.

QUESTIONS THAT WILL JOLT VAUGHAN'S CONSCIENCE

Published: 13 November 2004

Pity Michael Vaughan if he ever has to explain to a grandson the concept of "duty" forced upon him when he led a team of English cricketers to Zimbabwe in the benighted year of 2004.

Maybe it would go something like this . . .

Duty to what, Grandad? The duty of following your own instincts, not as a sports star, perhaps, but an ordinary man?

Not really, boy, I hated the idea of being in a country where human rights had been driven into the ground. No, I did it because if the game I played had any kind of future in our country and if it was to go on providing me with a living good enough to provide your dad and his brothers and sisters with a decent education and a good life, it was clear the team had to go.

But why did you have to go, Grandpops? Couldn't you have said, "Gentlemen, include me out?"

Well, some of us had to go and I was the captain. I couldn't stay at home and then expect to take over the job again when the team moved to South Africa to play the five big Test matches. You spend most of your life working towards a goal and then when you achieve it, it is not so easy just to walk away.

What was so wrong about playing cricket in Zimbabwe?

The feeling was that it would give something known as aid and succour to one of the most loathsome governments on the face of the earth, which at the time was saying quite a lot. Two of Zimbabwe's best cricketers, Andy Flower and Henry Olonga, were very much against it. They risked a bad conversation in the night by wearing protest armbands against the situation inflicted by the government of Robert Mugabe. Everyone, and especially our government, was very impressed by their bravery, at least at the time.

What did Flower and Olonga say was so wrong about that situation?

Well, they said that democracy and most other forms of decency had been put to death in their country.

What did our Government say about this?

Oh, quite a lot. Basically they agreed with Andy and Henry. They said we shouldn't go. We would be doing that aid and succour thing.

Didn't they order you not to go?

No. They said they would leave it to our consciences.

Why didn't they say, "Look Gentlemen, this just isn't on? You can't go there aiding and succouring a government that has turned a rich and fertile country back into the stone age, a regime which, in some ways, is as viciously racist as the South African one which was treated as a pariah for many years and, in the end, with excellent results." For one thing, couldn't the Government have said, "We're not going to let you?"

They couldn't do that. In fact if you had suspended every individual cabinet minister over a vat of boiling oil it seemed you couldn't persuade them to do it.

Grandfather, on what point of arcane principle did they stand?

It would have been far too expensive. The International Cricket Council – the game's ruling body – had said that if we didn't go to Zimbabwe we would be suspended from international cricket, and that would have been very costly indeed.

How expensive?

Well, when you added up all the lost revenue from TV fees and sponsorships, it would have been £50m in old British currency, and just for starters. Furthermore, one of the greatest incentives for my generation of English cricketers, a possible victory over the great Australian team the following summer, would have been swept away.

But, Grandad, didn't that particular government of ours cough up mounds of taxpayers' money on failed bids for World Cups and Olympic games and continue with the despised Tory practice of flogging off school playing fields? Didn't they squander vastly more on the building which used to stand on that waste ground on the banks of the Thames? And didn't they whip up huge parades and receptions whenever any of our sportsmen and women, rising above one of the poorest sports infrastructures in the developed world, managed to win something?

One small problem was that the Government couldn't very well order us not to play cricket in Zimbabwe, and provide compensation, if they were not prepared to do that to an army of businessmen still eager to do trade with people underpinning Mugabe's regime.

So you didn't pack up your togs and go off to Zimbabwe with any real appetite for the ensuing action?

No, not at all. In fact I said at the time: "We leave on Monday and I think it is clear we are making a stance in itself because we are not going to Zimbabwe until 24 November. We go to Namibia for our preparation and fly to Zimbabwe before the first one-day game."

As stances go, Grandpa, it maybe wasn't quite on the same level of the Spanish Nationalist general who, when told that the Republicans held his son and were about to shoot him if the garrison wasn't surrendered immediately, spoke down the telephone to his first-born, saying: "Commend your soul to God and cry Viva España."

Well, Grandson, the Spanish are quite a passionate people. Those were different times.

But don't you wish you had felt a little rush of the blood, that you had told the ICC where to go with their blackmail, and also told the Government that if they weren't prepared to react meaningfully to the difference between right and wrong as long as it wasn't spelled down the hot-line from Washington, there were still a few English cricketers who were?

When you put it like that, maybe I do. But then one day, you'll be an old man, too, and perhaps everything will not seem so wonderfully straightforward. In the meantime, while we're talking about cricket, how many times do I have to tell you to get your head in line with the ball?

A BETRAYAL OF CRICKET
AND HUMANITY

Published: 27 November 2004

We knew that David Morgan, the chairman of the England and Wales Cricket Board, was not exactly Dr Livingstone, and that when he was greeted at Harare airport by some stooge of Robert Mugabe there might be a certain shortfall in plain speaking.

However, no one could have been prepared for the toe-curling pusillanimity of this sports politician for whom a great door to decent behaviour had been opened – but who had neither the wit nor the conscience to walk through.

Eventually, he emerged with a handful of visas for cricket writers, a victory so derisory that the broad hint that he was rather pleased with himself was nothing less than breathtaking.

Indeed, if it is true that we still search in vain for a hero in this farrago of spinelessness – while saluting belatedly the principle of the BBC foot soldier Pat Murphy, who at the time of the World Cup last year said that he would rather walk on broken glass than report cricket in what Mugabe and his henchman had made of Zimbabwe – it is necessary to grade various levels of operational and moral failure.

Morgan and a government which includes in its ranks Peter Hain, the man who made his name as an anti-apartheid campaigner, who once urged that we should place barbed wire around Lord's or Twickenham rather than allow in cricket and rugby players representing the pariah state South Africa, surely contended hard for top place on the midden.

Hain made a serious run for it when he heaped all the blame on the feeble ECB. Here was the former young lion of human rights side-footing responsibility away from a government which disapproved of the cricket tour but refused to lift a finger against it, as it does in the case of all kinds of business support, from British Airways down, for Mugabe. But in the end Morgan brushed aside all opposition.

Even when Zimbabwe barred entry to the cricket writers – and plainly offered a huge loophole for Morgan and his colleagues to say, finally, that they were not to be blackmailed by the International Cricket Council into doing something that was deeply offensive to most of the nation – Morgan was quite indefatigable.

He would find a way to make the tour happen, he told us, as though he was offering a gift rather than a betrayal.

Yesterday he went into Harare Cathedral for, it might have been assumed, some moments of reflection about what he was doing, why he was re-treading the ground that so infuriated the former England captain Nasser Hussain and his players when they were holed up in a Cape Town hotel during the World Cup. However, this was no stop on the road to Damascus.

Morgan emerged preening himself on the approval for his actions he won in his own vox pop in the cloisters. Underwhelmingly, it consisted of two men, one black, one white, who according to Morgan were both delighted that the English cricketers had arrived, albeit rather in the fashion of a flock of weary sheep.

That would have been bad enough in its utter detachment from the reality of a once beautiful, and productive land, being systematically ushered back into the Stone Age, but Morgan was filled with conviction now. Here is what he said: "I have certainly looked at what is happening here. We have sympathy with the people here but the ECB is in business – our trade is cricket and the revenue part of our trade is international cricket. In order to trade internationally, we have to play by the rules of the ICC and the rules of the ICC are such that member countries are not allowed to avoid tours for moral reasons as part of the future tours programme."

Translation: Your hearts can bleed as long as they like, but I'm here to represent cricket not as a great game, one that the Caribbean Marxist philosopher C L R James rated as the most profound gift of the British Empire to his beleaguered countrymen in Trinidad, but a piece of merchandise, something to sell at any cost to human dignity.

Morgan may have felt he flew to Africa as a man of some stature. One day, though, he might just have to acknowledge that he got off the plane not as a statesman of cricket but a grubby little shopkeeper holding up cricket as nothing more than a bag of humbugs.

Meanwhile, we can only be ever more depressed by an affair that in the end has become rather more than just another episode in the losing battle to separate sport from politics. This is so even if you accept the broad argument that engaging in sport only with countries of impeccable regimes and stainless human rights records might just leave you with a World Cup final between two thinly populated dots in the South Pacific.

On these grounds, who would have taken a World Cup to Argentina in the time of the generals or voted for the Beijing Olympics in four years' time? However, what is specially jarring about the Zimbabwe business is the high visibility of the suffering in that country, the contempt the Mugabe regime has for criticism of the horror it is producing and the dogged refusal of the ECB and the ICC to accept that in certain circumstances playing sport is not only an irrelevance to all that is happening around it but also an obscene statement of disregard.

In this, Morgan's epistle from the shadow of Harare Cathedral was particularly numbing. Earlier in the week, as even the outrageously immoral ICC began to accept that trying to enforce financial penalties on anyone rejecting the conditions imposed by a regime plainly beyond reason or conscience would have invited not only defiance but outright scorn, Hussain was dragged back to what he described as the worst days of his sporting life.

He said: "Put to one side the overwhelming moral argument against playing cricket in Zimbabwe – and who can be unaware of the atrocities being committed by the Mugabe regime? Last time we players had moral objections but we were told we had to keep them to ourselves. Our only grounds for complaint, which could get the match cancelled without English cricket incurring huge financial penalties, were security issues – or so we were told. So we complied, pretended we were prepared to go because of security advice, and were branded shallow and insular sportsmen for worrying about ourselves.

"Nothing could have been further from the truth – we had genuine concerns about the morality of playing but we were under enormous pressure. Tim Lamb, then chief executive of the ECB, tearfully begged me to take the team. Chairman David Morgan promised me the trip was off, only to come back 12 hours later pleading for me to go. I told him where to go – he had been full of inconsistencies."

Hussain, of course, begs certain questions, as did his successor Michael Vaughan when he said that he felt the team were taking something of a stance this time when they insisted on delaying their arrival until immediately before the first one-day match. What is the point of concern without action? When does a man say he will do what is right simply for its own sake? These, no doubt, are questions easier to answer when your entire livelihood might depend on the strength of your convictions, but an awareness of such practicality is unlikely to lift the appalling sense of the abandonment of an entire, suffering nation when England walk on to the field at the Harare Sports Club tomorrow.

To get there you go down a broad avenue running by the presidential palace of Mugabe. I went there once to interview Graeme Hick before he took his place in the England team. China tinkled on the pavilion terrace at the tea interval. At Hick's old school you were told how young black players were coming through and on the drive down to the great young batsman's farming community the fields were full of grain and tobacco. At the Sports Club, cricket, like the still-fertile land, was changing, but it too seemed to have sturdy roots.

But that was before the crops were burned and the people driven into terrible hunger and pain. You could sit at the Sports Club, sip your tea and see cricket as a seamless part of a decent life. Now, we have seen this week, it is a miserable, unprotected pawn in a much bigger, grimmer game.

ONLY THE ASHES CAN
COMPLETE RESURRECTION

Published: 24 December 2004

So far there has been no mention of the appalling *déjà vu* which preceded England's record eighth straight Test victory in Port Elizabeth. This is odd because for any Englishman who cowered, shell-shocked and humiliated in Queen's Park, Port of Spain, ten years ago, it surely brought the sharpest edge to the celebrations which have been flowing all week.

The dreadful sensation came when Shaun Pollock sent down the first ball of England's second innings, when a modest target of 143 runs seemed like the most perfunctory of challenges.

Marcus Trescothick hung out his bat and the ball popped into a safe pair of South African hands. Pollock's face said a thousand optimistic things, including the improbable one that he and his team-mates might rise above not only the new weight of the English threat but the insanity of their own ruling body's selection policy.

That we were back in that dark hour in Trinidad seemed to be confirmed when Mark Butcher soon after, and quite unnecessarily, steered a delivery from Makhaya Ntini into the slips and the superb reflexes of the South African captain Graeme Smith.

Remember the denouement in Port of Spain? Mike Atherton, that most resilient of openers, went first ball to a rampant Curtly Ambrose, whose mother always ran into the street to ring a bell when her son claimed a wicket. That day she outrang St Clement's. Big Curtly, who had taken five for 60 in the first innings, destroyed England with figures of 6 for 24. He was cyclonic, awesome. England were shot out for 46, their lowest ever score in the islands despite the terror that had previously been inflicted by the likes of Wes Hall, Charlie Griffith, Michael Holding, Joel Garner and Malcolm Marshall.

Later, a grey-faced and bemused Atherton said of course English cricket would rise from the destruction – but it might take a little time. He was also asked to define the greatest attribute of a winning captain. He said, with impeccable logic: "Probably having a good team."

England have taken ten years to produce that good team, and if we are right to rejoice it is even more vital to keep some perspective. Thanks mainly to the phenomenally consistent Andrew Strauss, England avoided further disasters in Port Elizabeth. The ball which got the captain Michael Vaughan cheaply came from the hand of young Dale Steyn, but plainly via the heavens. He may spend the rest of his years yearning to repeat such a perfect delivery.

The perspective that is most urgently needed is the one that over the years has been such a stranger to the thinking of England's front-line teams.

When the obsessional Sir Clive Woodward guided England to their first World Cup rugby title in Sydney last year his achievement had only one parallel – the success of Sir Alf Ramsey in the football equivalent 37 years earlier, and we were bound to look for the similarities. The clearest one was the refusal of the men in charge to be touched by anything but the relentless need to improve performance – and maintain a degree of humility.

For matching effort England's cricketers must await next summer and the possibility of ending nearly 20 years of futility against the world champion Aussies. This is not to be churlish but realistic. In Australia England's progress has been noted with both respect and enthusiasm. They would like nothing better than a genuine contest with the Poms, who in recent years have provoked only weary derision.

The Australian captain Ricky Ponting certainly couldn't be accused of a shortfall in grace when he declared: "It's good to see that England are shaping up so well – and I'm glad to hear they fancy themselves a bit for the Ashes. But we have heard this sort of thing before and I guess we'll have to wait and see."

That is the proper reaction of the leader of a team who over recent years has made a formidable case that it may be the most dominant team in the history of the game. They have been the team of all seasons and all challenges and that they may still have quite a bit left in an ageing armoury is suggested by the pulverising of Pakistan. However, it is also true that defeat by Australia would do nothing to invalidate the praise which is being heaped upon Vaughan and his men.

Huge progress has been made since that annihilation in Trinidad and if being best in the world proves beyond England when the Australians arrive, it will remain an ambition founded on impressively solid ground with the potency of the pace attack of Steve Harmison, Matthew Hoggard and Simon Jones, the growing stature of Andrew Flintoff and batting strength represented by the relatively young Vaughan, Strauss, Trescothick, and the potential of an Ian Bell.

Bell's absence from the Test squad is one worry, given the rating he has within the game. It touches on the angst that must be felt when you consider the reason why the 27-year-old Strauss is now so central to all of England's hopes. It is not because of any clear-eyed appreciation of his potential but the mishap in the nets that kept Vaughan out of the Lord's Test match with New Zealand last summer. Misadventure is perhaps not the best foundation for team-building.

However, this is no reason not to celebrate striking evidence of an England team that is marching back on to ground that in the smoke and cordite of a damp evening in Trinidad seemed to be lost forever.

Mrs Ambrose would surely be the first to agree. So let the bells ring for English cricket's Christmas and, who knows, the first breath of summer.

EVEN IN A HOLE, REAL WINNERS KEEP DIGGING

Published: 07 January 2005

A team do not go bad in the course of one Test match but they can pick up a pretty serious infection. That has to be the worry about the all-conquering England of 2004, who have arrived in the new year dishevelled and, it seems, rather sorry for themselves.

Defeat is not the problem. South Africa, even one sliding down the world league table, are never going to be pushovers on their own soil, especially that of Cape Town, and any team who have fighters of the talent of Jacques Kallis and Shaun Pollock retain the capacity to come back in a formidable way.

No, the worry is not the loss of the winning sequence but the way it was surrendered. There are many ways of losing, but it is hard to imagine that England could have found a more discouraging one. In the crash-landing a lot of old baggage came tumbling out of the hold.

Most disconcerting of all is the sudden discovery that England have a tough itinerary, a rush of Test matches and little time to relax and play themselves back into form or a better frame of mind in some up-country game. Perhaps it was a completely wrong impression, but isn't this the way the modern Test cricketer wants it – all swift business without that time dragging them thousands of miles away from loved ones and home comforts?

Two points leap out of the debris of the slaughter of the English in Cape Town. One is that we didn't hear a peep about the draining schedule when the South Africans were destroyed in Port Elizabeth and pushed to the edge of defeat in Durban. No, all we heard then was how Michael Vaughan's team were getting ever closer to putting some genuine pressure on the world champions Australia before they arrive here in the summer.

The other worry is that apart from five days of wretched performance, England produced some of the most resigned and negative thinking ever seen on a cricket field.

Andrew Flintoff, a glory of England's renaissance, was ordered into a bowling line which would have been dismissed by his great predecessor, Ian Botham, as nothing so much as an outright insult to his ability to claim the wicket of a world-class opponent.

The big fear must be that England, their self-belief fattened on superficially impressive victories against New Zealand and the shattered West Indians, have made only a phantom leap into the highest class. Reaction to stiffening South African resistance at least points to this disturbing possibility.

England were outplayed and out-thought in every phase of the Cape Town action. The South African captain, Graeme Smith, did receive some cutting criticism from England's battery of former captains when his batsmen refused to take suicidal risks against bowling rooted in despair, but he had the reasonable response that his lead was approaching 500 with two days stretching out ahead.

Vaughan, whose own batting is in free-fall, correctly points out that England still have everything to play for at 1-1. He says that the last two Tests will see a ferocious restatement of the form and the commitment which made last year such a sustained march away from some of the worst of the nation's cricket history. For the moment he can surely be taken at his word; the light produced by his captaincy may be a little less brilliant after Cape Town, but it is hardly extinguished.

The England coach, Duncan Fletcher, was making similar noises in the Cape dusk but his mood, not surprisingly, was more sombre than at any time last year. Perhaps amid England's drooping body language, he was reminded of the reflections which darkened his brow the last time the Australians were in England. After Steve Waugh's men had retained possession of the Ashes at Trent Bridge, quite imperiously, he was asked what it was about his conquerors that most impressed him.

Now Fletcher's response echoes loudly in the wake of England's defeat and the latest piece of annihilation by the world champions against Pakistan at the Sydney Cricket Ground.

Said the coach: "Australia are a fine team, probably the greatest I've ever seen, full of experience and talent and success, but the thing that strikes me most is their enthusiasm, their togetherness, their absolute refusal to become jaded."

Fletcher said how impressive it was to see players such as Steve Waugh and Shane Warne and Adam Gilchrist at the ground so full of life and freshness hours before the start of play. "When you are near them you feel the buzz of their anticipation," he said.

It is maybe a point Fletcher might want to make on the journey up to Johannesburg. Winners don't talk about tough schedules, about running out of gas. They keep digging down . . . and they keep winning.

THE MIRACLE OF SPORT
SHOWS ITS HUMANITY

Published: 11 January 2005

According to some of the more breathless accounts it was possible to look down on a famous sports arena yesterday and see a miracle.

The miracle of Melbourne. There on the great green expanse of the MCG was the aristocracy of world cricket. Brian Lara, the greatest of West Indian batsmen, stood near to Matthew Hayden, one of the bastions of the champions, Australia, as Sourav Ganguly, the captain of India, drilled a ball fiendishly wide of the pride of Yorkshire, Darren Gough.

As the crowd of 70,000 cheered and the total raised for tsunami relief clicked past the £6m mark, even the most refined technology failed to pick up a whisper of the sledging that down the decades had crackled so venomously. Sledging is what rival cricketers say to each other when they are locked into almost any level of combat. They question each other's parentage, the fidelity of their wives and their girlfriends, and no one ever engaged in this bitter pursuit more relentlessly on this ground than Australia's Merv Hughes and Pakistan's Javed Miandad.

Most memorably, it occurred when Javed, whose coruscating batsmanship was always more easily appreciated than his generosity to opponents, was thrashing a perspiring Hughes to all corners of the field.

At one point, Javed, after cutting his victim to the boundary with ostentatious precision, announced: "Hughes, this just isn't good enough – you are not a Test class bowler, you should be working as a bus conductor."

The torture went on for some time before Hughes, ransacking his body for a supreme effort, delivered the ball that claimed his tormentor's wicket. Hughes' team-mates were stunned when he didn't rush up to Miandad in a rage of gloating. Instead, the bowler raced to the boundary gates, where he was able to say, with a perfectly straight face, to the departing Javed: "Tickets, please."

No, there was no sledging in Melbourne yesterday – and nor was there a miracle. It was simply sport, abused so often by the forces which seek to gain from it only monstrous profits, taking the chance to show the best of itself.

That it did so quite brilliantly shouldn't have been so much of a surprise. If we mock so many modern sportsmen, if we find ourselves railing against epidemics of greed and cheating and self-importance, we should perhaps take a look at our own lives and our own expectations of ourselves.

Most of all we should recognise that sport is like most other things in life in that it is shaped by the wider world in which it exists.

We should sometimes remember that David Beckham wasn't always a narcissistic celebrity butterfly. There was a time, before he was engulfed by showbiz values, when he was a hard-working young footballer of notable talent and ambition that was extravagantly fulfilled on the football field in the red shirt of Manchester United.

Sport, let's face it, is a magnet for both the best and the worst of the human spirit and if we douse it in hero worship and grotesque wealth, if profiteers are allowed to plunder its riches and pervert its spirit, and if one of its greatest institutions, the Olympic Games, is made to look powerless before the machinations of coaches and chemists without conscience, we should sometimes be more careful where we lay the blame.

The men and women who play sport, we were reminded in the MCG yesterday, have a capacity for hurting and caring and loving like any other section of humanity and sometimes, when the cause is striking enough, when they are put on their best behaviour by the force of circumstances, so many of them indeed rise superbly to the occasion.

We were also reminded of what they can do for our often otherwise humdrum existence in the course of one day's work.

Anyone who has seen Lara, who shook off the effects of jetlag to produce a brisk 50 yesterday, anywhere near the top of his game has something to keep forever. Yet so much of the prime of Lara's career has been conducted under a fierce and often critical spotlight. Wilful, self-indulgent, negligent of his supreme gifts . . . these are some of the criticisms.

But then you think of the force of his talent and his commitment which carried him so far from his modest, wood-built little house on the road up from Port of Spain. You hear his mother, sitting beside what used to be the family's most treasured possession, a Singer sewing machine, talking about how one of his brothers fashioned a bat for the talented toddler and how he could hit unripe oranges over the neighbourhood rooftops.

In one sweep of the eye yesterday we could see our debt to one sport and one group of young men.

We could see the pride of the controversy-racked Muttiah Muralitharan as he walked back on to the cricket field where nine years ago all his prospects in life, his chances of doing something to lift his family above the merest existence, were put in doubt when he was no-balled seven times. In the past the Aussie crowd had given Muralitharan the hardest of times but yesterday they applauded him warmly. He came from the heart of the tsunami tragedy, doing that which he does best and with more practical success than he could ever hope for back at home in Sri Lanka at his relief work.

The beaten Asian captain, Ganguly, was for once able to bury the strongest of his competitive instincts. On any day, even this one, loaded with so much significance beyond the column of win and loss, we knew that Ganguly would have ached to match the regal run-getting of the Australian captain of the winning Rest of the World team, Ricky Ponting, who effortlessly swept past the 150 mark.

But Ganguly agreed: "Though we would have liked to win the game it really doesn't matter. We all know what we are here for . . . it is a cause, and that is the most important thing. I hope we can raise as much money in our next game next month."

Kumar Sangakkara, the Sri Lankan wicketkeeper, said: "All through the day you couldn't take your mind off the people back home. I'd like to think this will do a lot for the whole region."

Steve Waugh, the great captain of Australia, was in charge of the Rest of the World team, and when he said it was an uplifting experience he didn't speak as a man new to the rawness of life beyond the cricket boundary. No one travelled more intensely in the tunnel of competition than Waugh, but when the battle was over he did more than go back to his hotel room and plug in the video machine. In India, the land of beauty and magic and pain, he came under the spell of the heirs of Mother Teresa, and when he put down his cricket bat he knew that a bigger game was just beginning.

Waugh said that he would be flying to India later this week. He has business there, and some of it is the kind of selfless work that we do not associate with mega sports stars in the 21st century.

It was something to think about as Ponting and Chris Cairns, the boisterous Kiwi, flailed sixes and Shane Warne, the former sun-bleached beach boy, turned his sorcerer's arm; something to feed into the stereotype of a world of sport shut off from the realities of a wider world.

What we had, more than anything, was a small but priceless insight into the value of sport, its power to lift and, so vitally at times, to distract. In

Melbourne, though, it has not been about the business of distraction. It has been saying that sport in the end does not have a life of its own. It cannot – or it least should not, as it did recently in Zimbabwe so shockingly – operate as though the real world doesn't exist.

Sport is part of that world and to a hugely important degree. As well as controversy and dismay, it has the power to provoke joy and excitement and sometimes even more than a touch of wonderment.

"Whatever you achieve in sport," says Steve Waugh, "when something like the tsunami happens, you know where you are – and what you owe." Yesterday, no one could doubt it, sport's account was in splendid order.

SELF-BELIEF FUELS ASCENT OF
STRAUSS THE MARVEL

Published: 15 January 2005

Nasser Hussain, no less, now speaks of Andrew Strauss as a potential England captain and it is not hard to imagine the clucking of agreement in the Long Room.

The boy, after all, is phenomenal. But then it is also true that as the level of praise threatens to leap off the chart – quite inevitably and deservedly as he tucks in behind the legendary Don Bradman and George Headley in the all-time league table of colossal first impacts on Test cricket – the English game is still required to answer the question that just won't go away.

How is it that Strauss, who is of course not a boy but a 27-year-old in the prime of his sportsman's life, had to wait so long to show what he could do at the highest level?

Did he simply burst brilliantly from his chrysalis that day at Lord's when England turned to him – without warning or planning – after Michael Vaughan suffered the misadventure of injury in the nets, or was his emergence part of the English cricket masterplan that the Australian captain Steve Waugh said a few years ago was an absolute prerequisite of any reappearance at the top of the world game?

We know the answer well enough. We know how much fledgling talent has perished in England over the last few decades and if we are ever forgetful of this we need only think of the haunted face of another captain of Middlesex, Mark Ramprakash.

Ramprakash announced a sweeter talent than Strauss's, and at an earlier age, but then we watched him suffer on and off the big stage for so long. You may say this was nobody's fault but his own. However, it is also a fact that he never enjoyed the certainties that Strauss has now won for himself.

One part of the problem, no doubt, was his brooding, self-doubting nature; another, it has to be suspected, was the old club environment and game-by-game judgement in which he found himself. If circumstances had allowed Ramprakash to bed himself into Test cricket, if his talent had flowered as so many shrewd judges believed it might with sufficient faith and patience, would he too have made a mark on history in the way of his successor?

None of this touches the brilliance of Strauss's achievements in scarcely more than half a year. He has taken his chances so well, and is ridding himself of flaws so relentlessly, like a sunny version of the young Geoff Boycott or Nick Faldo, that no one can argue with the assessment of Hussain.

Yet there is that other worry. How can Strauss have come so far so quickly without inviting questions about the waste that has gone on before and might just happen again in talent less securely housed than his own?

The wonder of Strauss is his marvellous temperament. When he was selected by England he said he was honoured and pleased but that he hadn't become a desperate shell of yearning. If the call hadn't come, he said briskly, he would probably quite soon have devoted himself more to the City of London and, doubtless, made himself quite a lot of money. He is, wondrously in this sporting age, a hubris-free zone. When he is out his instinct, however many runs are on the board, is to curse rather than congratulate himself and Hussain, tellingly, reveals that when at the start of the South African tour he whispered that there were maybe a few areas of weakness that might just be worked on, Strauss replied, in effect: "It's sorted."

It may just be significant that Strauss's character was moulded in Johannesburg and Sydney before the family move to London. Perhaps the competitive instinct benefited from some early honing. It is a detail, of course; Graeme Hick, whose youthful talent blazed across Zimbabwe, served possibly the longest ever English apprenticeship, but at Test level his flaws were played upon to devastating effect.

For the moment, Strauss looks as bombproof as any cricketer in the world, but then he knows as well as anybody that there are many trials ahead, not least when the Australians arrive here in the summer. That he has shown a superb aptitude for such an investigation of ability and character is being correctly acknowledged. However, not the least of his attributes appears to be a willingness to live no further into the future than from one day's work to another.

It was a concept that was always elusive for the gifted but flawed Ramprakash. After scoring a brilliant and potentially breakthrough century in the West Indies, he revealed how he had gone into the shower after his innings and felt a surge of relief. "As the water poured over me," he said, "I felt that this century was something I would always have – something that could never be taken away. I felt that all my doubts were being washed away."

Strauss is not likely to make a similar miscalculation and this is perhaps his greatest glory. Significantly, it is one over which he is entitled to congratulate himself – quite exclusively.

SEA OF NOBLE SWEAT PROVES ENGLAND'S CHARACTER

Published: 18 January 2005

It was perfect that Matthew Hoggard should be in at the kill. In the end, it was character that was going to do it and no one displayed more of it through the draining hours at the Wanderers stadium than the thatch-haired Yorkshireman – not even the South African captain Graeme Smith, who despite being warned off by the doctors went out to play a great innings with what must have seemed like an entire symphony orchestra playing in his head.

The requirement of Hoggard the infantryman was quite different. He just had to keep going, delivering more overs than any of his fast-bowling team-mates and digging deeper than anyone in the course of a superb Test match.

No one in the ranks of England's resurrection does it better. Maybe he isn't covered in the Bothamesque stardust of big Andy Flintoff, who brilliantly intervened when South Africa were just beginning to believe in the possibility of one of the greatest escapes in the history of Test cricket.

Certainly, Hoggard has never been lifted so high as Steve Harmison, who went to South Africa under-bowled and thus under-prepared for the five-Test challenge against opponents who may have lost a lot of talent over recent years but have not forgotten how to fight right up to the last rounds. But as Harmison limped on and off the field these last few days, it was Hoggard who kept pounding away in search of victory.

Yesterday, as the England captain Michael Vaughan faced the horror of seeing the prize slip through his fingers as it did in Durban – and went off to the pavilion to consult with his coach and guru Duncan Fletcher – it was Hoggard's kind of work, his type of challenge.

When it was over he could gather his figures together and carry them through the rest of his cricketing life so that whenever the going gets tough, when his captain tosses him the ball with a pleading look, he can tell himself that he has been to this sort of place before – and that he has emerged as triumphantly and as decisively as any Yorkshireman since Jim Laker, the off-spinner from the gritty environs of Bradford who ransacked the Australians by claiming 19 of their wickets at Old Trafford nearly 50 years ago.

Hoggard's statistics in Johannesburg may not have been so dramatic as

Laker's 19 for 90 in Manchester, but 12 for 205, with seven for 61 in 18.3 overs in the second innings, was so much more than scrupulously honest toil.

It was the work of a pure fighter who produced the best of his talent when it mattered most to his team.

In Hoggard's native county there is a hierachy of great and ageing cricketers who believe that for one reason or another they saw long ago the best of the game in which they became so distinguished.

They shake their heads often in their belief that the old county no longer has the instinct or the culture to produce world-beaters. Michael Vaughan is, of course, building a formidable body of work as England's captain and he came up through league cricket in Sheffield, but he was born in Lancashire of all places. Darren Gough engaged some of the old enthusiasm for a while but then he went off to live in the south and there was a feeling that he pursued his own celebrity profile a little too enthusiastically.

But who could point to a flaw in the profile of Matthew Hoggard, born in Leeds and as dour as a frosty morning on Ilkley Moor, as he slaved for an English victory over the last five days? Not Brian Close, the former Yorkshire and England captain, who once remonstrated with a fellow fielder who failed to catch a ball that had come rocketing off his own bald head and who merely giggled when shocked observers viewed the tattoo of bruises he collected from Charlie Griffith and Wesley Hall one day at Lord's. Not Ray Illingworth, the ultimately shrewd England captain who beat Australia in their own backyard. Not the once brilliant but endlessly vain fastman Freddie Trueman. Not even the ultimate critic of the modern game, Geoff Boycott, who was recently suggesting his mother had displayed better footwork than Vaughan.

Hoggard doesn't do much cricketing in Yorkshire under the terms of his England contract, but they know him well enough and have always been quick to recognise him as a worthy ambassador of their particular view of life. It is a hard one, hard on themselves and hard on the rest of the world and, in Johannesburg, Hoggard made relentless demands on himself.

Yes, there were some other massive contributions, notably by Andrew Strauss in the first innings and Marcus Trescothick in the second, but it was Hoggard who delivered the most consistent evidence that there is indeed a tough and winning streak in this new England.

As in all the Tests of this extraordinary series, there were many moments which utterly changed the momentum and perhaps yesterday the sight of Jacques Kallis, South Africa's anchorman, going with nothing against his name was the surest indicator that England would force the win. However, when Trescothick swooped to take the catch despite the desperate and ill-considered late attempt by the wicketkeeper Geraint Jones, we again had something vital to think beyond the euphoria.

The fact is that Jones is in the team not because he is the best English wicketkeeper. Sitting watching was Chris Read, a vastly superior operator behind the stumps but one who in the opinion of Fletcher is less likely to add a few more runs with a bat in his hand. When you consider the value of Kallis's dismissal, and how it was endangered, this is an argument that surely shrivels before your eyes.

More importantly, it would no doubt have done so in those of Matthew Hoggard, if his magnificent delivery had not met with its proper reward. This, however, is no doubt a debate for another day.

For the moment, Hoggard is one part of Yorkshire and England utterly free of angst. It was simply washed away in a sea of noble sweat.

McGRATH REDEFINES HIS ART ON DAY OF STUPENDOUS TEST CRICKET

Published: 22 July 2005

On a day of stupendous cricket and theatre it was possible to produce a sworn affidavit saying that elderly members of the MCC had been seen dancing in the Long Room.

But that was when England's young bowling Turks were strutting around Lord's as though 18 years of Ashes cricket under the heel of Australia was officially at an end.

It was before Glenn McGrath, aged 35, reminded everyone in the home of the game that there is nothing more thrilling – no partisan advantage for your team, no winning bet – than an old champion near the end of his competitive days finding the best of himself. McGrath, the hammer of the English for so long, made the Long Room celebrations as premature as they were inappropriate.

He defined the art of the thinking man's pace bowler. He placed the ball with an unerring, almost uncanny accuracy; he coaxed out every nuance of movement on a wicket which was supposed to be sun-dried of its menace before one of the most extraordinary passages of one-man dominance in the long and tumultuous history of Test cricket.

McGrath's details will stand in long memory – 31 balls, two runs, five wickets – but they will never be able to convey fully the feel of his performance, the authority and the majesty of it.

He was so deadly, so all-consuming, that long before he was stood down by his grateful captain Ricky Ponting, after 13 overs, those Long Room antics seemed to belong to another day, even another lifetime.

This was a career tragedy for Steve Harmison, nine years McGrath's junior and for most of the day a bowler who might reasonably have believed that he had utterly supplanted the old warrior in the world's bowling élite.

Harmison, such a miserable figure at the end of the tour of South Africa last winter, grew to huge proportions on the magnificent Lord's stage. He tattooed the aristocracy of Australian batting, Justin Langer, Ricky Ponting and Matthew Hayden, after such a roughing up not one of them was able to produce anything like the usual command.

Harmison, with admirable assistance from his lieutenants Simon Jones, Matthew Hoggard and Andy Flintoff, claimed most of the spoils with 5 for 43 and his own period of personal rampage, four wickets for seven runs in 14 balls.

The consequence was the most dramatic shift in the balance of Ashes power since Mike Gatting's England team last won a series in 1987.

The Aussies, with Shane Warne providing some of the most profitable resistance and finishing second top scorer with a mere 28, were shot out for 190. That's when the Long Room began to resemble an upper crust version of the annual barn dance at the Lazy Q. But who could know that Glenn McGrath was preparing one of his ultimate performances?

McGrath stunned England's front-line batting with a series of perfectly delivered blows, and suddenly there was the terrible spectre of another Ashes annihilation, one more painful than most that had gone before because of the huge weight of expectation that surrounded yesterday's first day.

Marcus Trescothick and Andrew Strauss, the giant of last summer and winter, were consumed in the slips; Michael Vaughan, apparently the world-class banker of English batsmanship, was shot out for three, the young hope Ian Bell could only chop the ball on to his wicket and Flintoff, towards whom we so often offer the encouragement that he may just be another Ian Botham, was so bamboozled by the old Australian fox he watched the uprooting of his off-stump.

This was an impact guaranteed to astonish even the most experienced denizens of the Test match jungle – a certainty readily confirmed by former England captains Graham Gooch and Mike Gatting.

Gooch, who was in the twilight of a great career when the young Australian was flexing his bowling muscles and developing his edge, said: "That was an astounding effort . . . I'm not sure I've ever seen anything quite so perfect from an ageing cricketer. He used everything at his disposal. He certainly changed the match. He may have changed the summer."

Gatting, the old conqueror of Australia, who was the victim of the outrageous arrival of Warne in Ashes cricket when he fell to the impossible arc of the most famous leg-spin delivery in the history of the game, was equally mesmerised by the perfection of McGrath's efforts.

"Yes, I was stunned when Warne produced that delivery . . . but no more so than today watching Glenn McGrath. The scenario couldn't have been more favourable for England. You had the sense that at last the pattern might just be broken, with the sun quietening down the pitch. Now McGrath has questioned all that optimism."

For England it was a day when hope had grown quite relentlessly. If there was an early tendency, particularly by Harmison, to send balls down the legside, there was also a compensating fire and optimism. It was impossible not to believe that there had been a real belief in the England dressing room that this was indeed the time to bring down the great Australian cricket empire.

Harmison's aggression, the jaunty confidence of Vaughan, fed on two years of growing success as he deployed his troops, might just have been the prelude to such achievement.

However, McGrath intruded into the plans with an unbreakable force. As one victim after another fell to his guile, the change in the Australian team's body language was extraordinary to see. When he claimed another victim, his team-mates seemed to run to him not so much in celebration as deliverance.

In the end, English joy had dwindled to the point of cheering the 58-stand resistance of Kevin Pietersen and Geraint Jones.

Before his debut the young Pietersen had talked of the new surge of English confidence – and his team-mate Hoggard had speculated that McGrath might be on the slow ride home to retirement. He said: "It will be tough for Glenn McGrath, and it will be interesting to see if he is still the world-class performer he was."

Thus provoked, one headline screamed that the Aussies in general, and McGrath in particular, were "Past It". If you happened to be English it was worrying to read that. It provoked visions of nightmare Australian reaction. It prompted fears that some of them, especially the older ones, might just be sufficiently irritated to put in a special effort. Naturally, Glenn McGrath did. He produced one of the great performances of his life. Even more remarkably, he stopped the dancing in the Long Room.

MERLIN OF SPIN BRINGS CHARISMATIC MENACE TO MUGGING AT LORD'S

Published: 25 July 2005

However hard the rain fell yesterday it could not wash away the extraordinary impact of Shane Warne here over the past few days, nor the supreme achievement of his team-mate, and the man of the match, Glenn McGrath.

McGrath was a classic warrior hero, leading the charge to the 239-run victory and claiming match figures of 9 for 82. He goes on the honours board here again for his five wickets in the first innings – a distinction that will now almost certainly elude his fellow 35-year-old Warne. But then some things can't be written on honours boards. You have to feel them as well as read them, and what you felt here this past week was that every time Warne touched the ball, alchemy was in the air.

It was not a wisp of it, but a whirlwind of both menace and charisma which will surely survive a late buffeting from his young Hampshire team-mate, Kevin Pietersen, whose undefeated 64 in the second innings was another reminder that here at least was one Englishman – sorry, that should be one South African playing for England – not paralysed by the presence of the Australian old guard.

Warne, pursuing a fifth second-innings wicket with some passion, bowled a bouncer at Pietersen when he refused to run the single that would put the England No 11, Simon Jones, on strike. So Warne sent one whistling past his young friend's head. It was a case of "no hard feelings, mate, but try a little of this".

Watching Warne, even at this late stage of his career, is to be overwhelmed by the sense of a sporting giant, a champion who, for all the indiscretions off the field, has never mistaken mere celebrity for any adequate substitute for the awesome levels of performance that have always been attached to his name.

He faces now the probability, if not the certainty, that this was his last Test match at Lord's and that he came out of it with six wickets and so much of his old aura was a hugely significant factor in Australia's dazzling reassertion of their status as the world's best cricket team.

He did it without the full range of his old powers. He has now – rather than the complete Merlin kit – formidable leg-spin, the shooting spinner, and the odd trick still to be found at the bottom of his well-travelled knapsack.

But then he has never needed to pack the most formidable asset of all. It is something he carries around with the permanence of his diamond earrings. It is the pride of a champion, an ageing lion who will retreat to the cricketing bush when the last of his powers are done.

Here they have been vibrant enough to render utterly impudent the pre-Test remarks of Matthew Hoggard, who had a match-winning performance of great commitment in the recent tour of South Africa but generally has no reason to address either Warne, or the other object of disparagement, McGrath, without doffing his cap.

Instead, Hoggard said that it would be interesting to see if McGrath and Warne were trading on anything more than their reputations. Interesting? Presumably interesting as in back-alley muggings, or showing jack-high against a royal flush when all the money is on the table. It was entirely appropriate that first McGrath, then Warne, chose the alleyway in the middle of the world's most famous cricket ground as the point of ambush.

Before the brief, almost formal rain-delayed action, Warne filled in some of the time with a brilliantly coherent account of his professional priorities.

Yes, he told the television audience, he had been through some of the worst of times. The collapse of his family life had been painful – there was no denying that – but in the pain and the dislocation, and maybe some considerable self-recrimination, it had been clear that for him to let his cricket slide would be the ultimate defeat. He could not let the cricket go because it was the best of him, the least complicated thing he ever did.

It means that in the age of sporting hype, of vast contracts based on image rights, Warne is the shining exception to the rule that celebrity can corrupt the competitive nature and absolute celebrity can do it absolutely.

Warne has preserved, quite superbly in all his teeming and potentially destructive circumstances, the essence of his being. He has remained one of the great competitors, a champion who can put aside everything that besieges him when it comes to play.

In boxing they say that fighters fight, it is their most natural condition, and it seems that in the case of Warne it is true that great cricketers play cricket of the highest order when all else is in disarray.

At Lord's, the sheer endurance of Warne has perhaps been his most dramatic quality, especially in the light of the angst-ridden retirement from international cricket of one of his more obdurate opponents, Graham Thorpe.

Like Warne, Thorpe has known domestic turmoil, and several times it brought the Surrey left-hander to a point of deep professional crisis. Warne has marched on, rarely more impressively than in the past few days.

Yesterday he said that he couldn't disguise the difficulties of his life, but what do you do? Do you throw everything away? No, you don't, you go to play as fighters go out to fight. You work, as Warne did for two hours on the eve of this Test with his coach, Terry Jenner – and you do little fine-tuning on the morning of the game. You go into a game knowing pretty much precisely what you can do, and what he did, on Saturday afternoon especially, was cut away any beginnings of hope that England might just make a serious effort to reach the winning target of 420 runs.

He grew before our eyes as he mesmerised, and then dismissed, such key England batsmen as Marcus Trescothick, Ian Bell and Andrew Flintoff. The more he dominated, the more the folly of Hoggard was exposed. It was exceptional cricket – and remarkable spirit, and most of all it said that the great sportsmen have about them something that can never be mistaken when the important action begins.

England came to Lord's with a light appreciation of this old truth, and they paid a terrible price. They thought they were too strong for old men such as Warne and McGrath, and yesterday they learned they were wrong. They were made to feel like boys in a man's world – at least we have to hope so.

FLINTOFF SMASHES HIS WAY TO A PLACE IN THE PANTHEON OF TRUE CRICKETING GREATS

Published: 08 August 2005

Had it been Andrew Flintoff rather than Steve Harmison delivering the decisive ball here on the sunlit, unforgettable high noon of English cricket, we would have been engulfed by a last flight of fantasy. Instead we just had to settle for a jewel of reality, a victory over Australia that could hardly have had a finer margin . . . or greater significance.

The second Test at Edgbaston was epic in almost every possible way and so whatever else the big man from Lancashire achieves in his explosive career it is hard to believe that he will surpass the influence he exerted in the most important English triumph in 18 years of Ashes cricket.

Australia's captain Ricky Ponting framed Flintoff's effort quite perfectly. "It was stand-and-deliver cricket from start to finish," he said, and what did that make Flintoff? It made him Dick Turpin and Ned Kelly rolled into one. As a batsman he was herculean. As a bowler he was awash with adrenaline and bad intentions. Indeed, he was so good, so overpowering in both his talent and his will, he took away any fear in applying the B-word burden that has bedevilled every aspiring English all-rounder through all the barren years.

Yes, of all the splendid things he was over three days and slightly less than two hours of play that did nothing less than define the often savage beauty and intrigue of Test cricket, Flintoff was Bothamesque in the scale of his effect.

Even now, with the milestone of a truly great performance gloriously passed, Flintoff is unlikely to warm to the comparison. He is on the record saying that his ambition is to be the first Flintoff, not the second Botham, but sometimes sporting history leaps out from the mothballs to make an unanswerable point.

Here it said that Flintoff has the supreme gift of a Botham and all the great all-rounders.

He can shape the mood and the outline of cricket's ultimate investigator of the highest talent, the Test match, and that he did it to this extraordinary one to such a degree means that he has set himself a standard of quite awesome proportions.

In the first innings he galvanised England with outrageous sixes in his 68, in the second he added with Simon Jones the 50 runs that stacked the odds hugely against the Australians, and then, when those odds were met with great control and confidence, ripped them apart. The deliveries that swept away Justin Langer, Australia's anchorman opener, and Ponting were the kind of shattering blows that in a heavyweight title fight announce that one man is heading inexorably to victory.

Another dramatic measuring of his impact here: only one member of the world champion Australian team was a serious rival for man of one of the greatest Test matches of all time. That was the working legend Shane Warne, who with Brett Lee and Michael Kasprowicz took Australia so agonisingly close to what would have been the most staggering Ashes recovery since Botham and Bob Willis struck back at Headingley in 1981.

Warne produced fiendish deliveries as he attempted to fill some of the void left by Glenn McGrath's mishap in the warm-up last Thursday morning. He was the supreme example of Australia's defiance of defeat and, as at Lord's in the first Test, he exerted a mesmerising power over key England batsmen. But not Flintoff. He was untameable. He was on his own, a wild and untrammelled spirit that was accompanied by the power to execute with deadly precision. He was a force of nature, a whirlwind presence.

Without that power, the improvement of English mettle from the first Test would no doubt have served them well. Kevin Pietersen showed again that his talent and his nerve come from an extremely deep well. Ashley Giles abandoned his training as a potential agony aunt and reverted to his role as hard-headed pro with conspicuous success. Given the scrappiness of much of his work behind the stumps, Geraint Jones showed stunning resolve to take the match-winning catch.

Harmison claimed that wicket, and produced a spurt of brilliantly conceived deliveries to remove the dangerous Michael Clarke at the end of the third day. But would England have fashioned this most vital, historic victory without the momentum Flintoff supplied at such hugely pivotal moments? It is hard to imagine.

Yesterday, with the victory gathered in under the most oppressive pressure, Flintoff admitted that the meaning of the defeat, and the nature of it, at Lord's had bitten into him deeply. He went home in a mood of the sharpest reflection and self-examination. If England had any chance of the Ashes, it had to come from the willingness of the players to look at their own performances and maybe some of their attitudes.

The results of such scourging were luminous here. This was an England team which refused to collapse, which was ready to fight to the last wicket, the last shot, and Ponting was generous in his reaction. "It was a Test match in every sense of the term," said the Australian captain, "and England deserve praise for the effort. We got close, but not close enough."

What he didn't say – but you could read it easily enough in his eyes and the body language of his players – was that few Australian teams will have carried quite the motivational baggage that will be taken to Old Trafford for the third Test on Thursday. The English victory may have been by a mere two runs, but in the end that was an insignificant detail. Indeed, never had the old mantra of the great American football coach Vince Lombardi rang truer than when England captain Michael Vaughan asked his men for one last push at midday yesterday. Lombardi told his players that winning wasn't the most important thing, it was the only thing.

Vaughan confirmed that such a sentiment blazed at the centre of his thoughts as Warne, Lee and Kasprowicz inched towards their target and a crowd which for three whole days had been in a fever of excitement became clammy with tension.

Nodding soberly, Vaughan agreed that there would probably have been no coming back from a second straight defeat, and especially in what would have been such demoralising circumstances. Winning, however it was finally achieved, was the difference between belief and a sad resignation that perhaps the other team were simply too strong in both their range of talent and their conviction.

Now England believe. They believe that maybe they can shake off their chains at the highest level. You could see some of that in the ferocious hugging of Harmison when the final Australian wicket fell. It was more than mere celebration of a great victory. It was a release from sport's most demoralising fear, the one that says whatever you do you will not find a way to win.

At Old Trafford the Australians will no doubt produce everything they have to reimpose such pessimism. They will plunder their collective memory for every edge. Every weapon in one of sport's most formidable armouries will be brought out. But for once they will not carry the old guarantees. The problem is that England do now truly believe – in themselves, and, most of all, in Andrew Flintoff.

AUSTRALIA SHOW HOW CHAMPIONS LOSE AS FLINTOFF GIVES LESSON IN RIGHT WAY TO WIN

Published: 09 August 2005

One of the more spectacular sights in the wake of Australia's astonishing Test defeat was Merv Hughes dining in an Italian restaurant on Sunday night.

His huge moustache, never more beautifully groomed, would have been the pride of an officer of the Hussars. Generally, and it has to reported that this was the case with most of his countryman, he looked about as cowed as the time in Melbourne when, having been described as a "fat bus conductor" by the abrasive Javed Miandad, he unfurled a killer ball and then chirped "Ticket please, mate." That is an old sledging story but so is the point.

There is rarely such a thing as a beaten Australian cricketer. He is merely temporarily inconvenienced and if we had doubts about this they were surely expunged by the epic resilience of Shane Warne, Brett Lee and Michael Kasprowicz on Sunday morning. It was this that made the triumph of Michael Vaughan's England team so especially heart-warming. At Lord's they surrendered. At Edgbaston they held their nerve, and they did it against cricket's most natural-born competitors.

In the two-run defeat Australia came so close to a victory that would have scorched the bones of Vaughan's men. They also reminded us how real champions lose. They resent the idea so much it is almost as though the worry is that it might just contaminate their blood.

England's achievement – and it was a stunning one – was to match that intensity in a Test match that had breathtaking dimensions. After Lord's the gut instinct here was to bring in an Australian supremo of English cricket, someone to lay down a new set of values – or maybe re-install an old one. It was a theory which retained a certain viability right up to the moment of England's victory, at which point the author of it had a flicker of apprehension that he might just be hauled off to the Tower and have his head stuck on a spike. We will know about the permanent nature, or otherwise, of England's resistance to the Australian way of playing cricket in the early going of the third Test that starts at Old Trafford on Thursday morning, but in the meantime we have reason to celebrate more than one unforgettable victory.

We have so many images of a high summer of English sport being ignited quite superbly. Perhaps the best of all was the sight of the conqueror, Andrew Flintoff, bending down to comfort the disconsolate Lee. That inevitably provoked a comparison with the behavioural patterns of football, where in Cardiff the Premiership had its dress rehearsal at the Community Shield game. Before the match Chelsea's José Mourinho and Arsenal's Arsène Wenger dazzled the television screen with something which eerily hinted at warm respect, even regard. It took the form of a handshake, but how soon will it be remembered as something closer to a Judas kiss? Certainly the bickering started soon enough.

Cricket, despite the glory of Edgbaston, is far from perfect. Passions have already run high with three Tests to go. Simon Jones was fined for his gesture of dismissal to Matthew Hayden and by all accounts some of the sledging has lost nothing in ferocity. However, when the battle was over there was no shortfall of respect. Flintoff made his gesture to Lee at a time when a football superstar would almost certainly have been running to the crowd – and the cameras – for a photo op of glory. Later the big Lancastrian confirmed the sense of a young man perfectly in tune with himself and his game. Some of his words may sound a little artless, but they are no less appealing for that.

Both captains spoke in a way that rang entirely true. Vaughan admitted that defeat would have been catastrophic for his team's morale, and that he had feared that a precious moment was slipping away. Australia's Ponting faced up to the fact that it was a killing mistake to put England in to bat. However, after praising the victors, he said he expected a massive response from his team. The margin of defeat was so slight that it dramatically reinforced the need to fight for every run, every little advantage. The third Test was still four nights away, but it was as though it had already started.

The gift to cricket, and its highest form, the Test game, is the greatest that any sport can receive. It is the fine edge of genuine competition, the uncertainty that enveloped Edgbaston as a physical presence. When you felt that you also thought of the claim of Peter Kenyon, the money man of Roman Abramovich, that the Premiership winners would come from a "bunch of one". It was a statement guaranteed to fill anyone who cares about sport with repugnance, and when you thought that it could come from the chief executive of the football champions of England it was to redouble the level of disgust. Watching the second Test, and anticipating the third, amount to a thrilling release. Cricket's most pressing need is maybe a tranquilliser or two. Football's? It might just try a little fumigation.

VAUGHAN'S CENTURY ADDS TO DAY OF ASHES MYTHOLOGY

Published: 12 August 2005

When Michael Vaughan is very old he may be asked to name the time when he finally knew he was the man destined to win back the Ashes for England. If it happens, the chances are he will say Thursday 11 August, 2005 – the day when a summer of trial turned into one of quite dazzling possibilities and when it seemed he could do no wrong

How immune was he to the worst of cricket fate? Well, perhaps he could say no more than that he eluded even the fatally brilliant traps laid by the greatest spin bowler in the history of cricket.

Shane Warne, inevitably it seemed, claimed his 600th Test wicket when he had Marcus Trescothick caught behind by Adam Gilchrist. It was the kind of mesmerising strike that has carried Warne so far beyond the partisan barricades of this historic series.

Old Trafford has been in awe of Warne ever since he produced the leg spin of the ages to dismiss Mike Gatting here 12 years ago, and now the old stadium rose to salute the fullness of his reign as cricket's principal sorcerer.

But if Vaughan nodded his support of the tribute, there was no doubt he was also making his own accommodation with cricket history, and for a while there was apparently nothing to stop him. Not Warne. Not the legendary Glenn McGrath. Not a single breeze of malignance on the hot summer day.

Not until 5pm, that is. Not until the gods finally convened to say that enough was enough. Vaughan could scarcely complain. Long before lofting Australia's occasional left-arm spinner Simon Katich down the throat of Glenn McGrath at wide long on – a shot that seemed utterly irrelevant to the grand design that in the end he fashioned so brilliantly – he just might have been excused for believing he could stroll unaided across the nearby Manchester Ship Canal.

The England captain was 166 not out at the time, the prime contributor to the potential stranglehold represented by a total of 290 for 2, and he must have been in some confusion about which point of good fortune to celebrate most.

There was certainly no lack of choice. Strategically, the winning of his first toss of the coin in three was a hugely significant factor. If Ricky Ponting, the

Aussie captain, had prevailed yet again – and been able to hold back McGrath and Brett Lee as crack troops poised just behind the front line after their astonishing recovery – there could well have been a grave English sense that the momentum of their victory at Edgbaston last Sunday was already beginning to dissipate.

Instead, Vaughan was able to burst out of his individual batting crisis – the shadow over the amazing fightback that levelled the series at 1-1 in Edgbaston – with a string of beautifully struck boundaries. But before that breakout, the surge of more confident body language and the subliminal sense that a storm of confusion and doubt had passed, Vaughan had to face a few more battles with the demons of his summer.

He was fencing somewhat tentatively with McGrath and Warne, and on a mere 41, when the worst of those torments passed. McGrath sent down a delivery of his most finely measured menace and Vaughan stood in a fever of doubt. The ball flew off his bat and into the reach of Adam Gilchrist, but not only did the Australian wicketkeeper fail to gather it in, he also made sure it would not pass into the normally secure hands of Warne.

Vaughan, no doubt responding a little glassily, was then comprehensively bowled by McGrath – a shattering blow that was relieved only by the no-ball signal of Steve Bucknor.

The England captain might not have been broken, but there was no question he had been undermined, as he had been for much of this summer of high tension, which had yielded to one of the world's most outstanding batsman the miserable total of 42 runs in four innings and a top score of 24. Now, though, Vaughan's reaction was one that might indeed shape the course of the series, despite Australia's late recovery.

At 341 for 5, England, with the force of Andrew Flintoff still to be applied, are still in a position of some advantage, but as it is measured now the debt to their captain becomes ever greater.

Vaughan had one more successful joust with benign fate when he was on 141. Warne forced him into a rushed shot and Matthew Hayden should have pounced at slip. Vaughan was serene in his belief that his day was to be untouched by the merest hint of a setback, and he had good reason for this.

When he sent that irresolute drive into the hands of McGrath he could believe that Australia had lost fresh ground after the crushing disappointment of defeat at Edgbaston. He had come into a critical situation as a captain and an individual cricketer and he had ridden his luck magnificently.

That is a trick he will now commend to his audience that distant day when he may be interrogated about how it was that the battle for the Ashes was turned. Of course, there is a vital element to make the most of your good fortune. You have to seize the moment and you have to believe in your talent. Vaughan had no reason to doubt himself when it became clear that this was a day which was prepared to anoint him. It was his fourth century against the Australians, the sixth since becoming captain, and the 15th of his Test career.

In that battery of statistics there was one diamond of a fact. It was that this could well prove to have been the most significant day in his cricketing life.

Of course, there is so much more cricket to be played and the Australians had recovered a degree of competitiveness before the end of play. They had been facing the prospect of a long and bitter stint in the field but they were alive again.

Vaughan's comfort is that, as never before, he had taken the chances that came to him.

WAS THIS THE FIRST DAY OF NEW WORLD ORDER, ONE WITH ENGLAND ON TOP?

Published: 13 August 2005

A thought that probably should be suppressed right up to the moment it is written up in the sky as the most unadorned fact finally burst into the late afternoon sunshine here yesterday. It was that the great Australian cricket empire might indeed be passing into history.

You do not rush into a theory like this. That would be too impudent, too risky, given all that has happened in the last 18 years of Ashes history.

But then sometimes there is evidence on a cricket field, as there is in a boxing ring or at a football pitch or an athletics track, that is just too compelling to ignore. In it, you see – just maybe – a moment of fate, a flashpoint of destiny.

It was hard not to see the dismissal of Ricky Ponting in that light when a delivery from Simon Jones flew off the splice of his bat and was gathered in almost nonchalantly by Ian Bell, one of the new wave of English cricket, at backward point. It was the first ball after tea and perhaps something a little more. Maybe it was the first ball of the new world order of cricket . . . the first ball of the new English cricket empire.

Outrageous, premature jingoism? That is the worry with Shane Warne and Glenn McGrath still plainly able to draw on the last of their genius and with batsmen like Ponting, Justin Langer, Damien Martyn, Adam Gilchrist and the young, but currently stricken hope, Michael Clarke yet to touch anything like the kind of form and inspiration that has marked their extraordinary careers.

There are, we have to remember, two Tests to go when we get to the end of this one which, if the first two are anything like reliable precedents, still has a minimum of half a dozen twists and turns left to go. But the evidence is more than fleeting and the weight of our suspicions has accumulated significantly in the last few weeks. Irresistibly, they came roaring into the open when Ponting once again crumbled at a crucial moment of this ultimately charged Ashes summer.

His latest failure with the bat – he was shot out by Andrew Flintoff when the pressure rolled into its first major crescendo at Edgbaston in the second, lost Test – would have been demoralising enough for his team, and his own leadership, had it come in isolation. But of course it didn't. It was part of a pattern, a relentless tattoo of disappointment and exposed nerve and judgement.

When he fell again at a critical moment, Australia were teetering at 73 for 2, a first dawning crisis in the pursuit of England's first innings of 444, and it was to get so much worse for them so quickly. But it was in the fall of Ponting that all those suspicions that we might be at the end of an era came rushing to a head. Inevitably, perhaps, because for Ponting this was so much more than a difficult day at the office. It was maybe the implosion of his life's work.

No one, certainly, at either end of the cricket world had ever chased so hard, so single-mindedly, the captaincy of his nation's team. This is true despite the fact of Ponting's wild youth, when he liked to drink and to bet, particularly bet, and was never too troubled by the title of "larrikin" which the Aussies reserve for some of their bolder spirits. He saw soon enough that there were greater goals than a thick head at the bar and a bad day at the betting counter. He declared his ambition, married a lawyer and elected himself into the highest company, most strikingly becoming one of just three Australians to hit four or more double centuries. The others are Greg Chappell and the late Sir Don Bradman. Ponting came here in the spring with the superior Test batting average of 56.50, but it has been the most dangerous of summers.

He wanted to step into the footprints of his great predecessors, Allan Border and Steve Waugh. Border built the foundations of the Australian empire and Waugh developed it with a relentless insistence on absolute commitment to the cause. Waugh had certain advantages, great players in the prime of their lives and a confidence in his own decisions that came with a run of rarely broken success. For Ponting, such seamless glory is beginning to look like a worn-out fantasy. Not only has he been outbatted here, and hugely so, by England's Michael Vaughan, he has also been outcaptained.

Vaughan has led his team with vision and a hard edge of opportunism and he deserves the greatest credit. However, even at this high point of an already distinguished career, he is no doubt enough of an old pro to agree with the point made by one of his predecessors, Mike Atherton, back in the wilderness years of the nineties. When Atherton surrendered the captaincy in Antigua after an ordeal of shot and shell at the hands of Curtly Ambrose and Courtney Walsh, he said: "One of the tricks of being a good captain is having a good team." Here last night the message could hardly have been more thrilling: Vaughan may just have more than a good team. He may have one young enough, vibrant enough to touch greatness.

There were other implications in the golden dusk for English cricket as most hopes of Australian resistance were harassed and then put down. Langer, Hayden, Martyn, Simon Katich, a hero of the Australian victory in the first Test at Lord's, the one that had seemed to condemn England to another spell of subjection, and Gilchrist all massaged Australian pain with the possibility of another astonishing revival.

England were not to be diverted from what they clearly saw as their historic course, however. Vaughan switched the point of attack; he maintained his faith in Ashley Giles, whose response was a ball of impressive, almost Warne-like creativity to dismiss Martyn, and Andrew Flintoff and Jones bowled with often biting intensity.

No doubt it was too soon to write all of this in the sky, but then there was no law against the sacrilegious thought, the one that just would not go away, the one that said that the Australian empire might just be over.

STRAUSS EARNS BATTLE HONOURS FOR REFUSING TO BUCKLE IN THE WARNE ZONE

Published: 15 August 2005

Andrew Strauss – one of the few English Test cricketers who had anything left to prove at the halfway point of this tumultuous Ashes series – joined the heroes of high summer yesterday. He did it with a superb and utterly vital batting performance as England sniffed the scent of the kill.

But then within that beautifully realised innings, Strauss had another, even more dramatic achievement. First, he had to win a private battle with Shane Warne, the man who has added cult status to his record-shattering total of 603 Test wickets in the last few weeks – and this after surviving a particularly ferocious delivery from Brett Lee which landed on his helmet at slightly less than 100mph.

Warne got to within ten runs of his first Test century as the Australians fought to stay in this pivotal third Test, but in the dusk he was more a broken man than a giant of the game he has dazzled for 12 years. He was broken, at least for a little while, by Strauss.

Despite all the mesmerising work which has triggered his love-hate – but recently mostly love – relationship with the English public, Warne is not always as cuddly and engaging as a koala. Indeed, in terms of amiability, sometimes he more resembles something that slithers around out in the bush.

However, Warne's venomous side no longer appears such a dire threat to the health of Strauss's still burgeoning Test career.

The 28-year-old's most important rite of passage came here in the late afternoon when he completed his first Ashes century, and his sixth overall, as England pushed hard to break down a little more of the spirit of the Australians. Those were the statistics, at least. The harder reality was that Strauss was stepping out of one of the darker spells weaved by the world's greatest-ever spin bowler.

Warne befuddled most of the English batting in the first Test at Lord's, but particularly Strauss, who while avoiding losing his wicket to the Australian at headquarters still arrived at Edgbaston for the second Test in a somewhat vulnerable condition. This was only heightened by the fact that Warne promptly bowled him twice. Not only that, Warne applied cricket's equivalent of the evil eye. His sledging line was that Strauss had replaced the South African Darryl Cullinan as his principal victim.

The Cullinan drama played out when South Africa were still Australia's main challengers for the status of the world's number-one team. Warne's intimidation became so effective, even profound, that at one point in the battle in the back-to-back three-Test series, Warne casually asked Cullinan about the colour of the psychiatrist's couch. In fact, the South African, a fine stroke-maker, had become so depressed and worried by Warne's ascendancy that he had consulted a sports psychologist. Warne naturally threw in the dart.

At around 5pm yesterday such extreme measures became utterly redundant in the life of Andrew Strauss.

He rushed to his century by first pulling Warne for six – earlier he had inflicted the same fate on Lee – and then Glenn McGrath for four. He was underpinning his right to an opener's role in the team making such purposeful strides towards upsetting the old Australian cricket empire, and in the clatter of impressive figures – two sixes and nine fours – there was a deeper reason for praise. Strauss's innings was perfectly judged in that it was a masterpiece of smooth acceleration. It absorbed the threat of early wickets by Warne, McGrath and Lee, and allowed England to chase securely the runs that would enable captain Michael Vaughan to set the Australians a target that offered only two possibilities; a draw or a defeat.

When Vaughan declared, and gave the Australians a 35-minute ordeal, Strauss had every reason to congratulate himself on his refusal to go the way of Cullinan. He was the latest England player to face the ultimate test of his career and emerge with battle ribbons of the highest order.

It was certainly not a formality when he walked to the wicket with his partner Marcus Trescothick in early afternoon. Warne's phenomenal performance with the bat, all the more remarkable on top of his prodigious bowling stints at the age of 35, had, with the dogged work of Jason Gillespie, reduced the England lead to a mere 142, a total which, while scarcely insignificant, would have shrunk dramatically with some opening impact by Australia's big three of Warne, McGrath and Lee. Warne must have reckoned that Strauss was a particularly inviting point of attack.

You had to consider the steep decline in Strauss's Test profile after coming into the Warne zone.

He arrived at Lord's last month with a magnificent body of work in 14 Tests against New Zealand, the West Indies, South Africa and Bangladesh. He had gleaned five centuries, including one in his first Test – at Lord's. In South Africa he had been tough, nerveless, amassing 656 runs in five Tests at an average of 72.89.

That was the formidable calling card he laid before the world champions in St John's Wood. But Warne was impressed least of all. In a burst of bowling that was as technically brilliant as it was bold, Warne stopped England in the belief that they had taken an early hold of a series that might just offer a first triumph in 18 years. He had Strauss and Trescothick groping in a thick fog on a summer's day.

Strauss survived the ordeal, at least in terms of missing a place on Warne's scalp belt, but there was no question that he had been shaken by the range of his virtuosity. One consequence was his double failure to cope with the Australian's wiles at Edgbaston and last week the failing hero of last summer and winter arrived here with an average of less than 20. From being merely sub-Bradmanesque, his figures had become, well, simply sub-standard.

It is just a fleeting memory now. There were moments yesterday when it could have been rather more than that, of course. It could have been a dawning sense that after the triumphs against lesser nations, lesser intimidation, Andrew Strauss had proved less a hero of the ages than a cricketer of brief times in the sun. That was the point Warne wished to inflict with crushing force, and there were times when all his wiles were applied. But Strauss resisted the worst of Warne – and of Lee, who also sent one delivery timed at 94.5 mph whistling scarcely an inch beneath his chin.

In the dusk once more Australian shoulders slumped. There were many reasons for this, some of them blows of the day, some of them cumulative. Not the least, in either category, was the final breakthrough of Andrew Strauss.

TRIUMPH OF SURVIVAL
ON DAY FOR AGES

Published: 16 August 2005

There may never be a day like this again as long as Ashes cricket is played.

In the end it came down to a battle between Glenn McGrath and Brett Lee, tail-end Charlies who will never be forgotten now in that secondary capacity, and the last that England, despairing England could throw at them.

When Lee raised his bat in the triumph of survival, he was merely finishing the epic work of his captain Ricky Ponting. But the nerve to withstand the last three balls from Steve Harmison – the man who broke Australia at Edgbaston last weekend – belonged in a category of its own. It was a dramatic capsule of the most draining kind, and to that Ponting, back in the pavilion after his superb day of personal resurrection, would no doubt be the first to agree.

It was already a day for the cricket ages. You could see that it would be before a ball was bowled and thousands streamed away from the old ground after being told every ticket had been taken.

Even the few among them in the blazers and the club ties had the faces of street urchins shooed from the glittering window of a five-star restaurant, and they were right to be so disappointed. Long before the final act of the day-long drama, the biggest crowd at Old Trafford since the Australians of Richie Benaud beat Peter May's England in 1961 – and the visiting skipper bowled the England captain for nought – knew it was part of one of the richest, most gripping passages in the history of Test cricket.

Some might have been inclined to talk, or at least think, of anti-climax after the drive to an apparently inevitable English victory foundered on the astonishing resistance of Ponting.

Yes, of course the national yearning was for a spectacular Ashes breakthrough by Michael Vaughan's young team – a team who for two years had been preparing themselves for this chance to break down 18 years of Australian domination – but sometimes the gap between what is desired and what is possible becomes simply Himalayan in scale.

That's how it began to look to the most passionate supporters of England as the old pavilion clock counted down the minutes, the overs and the light, and Ponting and Warne, who were alleged to have been at each other's throats in the bitterness of defeat in the second Test at Edgbaston, made an alliance that might just have saved the Australian cause in this staggering collision of entrenched power and thrusting ambition. Now the captain and his most celebrated player fused into an extraordinary block of unbudgeable Aussie will.

From Warne it was another example of his astonishing ability to roll back the boundaries of the possible on a cricket field – one made all the more amazing last night when he walked out at precisely the moment it seemed that England had once again broken down Australia's once legendary resistance to the idea of defeat. Ponting had gambled on the stonewall defensive technique of Jason Gillespie after Michael Clarke, hobbling in pain with a bad back for most of the match, fell to a beautiful Simon Jones delivery after supporting his captain quite superbly.

Gillespie, for once, found himself struggling to fend off the impassioned assault of hugely committed Test-quality bowlers. Matthew Hoggard did the damage when he got through the most obdurate forward defensive stroke in the upper echelons of tail-end batsmanship. This left us with the latest challenge to face Warne in the most dramatic autumn of his career. For so long – and in all the circumstances of his recent performances with both bat and ball, this wasn't the greatest of surprises – he was again staggering in his presence and his nerve.

Indeed, there was a sobering point for the English spirit when the unthinkable became something that could no longer be rejected out of hand. With Ponting reaching down for the innings of his career, might Warne just be capable of helping him to conjure the runs for the most unlikely Test victory of all time? That idea, which would have been so fanciful when Australia faced the mountainous task of surviving three sessions and 35 minutes beneath the shadow of a target of 423 runs, was growing hugely right to the moment when he lost his wicket in another moment drawn from cricket fantasy.

That Geraint Jones, the embattled wicketkeeper who is fighting for his place in this England side, should make the crucial catch, and that it should be one brushing the miraculous, was in the end simply consistent with all that had flowed from the moment the action unfolded at Lord's last month. Andrew Flintoff, who had done so much to drive England to this point of dominance, delivered the ball that squirted off Warne's bat and into the slips. There it flew off Andrew Strauss and was picked up an inch off the ground by Jones. On Saturday night Jones had missed a stumping off Warne, then dropped a simple catch. In 48 hours he had travelled as far as is possible in the upper levels of sport. It was then almost a formality that he should take the catch, off Harmison, that sent back the ultimately heroic Ponting.

There were four overs left when one of the greatest acts of defiance ever seen on a cricket field was brought to a close. Ponting scored 156, but that meant virtually nothing. He batted for the longest day that Australian – and English – cricket will ever know; and the fact that England, this battling, fighting England, could not break down the resistance of a team who are supposedly heading into the sunset makes the rest of this Ashes series into a class of competition entirely of its own.

PONTING RETAINS HEROIC BOTTLE SO PUT THE CELEBRATIONS ON ICE

Published: 17 August 2005

It may well be that the Ashes are about to become English property again, but before it happens maybe everyone, from the team captain Michael Vaughan down to the newest cricket fan caught up in the magnificent frenzy of this astonishing Test series, should make a solemn vow. Perhaps we should not forget the unswerving dictate of the great winemakers. No vintage should be taken before its time – no triumph should be anticipated before it is a reality.

That surely is the lesson of Old Trafford, where the the glass slipped so devastatingly. It is one that in the aftermath of the Australian defiance was utterly ignored by Vaughan's predecessor, Nasser Hussain. Here is an English cricketer, and leader, with much credit in the bank. If it is Vaughan who has carried the team to the edge of a great victory, if he has at times engaged the challenge of beating Australia so brilliantly, he would no doubt acknowledge that Hussain did much to instil a set of tougher values in a team for whom surrender was too frequently far from the last option.

But then the job isn't done – not quite yet, a fact which you wouldn't have gathered from Hussain's post-match declaration in the Manchester dusk. He said: "Heroes. Absolute heroes. Each and every member of the England team was absolutely brilliant at Old Trafford. People may analyse the ifs and buts and may wonder what might have been, but the bottom line is that this was another remarkable performance."

Nasser is right about the remarkable performance; wrong about the bottom line. The bottom line is that Australia stole the draw with the fantastic commitment of bone-deep champions. They may not be what they were, they may be heading for the shadows that sooner or later come to even the greatest performers, but the heroes of the third Test at Old Trafford – in absolute, bottom-line terms – carried the names Ricky Ponting, Shane Warne and Brett Lee.

No doubt it's true there were performances of deep talent – and character – from Vaughan and Andrew Strauss, Andrew Flintoff and Ian Bell. Simon Jones bowled himself into centre stage as the series moves towards its climactic phase.

But absolute heroes are heroic absolutely. England didn't win the Test they had dominated for four days. Why? Because they could not find a way to put away champions who refused to accept something that the rest of the cricket world thought was written plainly in the sky. They could not accept they were beaten.

The absolute hero of the Old Trafford Test was unquestionably Ponting. He did not perform forlorn gallantry. He moved a sporting mountain. He got from under an avalanche of circumstance that seemed determined to bury his ambition to join a tradition of successful Australian captains such as Allan Border, Mark Taylor and Steve Waugh, and he played the innings of his life. This is saying so much about a man who came into this series with a huge body of work, one of just three Australians to produce four double-centuries in Test cricket – Sir Don Bradman and Greg Chappell were the others – and with an average of 56 at the highest level of the game. However, that mountain of achievement was being scaled down before our eyes. His team-mates were said to be dismayed by some of his decision-making. There was talk of rebellion in the air. His work at the batting crease was haemorrhaging authority.

That was the oppressive weight he carried to the wicket seven balls into the last day of a Test match which seemed a certain candidate to be one that marked the loosening of Australia's iron grip on world cricket. That was the mountain of doubt he eroded, ball by ball, over by over, session by session.

Where did Ponting's work leave Vaughan's England? At 1-1 in a series that at the dawn they seemed to have at their mercy. That, Nasser Hussain should know, is where the bottom line starts and finishes for the moment. The former captain may prove right in his theory that the knowledge that they have now twice outplayed the world champions will serve England well in the fourth and fifth Tests, at Trent Bridge and the Oval respectively. Maybe it is true that the psychological battle is all but won by this England team.

However, there are no prizes for guessing which team felt the rush of elation in the Old Trafford pavilion on Monday night. It wasn't Vaughan's England. It was the team who yet again had refused to quit.

This is not to belittle the efforts of an England side who have grown superbly during this summer. It is just to say that if the Australians are indeed going down, it seems certain now that even in defeat they will surely define the nature of champions. For this reason alone, the cork should stay in the bottle. That way, if it is due, the wine will taste all the finer.

CRICKET IS JUST A FABULOUS FAD

Published: 07 September 2005

Where will the English – and maybe even British – heart beat most strongly over the next few days? Unquestionably at the Oval. Cricket, with England performing so heroically against the ancient foe Australia, has never been lovelier in the public mind than any time since the fifties, when enchantment came with a calypso celebrating the mesmerising spin bowling and modest demeanours of the West Indians Sonny Ramadhin and Alf Valentine.

Yet the rush of acclaim for England's other national game – and the accompanying rage that, when the drama of Kennington is done and we know if England has won its first Ashes series in 18 years, the game will disappear from terrestrial television screens – should perhaps not provoke too much giddiness in the committee room of the England and Wales Test Cricket Board.

Cricket reigns for the moment, and for the most glorious of reasons, but an intriguing question remains. Has it truly re-established itself as the nation's most compelling sport? Or is it providing passing relief from some darker developments in the real national game, King Football? Is cricket, when set against the universal appeal of the big round ball, really anything more than a fabulous fad?

It is the harsh but maybe inevitable call on a classic of sport. England cricketers have played the world champions Australia – widely considered before the onset of this extraordinary Test series to be one of the toughest, most accomplished teams ever assembled in any branch of world sport – to their very limits.

They have demanded from the Australians in the baggy green caps every scrap of skill and resilience; they have provoked stupendous performances from legendary players like Shane Warne and Glenn McGrath, but still the English nerve has held. Andrew "Freddie" Flintoff has become a giant, an authentic rival, to the beloved Ian "Beefy" Botham. The matches have been riveting to an almost excruciating degree. An Englishman sailing down the Grand Canal in Venice called home on his mobile phone and demanded to know the score, and was immediately surrounded by some fellow tourists. Cricket, plainly, has hit a main vein of the nation.

So what is there, then, to cloud the new and exciting vision of the cricket administrators, one of the green fields being re-colonised by a game that had been almost completely abandoned by state schools? It is the fear that, at least to some degree, cricket has captured the imagination by default, by the failures and the betrayals of the real national game.

The truth is that cricket is shining so brilliantly this summer because football, which over recent years has crowded the summer game into the smallest pockets of public attention, is seen by so many to have squandered its intense appeal in the most tawdry fashion. Cricket, whose administrators were accused of madness when they scheduled the climax of the Ashes series deep into a new Premiership football campaign, is being seen as a new force of sporting light.

While big Freddie Flintoff commiserated with his beaten opponent Brett Lee in arguably the most uplifting sports cameo of the year at the end of the white-knuckle second Test at Edgbaston, Manchester United's England centre-back Rio Ferdinand, a footballer who had been suspended for eight months for failing to take a drugs test, was concluding negotiations for a salary that dwarfed those of his cricket rival – £100,000 a week.

While footballers continue to dive and feign injury, while leading managers turn their eyes away from the most egregious behaviour, the Australian captain, Ricky Ponting – embattled, but also heroic – is fined for a brief burst of invective. Inevitably, comparisons have been made.

If cricket is for the moment the hands-down winner, does its future stretch out untrammelled by doubts about its new prominence and regard? For the men in the egg-and-bacon ties of the Marylebone Cricket Club, it is the prettiest of notions, engagingly promoted by English life-affirming characters like the commentator Henry Blofeld.

There is another reality, however, and it is that ultimately cricket cannot hope, any more than any other team sport, to eclipse the elemental appeal of football. Football may be having an extremely dangerous summer, it may have blurred, in this country at least, the appeal that has carried it triumphantly into every corner of the world and culture, but it retains the ability to touch every class and creed.

Cricket, still bounded by the borders of the old empire, cannot begin to make such a claim. All it can truly say is that for some little while now it has delivered, quite magnificently, the best of itself – and how many millions would football give to be able to say that?

DEAR SHANE ... I LOVE YOU

In an open letter to Shane Warne, James Lawton pays tribute to
a departing legend who has hit new heights this year

Published: 08 September 2005

Dear Shane,

You may feel this is a little abrupt, and perhaps not the way you do things down in Oz – give or take the odd dodgy text message – but I do have something important to tell you on the dawn of your farewell to Test cricket on English soil.

I love you. Not all of you, of course. I'm not crazy about the peroxide and the diamond ear studs, but then I'm old enough to know that no one's perfect, not even you, Shaney.

But love, albeit of a specific kind, it is, and I have more than a hunch that I speak for much of the Pom nation willing you to fail at the Oval over the next few days as spectacularly as you succeeded with your first delivery in the Old Country.

We love you, at least I do, because you have carried us so far beyond the turgidly embittered rivalries of big-time sport, the banal chanting and the booing of national anthems, and not least because you have made it so much easier to be thrilled, even awed by the achievements of the England side. You have stood and fought, at the age of 35, quite beautifully. You have set a standard for the ages.

Even as we hope, and in extreme instances, pray for the demise of you and your team-mates, we glory in your defiance and what you have been asking of Englishmen like Freddie Flintoff as he explores new areas of his talent and his competitive character.

With both the ball and the bat you have defined the way it is when true champions are required to respond to the first fading of the light that has bathed them for so long.

We were privileged to see this in Muhammad Ali one night in Madison Square Garden, when a big, younger man from Ohio, Earnie Shavers, hit him so hard it was easy to imagine the building was shaking. We saw it in Jack Nicklaus when he almost won the US Masters in the shadow of his 60th year and on a wet day at Leicester racecourse ten years ago when Lester Piggott was asked what technique he would bring to one of his last rides. "I suppose I'll put one leg each side," he said with a chilly smile glinting with battle.

We saw it when one of Michael Vaughan's recent predecessors, Mike Atherton, batted for an age in Johannesburg, and when your own embattled captain, Ricky Ponting, put down the anchor at Old Trafford a few weeks ago.

Endlessly, Shane, we have seen it in you this unforgettable summer.

This is where the love is, Shane – the love of sport's ability to bring the best out of a man, to allow him to put aside all the screw-ups he shares with much of the rest of humanity, and say: "This is something I can do, maybe better than anyone else."

It is the beauty of great games when they are played at their highest level and the extraordinary thing now is that we do not have to trawl back through all the years of your inexorable progress from feckless beach boy to master sportsman. We don't have to begin to itemise the record wicket haul, except maybe that first one in England at Old Trafford which rearranged both Mike Gatting's stumps and his understanding of what was possible on a cricket field.

No, the wonder of your effort this summer Shane, at such a venerable point in your career, is that you have managed to produce, in one form or another, almost everything you had, and, at times, given the growth and the passion of an England team that has thrilled the nation to its bones, maybe even a little more.

You even gave us a passable facsimile of the Gatting Doomsday ball – the one that shot out one of the new, authentic English heroes, Andrew Strauss, clouding his face with a disbelief that rivalled Gatting's 12 years ago.

Your bowling at Lord's on a Saturday afternoon was transcendent. You mesmerised both the English batsmen and the headquarters of cricket. You were the not quite superannuated Merlin of the game.

I could go on in this vein for some time but maybe the *billet-doux* has already created enough titters in your dressing-room.

I know to my cost it is not a place normally suffused with sentimentality. One of your compatriots, the former captain Ian Chappell, made this clear many years ago when I made a soft entry into what I reckoned was quite a biting question. "Let's cut the bullshit, mate," he said, "what do you want to know?"

Another of your compatriots, the fighter Jeff Harding, was even less patient with one colleague who repeatedly failed to gain a response from a leading question. He tried one last time, only to be told: "I heard your question the first time, cobber, and you can still stick it up your arse."

So maybe we ought to put away the pleasantries and cut to the point. It is simply this: if Michael Vaughan's England carry the highest hopes – and respect – of their country to the Oval this morning, if their deeds have so superbly coloured the nation's life this last month or so, if Flintoff is indeed the new Botham, you are, mate, a huge part of the reason.

You have provided an edge of fight and skill which has required every member of Vaughan's team to dredge from deep inside himself the best of his talent and character. This has enabled England to match, and so often outplay your team, which carried such awe when you arrived, and in the last act it could be they will finally go beyond the demands placed upon them so magnificently.

This is not what you had planned for your last sweep through the Old Country. You imagined you would be trailing glory yet again. But then, of all people, Shane, you know better than most that, on and off the field, life has a tendency to pop up with a kick in the groin. The most important thing, as you have proved this summer, is to remember what you have achieved in the past, who you are, what you are, and then maybe what you can do today.

One of the less significant disappointments of the summer was that you were one wicket short of getting the "fiver" bowling statistic that would have been put up on the Lord's honours board. You shouldn't worry about that, Shane. Your name is etched immovably in a rather more important place – the heart and the respect of an entire nation.

Yours, can I say, affectionately,
James Lawton

PS The flowers are on their way but in the circumstances I quite understand if you decide to put them through security.

CLASH OF TITANS ENTHRALS AS FLINTOFF CARRIES THE FIGHT TO SERPENT OF SPIN

Published: 09 September 2005

There have been so many pivotal moments in this summer of the ultimate Ashes they go beyond record. You might almost as easily separate grains of sand in a desert storm.

Yet when the final accountancy comes in the next few days here is one that might prove to be the most decisive of all: it is 1.40pm and the Australians, caged and desperate for so long, have the old sniff of English blood.

They have taken – or rather their talisman genius Shane Warne has – four wickets and there are just 131 runs on the board. The gold of England captain Michael Vaughan's winning call of the toss has become very shoddy metal indeed.

The dramatic point is that suddenly Warne is bowling and Freddie Flintoff is batting. The long dangerous summer has come to a head, as it did when the great matadors Luis Dominguin and Antonio Ordonez fought hand to hand across Spain.

Here, nearly 50 years later, we have cricket's high summer equivalent. Flintoff the lion against Warne the serpent of spin; brave youth against the subtlety and cunning of age. The Oval, splashed in vivid sunshine, is so quiet you can hear fevered breathing seats away. Is this the most telling phase in the latest and most extravagant, unlikely drama of more than one hundred years of fierce rivalry?

We didn't quite know then – and we still don't, not in the cool and reflection of evening, but one thing is certain. If Flintoff, the heart and the sword-striking arm of England, had faltered when Warne was taking on powers of intimidation remarkable even in the weeks of stunning farewell at the age of 35, what we would be discussing now would not be the possibility of a four-day extension of the knife edge on which the previous four Tests had been conducted.

We would be saying that the Aussies, harried and challenged at almost every stage in the only series in which they had been properly challenged in 18 years, had finally got us in the end. After all the glory of Vaughan's men, the power of

Flintoff, the big innings of Strauss and Trescothick and the captain, they had conjured some last burst of killing resistance, enough at least for them to hang on to the Ashes.

Sobriety insists that such is still the possibility. At the close of play, England could certainly not be overjoyed at the fruit of Vaughan's third successful call out of five: 319 for 7 was only a slender downpayment on the price of shutting out the Australians from the victory which they must achieve to keep the Ashes. But then when Flintoff came to the wicket to face Warne it could suddenly have turned so much worse. Warne long ago established in English cricket hearts and brains the capacity to strike in the most devastating, even unworldly fashion.

But here, jogging in endlessly once it became clear to his captain, Ricky Ponting, that the sky, clearing to a bright blue, and the flat track, offered no assistance to his fast-bowling team-mates, he seemed to take on still another new dimension. He moved the ball certainly, at times quite sharply, but this was a story of the technique of leg-spin. It was a lesson in inflicting what you have left of your aura. Warne, as the great throng who choked the streets around the Oval before play suspected he would be, was yet again laden with it.

So if it wasn't Warne the Saviour of Oz it wasn't going to be anybody, not on this day when almost everything could be settled. He had sent back Trescothick, Vaughan, Bell and Pietersen by a weird alchemy of menace and maybe even auto-suggestion. Was it the fabled sight of Warne running in to the wicket that induced the poor, nervy, shots? It was a purely academic question once Flintoff engaged the problem of dwindling England nerve.

With Strauss once again reminding us that he is a not-so young Test batsman of deep substance, one whose late arrival on the big stage is another reflection of an old, and, we hope, extinct way of doing things in English cricket, it was a crisis that desperately needed the new confidence, even bravura of Freddie Flintoff.

He did not disappoint – at least not for two hours and 41 minutes which spoke of the best of England's assault on these world champion Australians. Flintoff, massive and fiercely concentrated, hit Warne for three fours in one over. Each one was a small essay in easily gathered, almost insouciant power. Once he drove Warne through the covers as a maharajah might swat a fly. Finally, he straight drove the Australian virtuoso for six runs. It was a towering shot, the moment when the impressionable might have believed that the Ashes had once again become English property.

In all, Flintoff hit 13 boundaries, 12 fours. His total of 72 may yet be the difference between huge glory and the most bitter of disappointment, but as the crowd left the Oval inevitably there was the sense of choked euphoria. Flintoff's glory this summer has been to excite the highest hopes. If Warne is Merlin, Flintoff is surely an amiable Sir Lancelot, and for a little while yesterday it seemed that he would once again carry not only the day but England's Ashes destiny.

That was the disappointment that caught the Oval by the throat – and reignited Australian belief that they might indeed escape from England without the pain of shocking defeat. Warne, inevitably it seemed, played a part in Flintoff's downfall. McGrath delivered a fine ball; Flintoff, who had become becalmed, played it with low-level conviction and Warne swooped at slip. The spinner's bowling figures were another gift to legend . . . 34 overs, four maidens, 118 runs, five wickets. He had bowled for most of the day and hugely extended Australia's debt to his willingness to fight through to the last round.

Flintoff, who had met his challenge spectacularly enough, was also due his nation's thanks. He had, for a little while at least, faced down the man who is fighting the hardest, and most brilliantly, to save the Ashes.

REALITY BITES AS AUSTRALIA'S GRANITE WILL FIRES PURSUIT OF REDEMPTION

Published: 10 September 2005

All summer long we have been very English, in a certain gracious way, about the decline of maybe the greatest cricket team the world has ever seen. Yes, we've pounded Australia to the very edge of their professional reputations, but, heaven knows, we have been generous about it.

Remember – and surely who can forget it – the image of Freddie Flintoff bending to console the fallen Australian hero Brett Lee on that astonishing Sunday of the second Test when England's ability to once again beat Australia in a match that mattered was a fact radiating across the nation like some monster sunrise?

Remember the standing ovation for Shane Warne when he claimed his 600th Test wicket at Old Trafford, and how, moved almost to tears – almost is, of course, a relative term – he waved his floppy hat in appreciation?

Yes, even while we have attacked them, we have nourished their finer feelings.

Warne, we have allowed, is a phenomenon of competitive zeal and imagination. His fellow 35-year-old, Glenn McGrath, is another legend still capable of springing deadly ambushes. If batsmen like Matthew Hayden and Justin Langer were living deep in personal nightmares of lost form and belief, they still had the capacity to build the foundation of a comeback victory. We kept saying all of this rather like apprehensive boys whistling in the graveyard, but did we really believe it would prove true after the great eruption of English cricket?

The question became academic here yesterday when most of a crowd of 23,000 stood staring at a glowering sky – and praying for rain.

All that brash certainty on the approach to this final Test match – all those conversations with the office of the Mayor of London and the Met Police about the staging of a massive celebration in Trafalgar Square, win or draw the series – came down to umbrellas waving as though they were so many white flags.

At first it was a confusing situation filled with mixed messages. For four hours the Australians had fought their way into a position to save the Ashes –

an astonishing possibility after England's summer of growth and power with both the bat and the ball. Then, immediately after the tea interval, Langer and Hayden were invited by the umpires to return to the pavilion because of bad light. They accepted and it seemed that a large part of Kennington gasped with the purest relief.

For a little while there was bewilderment. How could the Aussies, so cold-eyed in their pursuit of redemption on the back of Warne's brilliant aura for the best part of two days, break off in their pursuit of an astonishing recovery?

Again you had to believe that it was another example of the Australian instinct to take all of the blows while preserving their chance of some great escape. Langer was 75 not out, Hayden 32 not out and Australia had knocked 112 runs off England's disappointing first-innings total of 373. If the weather forecast was discouraging for now, there was a strong belief that Sunday and Monday would see long days of testing action after some sporadic play today.

So what did Langer and Hayden do? Did they wing it in the gloom, hope to continue the arc of Australia's growing ascendancy – and risk the loss of one or two wickets under an assault led by Steve Harmison, the man who first broke through Australian psychological defences in the first Test at Lord's with his bodyline assault on Langer?

Langer and Hayden decided to bat only under optimum conditions. They had fought for an advantage that might still permit the chance of a strike for victory tomorrow and on Monday. They had come from a place of extreme pressure and with ten wickets standing Australia were in so much better shape than they could have hoped for when their captain, Ricky Ponting, lost potentially the most important toss of his career on Thursday morning.

That was how it was when pause came to the epic Ashes battle last night, and it was another extraordinary place for it to be. If Langer and Hayden had gone in a brief flurry of action before play was abandoned finally, we might have seen another swift change of momentum. It is not what champions like to risk, and certainly not encourage. They like the development of certainty over any contest, and that is what was happening when a blue sky slowly turned to grey.

Before the action, Langer's father revealed that when his son goes in to bat he lights a cigar and smokes it for so long as his boy is at the crease. Recently he could have got by with discarded cheroots in some Tijuana bodega but yesterday's ritual required a two-and-a-half-hour puff. The wise move for him now might be to lay in a supply of some of the best of Havanas.

Before this series Langer had the reputation of being Australia's ultimate grafter, a man of steely purpose and great patience. Yesterday he showed quite a lot of those qualities in subduing the early menace of Matthew Hoggard, but soon enough he was digging deeply into the confidence of one of England's key men, the spinner Ashley Giles.

When Giles, a vital component in England's gamble to pad their batting with Paul Collingwood and rely on just four main-line bowlers, was introduced by his no-doubt-concerned captain, Michael Vaughan, Langer's resolve was as brutal as an old gunfighter's.

He smashed Giles for two massive sixes and a total of 14 runs in his first over. Vaughan cleverly regrouped, moving Giles to the Vauxhall End and having him bowl with the protection of much deeper boundaries at that end of the field. That briefly troubled Langer – and preserved Giles' presence in the match that will decide the Ashes.

However, when the teams walked off Langer was in control again. His jaw seemed to be made of granite and no one, least of all anyone English, was mouthing platitudes about the fighting instincts of the Australians as they went down. Kind words had become a hard reality.

FLINTOFF IS MAN FOR ALL SEASONS, EVEN IN AUTUMN

Published: 12 September 2005

With good, endlessly recurring reason, we talk about the glory of this Ashes summer but the fact is that we are now just a little short of a Freddie Flintoff stride into autumn, a fact presumably mislaid by cricket's administrators as they snapped to attention when the television men first laid down the schedule.

The gut-wrenching result, while doing nothing to compromise the glory of England's achievement in coming here with a 2-1 lead over the world champions Australia, and the moral high ground of outplaying them in three of the previous four Tests, has made a parody of balanced competition in what should have been the last act of a true sporting epic.

Was it too dark for Michael Vaughan and Marcus Trescothick to face the spin bowling of Shane Warne and Michael Clarke – even though it's true that some would say on his best days the former would be a handful on a featherbed in a brightly lit furniture store?

Was it an uplifting statement about the national sporting psyche that after hearing hired opera singers lead stirring versions of *Jerusalem* and *Land of Hope and Glory*, more than 20,000 Englishmen and women spent most of the day cheering the fact that their land in late summer is a place of mists, low cloud and, almost certainly, Ashes-bearing fruitfulness? In other words, a season fine for the poet Keats and cricket captains eager to accept an offer to return to the pavilion because of bad light – eager not to face the best spinner the world has ever seen. The short answers are no and no.

But then nothing is simple in England's last reach for the Ashes. Apart, that is, from the fact that, as though it was really necessary, Flintoff, the revelation and the inspiration of England's sporting year, has once again announced that he is a truly great cricketer.

On the first day here he scored a magnificent 72 that was, along with Andrew Strauss's second century of the series, the most brilliant check on the rampant artistry of Warne. Yesterday, again with just one significant ally – this time the tough fellow northerner, Matthew Hoggard – he insisted that the Ashes would indeed become English property again after a break of 16 years.

The details of Flintoff's latest eruption are dramatic enough as he bowled through the murk which Australia's circumstances dictated their batsmen had to brave, but as he added four more victims to the scalp of Australian captain Ricky Ponting, which he had claimed on Saturday night, it was again his sheer presence that yet again filled and spilled over one of England's great cricket grounds.

Flintoff's supreme moment yesterday came when he claimed the wicket of the one man to seriously challenge his ownership of the summer – Warne. It wasn't his finest delivery – and Vaughan pouched the catch as though he was handling a Molotov cocktail – but it had symbolism extraordinary even by the standards he has created so quickly, so profoundly.

He had struck another blow at the monstrous prospect of England having to face Warne this morning under the weight of a first innings deficit that, everyone knew, he was capable of turning into an Ashes-denying innings victory. Instead, England, having lost just Strauss to the cunning of Warne, are 40 runs ahead going into a last day that will inevitably be foreshortened.

Here we have the offence against sport at the Oval – one that cannot be blamed, in a world where winning has become the ultimate, and perhaps only, permanent measure of performance, on anyone but those administrators who agreed to an orgy of knockabout one-day cricket in mid-summer. That is, the placing of the climax of the Ashes at that time when any club cricketer will tell you that the only sensible option is discussing the summer's events over a pint in the local.

In a more romantic age, maybe Vaughan, having just been utterly hoodwinked by a Warne delivery, would not have made so obvious to the umpires his distaste for the action, even after his rival Ponting had been advised that he had to proceed without his pacemen – Glenn McGrath, Brett Lee and Shaun Tait.

He might have said: "No thank you, gentlemen, I want to win these Ashes in the purest way . . . I believe in my players, my ability to deliver this famous triumph out here on the field and not in the pavilion looking out on an empty field, it is something I owe to cricket". Vaughan could have said that, but only in the certainty that he would have been laughed to scorn all the way from Kennington, this place of stygian gloom, to the early spring sunshine of Bondi Beach.

No, Vaughan made the cold, professional decision – as he had to – in the way Ponting did when he twice accepted the offer of bad light as Justin Langer and Matthew Hayden so superbly laid the foundations of what seemed, with reasonable conditions, a rock-hard foundation for victory. This was neither Vaughan's nor Ponting's tragedy, but cricket's.

Why? Because everything that had gone before, demanded, emotionally at least, more than this wearisome ritual of retreating players and hollow triumphalism. In one of their wittier phases, the Barmy Army sang: "We're singing in the rain, it's a glorious feeling and we're happy again."

Glorious was though, plainly, the wrong word. If the Ashes do fall to England today, as both the odds and natural justice say they should, it will unfortunately do little to take away the sense that much of this final Test has been a perversion of what has gone on before.

However, the grace, and the brilliance and humour of the players of both sides survived, with heart-warming force. Ponting and his men came into the last session of play wearing sunglasses, sardonic cricketers playing the Blues Brothers for comic effect. It brought plenty of smiles, but they were of a rather shallow kind.

It was, after all, nothing so much as laughter in the dark.

PIETERSEN FOLLOWS IN BOTHAM'S SHOES

Published: 13 September 2005

You had to go back 24 years here yesterday to find something to compare with the brutal yet sublime, Ashes-bearing violence Kevin Pietersen brought to this old ground which has seen so many points of astounding cricket history. But really, and with great respect to Ian Botham, maybe that wasn't quite far enough.

There is a compelling argument to say what happened here over the last few days, and indeed the entire Ashes series, has simply been beyond compare.

But when a game reaches the height it has achieved all summer, history inevitably presents us with a point of reference, and the obvious one as Pietersen settled the last of the doubts, was the heroically battered century by Botham at Headingley in 1981.

Botham stopped the Aussies of Dennis Lillee, and there was an astonishing symmetry in the fact that such similar young men found a way to conquer the game's master race at an ultimately pivotal point in a collision between the oldest foes. Both have provoked questions about their understanding of the true nature of the game. Both have been seen as the most overtly ambitious of young adventurers in a game which was always supposed to be about a sense of team and tradition. Both might still struggle to earn a benevolent look in the Lord's Long Room. But, 24 years apart, both have made the same point. It is that, ultimately, talent means little if it is not accompanied by an abiding belief in your ability to take hold of a cricket match by its heart and its throat.

When Botham pulled his team up so sensationally, the Aussies sneered that he was the author of a "slog".

"They were quite right," said Botham. "It was a slog – a glorious slog." Ditto, Pietersen's astonishing break-out here yesterday just when the Australians, led again by the most durable and brilliant veterans cricket has ever known, Shane Warne and Glenn McGrath, had conjured the shocking resistance to the rise of England.

Pietersen was twice dropped when the match still had the properties of an emotional powder keg. Adam Gilchrist fumbled a chance off Warne which could not be quite retrieved by the normally hawk-like Matthew Hayden. Then, of all people, Warne dropped him off McGrath. Pietersen's innings was still in its infancy, as it was when Brett Lee launched an assault, at speeds of up to 94mph, which was quite astonishing when you considered it came from an essentially amiable man.

Lee, though overshadowed by McGrath, has bowled superbly at times this summer, and he has laughed in both glory and pain. Now he had the smile of an assassin as he bowled head and throat balls at the man who represented the last serious English threat to an unforgettable Australian recovery. Pietersen not only survived, he assumed the status of a bludgeoning giant.

Some say he is not a young cricket star fashioned in the heavens. His self-interest is palpable, his love of the glory comes without apology. With his dyed hair and his love of bling, he is the antithesis of his team-mate and massive folk hero Freddie Flintoff. But, of course, he shares something quite valuable in a burgeoning sports star. He has talent that you could throw on a bonfire without burning it all away.

His seven sixes smashed the Ashes record, and guess who was supplanted? Yes, Botham, the supreme extrovert whose like some argued would never again appear in an England team. Now England have two men of such explosive performance – Pietersen the herculean egoist, Flintoff the great heart.

They also have in Michael Vaughan a forceful captain of high intelligence who – now that he is so utterly secure in his job – may again be a batsman of classic technique and outstanding performance. They have a pace bowling attack which can bring a surge of concern in any corner of the game.

We saw here again the quality of these deposed champions. We saw Hayden and Justin Langer scoring centuries from the tightest of corners. We saw Warne, who took 12 wickets in his last Test on English soil, and McGrath fighting with the intensity that made them champions.

Yet nothing they did could stop the English tide, one that, long after the issue was closed, was still being expressed by Steve Harmison in a burst of bouncers.

The point of supremacy had been made dramatically enough, and most crushingly by Pietersen. That he belongs to a new age, and another dimension, was maybe underlined by another remnant of history. Sixty seven years earlier, Sir Len Hutton had scored a world record 364 on this ground. He batted for more than than two days and scored 35 fours. He didn't score a six. He belonged to another age, another world.

MICHAEL VAUGHAN: 'IT'S ALL ABOUT THE FUTURE'

Published: 17 September 2005

Michael Vaughan says that one day he will re-create, as perfectly as he can, all those feelings that required him to fight back the tears – "I was closer than anyone could have imagined" – in Trafalgar Square earlier this week. But when it happens the odds are he will be an old man.

His priorities for a long time, he declared yesterday, are to do with the future and not the astonishing glories of the past summer when the Ashes became English property again. "More than anything," the England captain said yesterday, "I want to keep my team honest. I want them to focus more on what they can do in the future than what they have already achieved. I know that's a lot, in some ways they exceeded all my hopes, but great teams have a hunger which the Australians displayed for so long – and I think they will show that again when we go there in 18 months' time. It means that starting this winter in Pakistan and India we all have one great obligation. We have to grow. We have to believe that we have started a job that we must finish."

As the "boys of summer", including new legends like Andrew "Freddie" Flintoff and Kevin "KP" Pietersen, relax away from the front line, their captain has spelled out the imperative that must stay at the front of their minds. "They have created huge expectations in the nation and they must meet them. We all have that duty," Vaughan said.

As Vaughan relived the Ashes campaign – he told of how he delivered his version of the "England expects" speech to the young hero Pietersen in the Oval pavilion last Monday, how he and the coach, Duncan Fletcher, forcefully reminded the players of the challenge they faced on behalf of the nation and themselves as they gathered in the Edgbaston committee room for the critical second Test following a savage defeat at Lord's – his thoughts invariably turned to the future.

At times he echoed the speech of Britain's most successful golfer, Nick Faldo, after he won back-to-back US Masters titles. Then, Faldo said: "The British public may understand how hard it is to get to the top of the world in any sport. What I sometimes doubt is if they know how hard it is to stay there."

Plainly, it is a problem Vaughan has already engaged, even before the Oval cheers and those of the great victory salute in Trafalgar Square have lost their resonance.

After working with young competition winners at his county Yorkshire's indoor academy, and for his sponsor, Quorn, Vaughan would make only one firm promise to the team which he led into history. "Their places in the team are guaranteed only by their hard work, their willingness to do again what they did so magnificently when it mattered this last summer.

"What's most exciting of all to me is the possibilities of the future. The [possibilities] have to be so good when this young team have beaten the number-one team in the world in the most incredible circumstances.

"The pressures and the challenges went way beyond what we expected with the levels of expectation going into the last game at the Oval . . . and they were asked to bat the last day out, and they did it so convincingly. That told me I had so much character at my disposal, but then I also know that you are only as good as your back-up . . . It means that you have to keep building and it's so important we keep getting young players pushing the team and making sure everybody stays honest . . . That is what it is going to take to stay in the team."

For Vaughan, the moment of everybody's truth came in the Oval pavilion at lunchtime on the last day of the final Test of the series, which was played as though it was the last will and testament of one great team against one that aspired to be so.

He took Pietersen to one side for the one-on-one that provoked the innings that finally delivered the Ashes. "In the morning I told everyone that they just had to bat as if was not the last day but the first. We had to score runs, we had to get some distance on the Aussies. At lunch Kevin had just been peppered by Brett Lee in one hell of an over, but I sensed that he had survived not playing his way. So I just told him to go out and play positively because we knew an hour and a half of Kevin and everything would be ours anyway."

That was the last stroke of the leadership that some of the old guard of English cricket, most notably the former Ashes-winning captain and chairman of selectors Ray Illingworth, openly questioned when Vaughan was appointed captain in place of Nasser Hussain two years ago.

Vaughan grins when he is asked if his mail has been filled with distinguished apologies. "No, I haven't had too many responses from those who said I was maybe too soft for the job, that my body signals on the field were not tough enough. I did have a wry smile when I heard that because I've always had the confidence to believe that good comes through in the end, and it's been the same with my batting. If I have a few bad scores, I do know I'm good enough to score runs and I back myself.

"It's the same with everything, you are judged on your results and that's what I've tried to hammer home to the team. It's all very well talking about the confidence that comes with consistent selection, and the Australians talked a lot about that . . . but that's okay when you're a winning team. When you lose, you have to accept your position is in doubt if you're not playing well."

In all the glory of the Oval triumph, the personal agony of Ian Bell did not escape the captain. "I told him he shouldn't be too hard on himself. If you're going to have a pair you might as well have them against Shane Warne and Glenn McGrath, the best bowlers in the world. I told 'Belly' that he should draw confidence from the fact that he has played seven Tests and that, anyway, you generally learn more from your failures than your successes. The fact is he did some valuable work in the series and he is clearly a fine player."

For himself, acclamation from the game's Old Contemptibles can wait. "My emotional moment came when we pulled up in Trafalgar Square. Then it hit me that we had carried cricket to a level in this country which I had not really thought was possible. The wonderful thing was that in my bones I always felt we could beat the Australians, and that's what was so painful about the first Test at Lord's. It worried me that we had been beaten not in performance but mentality.

"Before the second Test at Edgbaston a lot of hard talking was done. I said that all the achievements of the previous two years would be wiped away if we couldn't beat Australia. I said that of course they were a great team, they had so many champions, but we had the potential to be great. It depended on our mentality, our willingness to take ownership of some of the most vital decisions, and not just leave it to the coach or captain.

"If we could beat this team, we would have something to build on in an unbelievable way. And then what we did at Edgbaston and Old Trafford and then Trent Bridge was win the respect of the Australians. They already had ours, but we had to win theirs and we started right from the one-day games. At the end, they were fighting with everything they had. There was a tremendous feeling between the teams, but at the vital points – and there were so many through the summer – all the old edge was there.

"For example, Warney gave Paul Collingwood a real sledging when he came out to bat. He said that the only reason Paul was in the team was that he caddied for the captain. It meant that the only time we could relax and say the game and the series was ours was when we got to 270 runs ahead and 'KP' and 'Gilesy' were batting, and you could sense this tremendous relaxation spreading along the balcony. Twenty-five thousand fans were singing that we had won the Ashes.

"It was the greatest feeling we had ever had as cricketers, and when I embraced the team I said that we should never lose sight of what had taken us to this time and place. I said that players like 'Freddie' and 'KP' had stuck their hands up when everything had to be fought for and won, and that no one had let down the team.

"That is a wonderful thing for a captain to be able to say." It is also, Michael Vaughan made clear yesterday, highly addictive.

VAUGHAN'S NEXT TRICK SHOULD BE TO BRING ENGLAND BACK FROM CLOUD NINE WITHOUT CRASH LANDING

Published: 25 October 2005

It may not be the fault of the Ashes heroes that their achievement turned the nation so giddy, but it could very well be their problem when they step off the plane in Pakistan later today.

Nearly two decades of comic ineptitude by many of their predecessors, not to mention the England football team, provided much of the fuel for the extraordinary celebration that has flowed more or less non-stop since those last epic hours at the Oval six weeks ago. It means that Michael Vaughan is now required to play the ultimate trick of any significant captaincy.

The challenge is one, he can point out gently, that never confronted all those Aussie captains who kept English cricket in serfdom for so long, men like Allan Border, Mark Taylor and Steve Waugh. They didn't have to frogmarch their men off cloud nine. In their winning moments they could luxuriate in the knowledge that for their teams winning the Ashes, reminding the world that they were the best team around, was a professional chore rather than an out-of-body experience.

This state of mind became embedded between the years 1987 and 2005. It became the Aussie code, one familiar to all the great champions of any sport. You win and then you put it aside because suddenly the most relevant victory is not the last one but the next.

England do not have this underpinning of long experience of winning as they engage the first days of the rest of their cricketing lives, but undoubtedly there are reasons for optimism. Ashes victory did represent the climax to a trend of increased success and efficiency. It wasn't quite the miraculous transformation it was often painted.

It is also true Vaughan was talking about the need for his team to "stay honest" when the rampage of glory in Trafalgar Square and the Prime Minister's back garden was just a day or two into a foggy past.

This week the great hero of the summer, Andrew Flintoff, turned clear eyes away from the best-seller list and said: "Our profiles have gone through the roof after the Ashes triumph but playing in Pakistan will be totally different for England and will be quite a challenge."

No doubt helping to sober Flintoff was the first delivery he received from the "Rawalpindi Express", Shoaib Akhtar, in the nets while on duty for the Rest of the World team Down Under. It flew viciously shoulder high and it said: Welcome back to Earth. That may have been a gratuitous gesture considering Flintoff's so far wholesome reaction to instantly huge celebrity, but it would be naïve to believe that for some of England's team this week the return to the workplace will not have its jarring moments.

How, when you consider the scale of the distraction over recent weeks, the TV interviews, the book signings, the personal appearances, the clatter of cash registers, could it be otherwise? Pakistan's knowing old coach, and former England batsman, Bob Woolmer, has certainly not been slow to cast doubts about his opponents' ability to hit quickly the straps which left such weals on Ricky Ponting's back – and soul – in the English summer. He says he is intrigued by "post-Ashes England".

That seemed to be a question mark not against a set of cricketers but a euphoric state of mind. He said: "England will either continue on a roll and be very difficult to beat because they will be so good or, and they won't know it is happening even if they discuss it, they find it difficult to get up for Pakistan in the same way as they did against Australia.

"I'm not underestimating them, but I'm interested to see if they can motivate themselves the same against us as they did against the Australians, as much from a coaching viewpoint as anything."

Round about the time Woolmer was saying this his opposite number, Duncan Fletcher, a man of a legendary restraint in the matter of personal projection, was sitting down with a representative of the second national newspaper to have bought rights to a memoir apparently so anodyne it makes the average football recollection seem like a cross between Ian Fleming and Raymond Chandler. But there it was all over our breakfast tables, another recounting of cricket's version of Trafalgar.

No, you cannot blame the boss and the boys for the "greening" of the Ashes. The time of their financial lives had come, and if the result was some of the most benign literary endeavour since Barbara Cartland, only a churl would carp at the rewards of real achievement in this age of contrived celebrity.

However, this doesn't answer the question posed so cunningly by Bob Woolmer.

Will England leave the glory of an unforgettable English summer on the cutting room floors of book editors and TV hosts? Or will they remember the truth that made the men they conquered champions for so long, the one that says the real winners move on to the next challenge before the smoke of battle has cleared. The latter question is no doubt the one Michael Vaughan will be putting to his men with most force in the next few days. Let's hope, for the sake of the national conscience if nothing else, he gets the right answer.

CRICKET'S DARKEST HOUR

Published: 21 August 2006

A Test match died at the Oval yesterday for a lack of trust between those who play cricket and those who administer it. But for those who simply watched, with equal disbelief and dismay, a much wider question was provoked by the cheating dispute between the Pakistan team and one of the game's senior umpires, the Australian Darrell Hair.

It asked if the collapse of a single match, shocking enough in itself, was not simply another pitiable example of a wider death throe.

Were we seeing still another blind march to the point where the very meaning of sport falls into the most painful of ridicule? As the chairmen of the English and Pakistan cricket boards fought desperately for a compromise which might rescue, if not the final Test, a lucrative one-day series, as a tide of boos rolled down from the terracing of the famous old ground which just a year ago was enchanted by seeing England regain the Ashes, those simmering questions inevitably gathered still more force.

This weekend it seemed that the start of a new Premiership season carried most threat to sporting values which have been so relentlessly undermined this disquieting summer.

Endemic diving and steadily eroding discipline in football is seen as a huge threat to the popularity of a billion pound-plus industry – a fear encapsulated in the fact that the most brilliant young player in the English game, Wayne Rooney, a two-goal hero for Manchester United yesterday, is about to start a three- match suspension for a red card received less than a month after he was ejected from England's most vital game in the World Cup.

But such concerns were enveloped in the crisis that overwhelmed the Oval yesterday. If a Test match could suddenly become so completely unhinged as it did when, without warning, Hair in effect announced that the Pakistanis were cheating by tampering with the ball, where were the limits to the disintegration of classic sports values?

Perhaps the idea that cricket was sacrosanct was quaintly anachronistic – the old empire was once threatened by the Bodyline series when Sir Don Bradman was targeted by English bowlers and charges against Pakistan bowlers are not new – but it was the speed and the chaos of the Oval denouement that went to the heart of fears about sport as we like to think we have known it.

The Pakistani captain, Inzamam-ul-Haq, a fiercely proud character, later said that he was merely protesting against the arbitrary branding of his team as cheats by Hair, an Australian official deeply unpopular in Pakistan, but by then there was a sense that cricket had been swept into a crisis that would bring wounds not easily healed.

For the wider image of sport the timing could scarcely have been more disastrous on a weekend when Marion Jones, the American sprinter who six years ago was hailed as the superwoman of the track, was reported to have tested positive.

Track and field has long operated under the darkest of clouds but Jones was said to be intent on redeeming her sport, one which was besmirched again last weekend when Darren Campbell, a member of the gold-medal-winning British sprint relay team at the European Championships in Gothenberg, refused to take a lap of honour with his team-mate Dwain Chambers, who was banned for using drugs. That controversy was fuelled further by suggestions that Linford Christie, the Olympic gold winner who finished his career under a suspension for testing positive for nandrolone, would be the mentor of the nation's young sprinters.

The list of disillusionments scarcely needed to be augmented by the final days of a Test series which had featured some outstanding performances.

Last month the Tour de France stripped the yellow jersey from American winner Floyd Landis. He swears he will prove himself innocent of doping, but the cynicism of his sport has become a lurid joke.

Most disastrous of all was the collapse of fair play in the World Cup in Germany in June and July. The most watched sports event of all time produced passages of brilliant play and was then consumed by a spate of diving. Thierry Henry, the hero of Arsenal and France, was caught in a gut-wrenching dive to win a crucial free-kick and then there was the ultimate horror . . . the great Zinedine Zidane head-butting Italian rival Marco Materazzi in the World Cup final in Berlin.

Zidane reported that the Italian had insulted his sister, a not uncommon occurrence at the highest levels of football, but the president of France, Jacques Chirac, was among those who appeared to condone the fêted player's act of shocking violence.

Yesterday former British Prime Minister John Major, like Sir Mick Jagger and the late Welsh poet Dylan Thomas a devotee of a game which used to be known as one of manners, was among the crowd at the Oval. He is one of those who has always argued that cricket provided a refuge from some of the worst pressures and cynicisms of modern life, but there was little protection in Kennington yesterday.

As former England captains David Gower, Mike Atherton, Ian Botham and Nasser Hussain grappled to come to terms with the worst crisis since the International Cricket Council insisted on a World Cup staged partly in Robert Mugabe's Zimbabwe, Major's face spoke of shock and incomprehension.

The reaction was of men watching something they considered extremely precious break apart before their eyes.

Yesterday it was cricket's ordeal, cricket's pain. Tomorrow no doubt it could be almost any other sport's. One by one the games we play are falling into disrepute. One by one they are inviting the big question: how long can sport, in its present form and morality, survive?

HAIR'S 30 PIECES OF SILVER SMALL CHANGE NEXT TO £10M FOR PUTTING TRUTH ON HOLD

Published: 26 August 2006

Given inflation rates over the last 2,000 or so years, some will say that Darrell Hair asking for $500,000 worth of walkaway money equates roughly to 30 pieces of silver, and presumably, no one at the International Cricket Council will complain – least of all the chief executive, Malcolm Speed, who stopped short only at producing the water and the towels yesterday when he announced the contents of the letter in which the Australian umpire made his request.

Forgive the hint of cynicism, but if Hair's reputation is to be slaughtered publicly because he made what the charitably inclined might just say was an opening gambit in negotiations for a conveniently timed retirement deal, it seems only fair to say that in these days of cricket's crisis after the collapse of the Oval Test, he has hardly been the only one with money on his mind.

Indeed, we can be sure celebrations within the ICC, the England and Wales Cricket Board and its Pakistan counterparts at the rescuing of the one-day series starting next week have rather more to do with the resulting income of £10m than some magical restoration of sporting values – and relations – out on the old green square.

The complaint against the obdurate Hair, certainly in this quarter, has thus far been the relatively minor one that at the very least he was insensitive to the pride of the Pakistanis when he so brusquely, in effect, accused them of being a bunch of cheats. Rightly or wrongly, Hair believed that Inzamam-ul-Haq's team had been tampering with the ball, and if there is another valid criticism of the official it is that he could have been more susceptible to compromise when the seething tourists prolonged their protest after the tea interval.

However, laws unquestionably are laws, and the greatest cause for indignation now must be that the show will continue next week without any of the questions provoked by the scandal of the Oval being officially investigated. Not, that is, until the games, surely utterly meaningless in any spirit they might generate after the betrayal of the public witnessed in Kennington, are played and the money is gathered in.

Speed quoted three lawyers in his decision to go public with Hair's letter, which the author revoked two days after writing it "under great stress". But then legalities were much to the fore when England's cricketers were almost browbeaten into making an appearance in a World Cup game in Harare at a time when the policies of the Zimbabwe government were causing waves of revulsion around the civilised world.

Why has the official inquiry into the dire Oval episode, and the charge against Inzamam that he brought the game into disrepute when he forfeited a Test match – the first time that happened in cricket history – been postponed? It is, we are told, because the one ICC official who could apparently be trusted by all parties was beset by a family crisis. Are we supposed to take this absurd proposition seriously, accept that the game which used to be known as one of manners, which generates millions of pounds of revenue across the world in a quite relentless manner, which burns out its star performers on a routine basis, has just one figure of sufficient, undisputed honour to get to the heart of this matter and reach his conclusions without the taint of bias?

If it isn't an absurdity, it is a shocking statement on the quality of the men who administer a game that in recent years has lapsed into one moral crisis after another.

The World Cup affair was the worst, but then how resolutely did cricket tackle the consequences of the betting scandal that brought down the South African captain Hansie Cronje and asked questions about the honesty of cricketers in every corner of the world? How has it dealt with the game's degeneration into wholesale cheating, including spurious appeals and a blank, uncomprehending stare at the possibility that a batsman might walk when he knows himself to be out?

We know the answers to all of those questions. Now we have to stomach the conveniences of fate which have cleared the way for the cash bonanza which comes in the wake of a Test match – still by far the most superior form of the game – that died because not enough of those involved accepted their responsibilities to the game that has nourished them and the public who so faithfully fund it and then hope for the best.

Darrell Hair has the reputation of a curmudgeon and in parts of Asia they say worse of him than that.

But no one has impugned his honesty thus far, only the wisdom of having him stand in the company of the Pakistanis. Now there may be fresh accusations, at the very least of opportunism. How convenient it is for the game which has just saved itself £10m while putting the truth on hold.

SELECTION WAS A RISKY ROLL OF THE DICE THAT HAS BACKFIRED ON ENGLAND

Published: 15 November 2006

Marcus Trescothick's flight home before a single ball is sent down in the Ashes series that has come to challenge the fibre and will of English cricket is shocking at every level.

In personal terms the call can only be one of compassion. Trescothick for so long was no fragile vessel, likely to shatter at the first serious investigation of his competitive character. At 31, he should be at his peak, a weathered pro boasting 5,825 runs in 76 Tests at an average of 43.79. The benchmark average of a significant Test career has, after all, always been set at 40, a fact that could only have accentuated the pain of the Somerset opener's lonely, angst-filled journey home from Sydney.

Yet if sympathy for a man who was forced to retreat from India and its teeming pressures last winter – and was then advised that he had not recovered sufficiently from a stress-related illness to take part in the recent Champions Trophy in the same country – has to run deep, there is also bound to be another reaction.

It was one merely hinted at by English cricket's ultimate swashbuckling and apparently carefree hero, Ian Botham, yesterday when he said that plunging Trescothick back in the cockpit of Ashes cricket with such slender reorientation always carried high risk.

In fact, some would say that it was one of the most desperate rolls of the dice ever seen at the highest level of world sport.

Supporting evidence for this theory was provided yesterday with re-runs of Trescothick's recent first high-profile television interview since he emerged from his illness – and the mystery that cloaked his earlier flight home from the subcontinent.

Trescothick claimed that he was eager for the Ashes battle, relishing the prospect of building on his success in the summer of 2005, when England won back the prized urn and he made the major contribution of 431 runs. But then there was some hesitation in his voice, and on one occasion he felt obliged to repeat himself.

He also said of the unfolding challenge in Australia: "We will cop it, that's for sure, from the home crowds, the media and an intensely focused opposition."

Focused opposition? That was euphemistic shorthand for the most accomplished and often vicious sledgers in cricket. Shane Warne did give a public assurance that there would be no attempt to apply special pressure to Trescothick, which was a warming thought before the first shot had been fired, but not something to convince old warriors like Botham.

The consensus was that when the pressure was on, the kid gloves would have been casually tossed aside. This, it was pointed out, was the historically ferocious series that once threatened to break up the old Empire when the England captain, Douglas Jardine, ordered his fast bowler Harold Larwood to attack the bodies of key Australian batsmen such as Don Bradman. Such memories are fused into Australian blood and were not likely to be suppressed for too long when a potential mental weakness was there to be exploited – especially when the obligation, after nearly two decades of success, was to win back the Ashes.

At its very highest, the selection of Trescothick was a calculated risk as it ignored certain basic sporting realities. The most important of these is that playing world-class sport successfully is almost always the result of an ability to suppress the pressures of personal life and for a short but intense time commit everything to the challenge of producing your best.

In terms of his status as a cornerstone of the England team, Trescothick failed catastrophically to do this in India and months later he was deemed by his consultant not to be ready for the relatively low-key challenge of the Champions Trophy.

Projecting that vulnerability, so quickly, into the maelstrom of an Ashes series can now be seen as reckless to the point of irresponsibility.

Despite the impressive century of Kevin Pietersen this week in the warm-up game against New South Wales, and the revival of the form of the paceman James Anderson, the psychological cost of Trescothick's relapse is clearly immense. For the moment, though, this particular accountancy is bound to sound heartless. England may just recover from the disaster. There is no such guarantee for the man on whom England gambled so wildly – and lost.

DISSENTING VOICES UNDERMINE TIMELESS AURA OF PONTING'S AGEING ASHES WARRIORS

Published: 21 November 2006

At the Plaza Monumental in Madrid they brush the sand with the reverence you would expect before any episode of pride and danger. This week it is pretty much the same here in Brisbane along Vulture Street.

The Gabba is maybe no longer recognisable as the scene of English terror 32 years ago when Jeff Thomson and Dennis Lillee unleashed a terrible, brilliant fury, but in the modern stadium glinting in the early summer sunshine yesterday you could still feel the old chill. Indeed, what you thought you could taste might well have been a reawakened blood lust.

Behind a tight wall of lock-out security the groundsmen were manicuring what is still the "fastest, bounciest" track in Australia. That was the former Australian captain Ian Chappell's assessment at the weekend when he urged the release of the raw pace of young Shaun Tait in an opening assault on the England psyche which the old warrior believes could well establish an unbreakable home advantage over the next few months.

For the moment Chappell's call is one reinforced by a barrage of Australian belief that the Ashes series which opens on Thursday will quickly prove a ritual more than a contest, a repossession not of a gift but a right.

Even in a distinctly strident history of self-belief, the local desire, even insistence, for the avenging of last year's debacle in England is touching daunting levels of the shrill. It is universal and fierce as it relegates all other issues to the margins of debate in a nation which, perhaps not idly, has come to believe itself to possess the best pound-for-pound sports people on earth.

Certainly the varying fortunes of the rugby union and rugby league teams have never been less significant. Even the crisis of Ian Thorpe, so recently a cornerstone of that Australian belief that they can take on the world and thrash it, is only of fleeting interest. The great swimmer's retirement announcement, despite the incentive of millions of dollars worth of sponsorship at the Beijing Olympics, was expected earlier today. But no one was holding their breath. That will await the first explosion of action here on Thursday morning.

Thorpe is suffering a failure of ambition that is being put down to too many years on the world-beating job. In this the contrast with Ricky Ponting's cricketers could hardly be more extreme. Thorpe at 24 is said to be suffering from ennui. Ponting's team, average age 33, declare themselves aflame.

For Andrew Flintoff and his team it means that if the Gabba truly represents the greatest challenge of their careers – and for the captain the extent of the trial can only be deepened by the fact that this is his first Test on Australian soil – it also offers the chance of a psychological riposte that might just be unprecedented in the history of the Ashes.

Here, you see, the prospect of an English victory in Brisbane or anywhere else is considered utterly outlandish. You have to put down nine dollars to win two unless you are crazy enough to believe that the Poms can retain the Ashes. You also have to wade through a tide of opinion so loaded against English chances that any success this week will produce a mood swing of astonishing proportions. Vulture Street might just tremble. More likely, Ponting's men might just grow old before our eyes.

That certainly is the possibility, however distant, that all of Australia is currently talking away. Here is one morning's sample . . .

"Ashes Warning . . . Shane to bring back the Flipper! Full bag of Tricks!" This is an Aussie theory that the 37-year-old Warne, not content with taking 40 English wickets at the last attempt, has ransacked the best of his amazing career and has emerged with every weapon employed in the best part of two decades of rampant sorcery. Overkill, perhaps, but also in line with the belief here that Warne has only to approach the delivery crease to sow untold panic in English hearts.

"Tait perfect for Gabba." Chappell's belief, offered to his London news-paper, that Tait can re-create the menace of Lillee and Thomson and shatter what is left of England's self-belief at the first time of asking, was given massive play yesterday. Sober judges see only a minor thrust in the propaganda assault, believing that while Tait is quick and promising, we have been asked to consider different species. Lillee and Thomson were of the ages, Tait might just do damage on the best of his days.

"Fletcher Helping Aussies." The former England captain Mike Atherton's view that the coach Duncan Fletcher's rough (some would say brutal) treatment of the wicketkeeper Chris Read is destructive of team spirit has been eagerly seized upon. Divide and conquer the tottering Poms is the thinking here.

"Out of Order. England is taking the timid option shielding Pietersen at number five." This is an attack on the man the Australians see as the most serious threat to their formal repossession of the Ashes. Despite his century last week, Pietersen is being categorised as vulnerable against quick bowling.

It may be of some comfort to Flintoff's men that for some an unflattering picture last week of the spinner Ashley Giles, accompanied by the headline "How did we lose the Ashes to this lot?" was a reminder of the peak of hysterical aggression mounted by the Australian media three years ago when England's rugby union team faced the local heroes in the World Cup final. Then there was the picture of Martin Johnson and his men pounding the beach beneath the question "The most boring team in the world?" Can Freddie Flintoff and his men take similar revenge for potential death by a thousand sneers and cuts? You could trawl Australian opinion from dawn to dusk without gleaning a grain of support for the idea, but then again you might just stumble on the view of a certain Len Pascoe.

It is one which in the present climates may impinge on full-scale treason but Pascoe is something more than a random maverick. He played 14 times for Australia and was considered a sure-fire presence in the pace attack before Kerry Packer's World Series cricket changed the face of the national game. Now, rather like the boy who noted the King was naked, he believes that Australian euphoria may just be built on sandy ground. He points out that Australia are likely to go into Thursday's action with just one player under the age of 30, which would make them the oldest team in 80 years, with an average age of 33.

"I really feel there is a possibility that we will lose this series," says Pascoe. "If we lose the first two Tests, say, the selectors will have no choice but to tap blokes on the shoulders – guys like Justin Langer, Matthew Hayden and Damien Martyn." Pascoe's picture of doubt is in stark contrast with the the one being painted by Ponting.

The Australian captain says that talk of age is nonsense. His team are primed to produce the performances of their lives. His vision of the Australian summer was bullishly encapsulated in one headline: "The old gang is back and ready to roll: bring on England."

Given the records of men like Ponting, Hayden, Martyn, Langer, Glenn McGrath, and, above all, Warne, it is an assertion that only helps along the flow of Australian confidence. But then the old soldier Pascoe and, maybe unconsciously, the superb swimming coach Don Talbot are voices that may just have an encouraging tone for embattled England.

Talbot was asked about the dilemma of his protégé Thorpe, the most phenomenal swimmer the world has ever seen. It was suggested to him that Thorpe's mood may change and that once again he will be talking about beating the world. "Yes, maybe," said the super coach, "but you know at the highest levels of sport talk doesn't do it. You can talk about what you're going to do all day long but it doesn't matter unless you are able to do it, unless you can still deliver."

Talbot's audience was not as attentive, or as reverential, as it might have been before the onset of Ashes fever. But as they groomed the Gabba in the bright sunshine he raised questions that might yet come to haunt the nation who believe, as never before, that it is their destiny to win. This may be thin encouragement for Flintoff and his troops but for the next 48 hours, at least, they cannot hope for anything more.

PONTING HAS THE STEELY RESOLVE OF A CAPTAIN IN SEARCH OF REDEMPTION

Published: 22 November 2006

It may be possible to take the devil out of Tasmania, and even make him the most successful captain in the history of Australian cricket, statistically speaking at least, but there is a limit to the transformation of Ricky Ponting, former brawler and ferocious betting man. You could see it in the hard cast of his eyes on the eve of an Ashes series potentially the most explosive since those sepia days of 1932 and '33 when the Nottinghamshire miner Harold Larwood was instructed to bowl at the head of Sir Donald Bradman.

When an Englishman pointed out that in a certain light you could still see the scar he received when Steve Harmison sent him to the deck at Lord's the summer before last, and the rival captain, Michael Vaughan, instructed his men not to give aid or comfort as he writhed in agony, Ponting smiled in a way that managed to be both exultant and cold.

He said that he loved that day of steamy action at Lord's – and he could not wait for it to be reconstructed on the fast, bumpy track of the Gabba tomorrow morning, when deliveries, as surely as the heat generated by the rising sun, would again fly around the heads of the batsmen.

There was a blaze in the dark eyes now. "It's Test cricket – it's Ashes cricket, isn't it? It's what it's all about. Yes I loved that day, going down to hostile bowling was only part of it. It's the reason you play Test cricket, to be involved in those sort of battles.

"I made no secret of it at the time. That was probably the most intense couple of hours – or day – probably we've all been part of. To be bowled out as we were, and then take those wickets late in the day was just brilliant Test match cricket. On Thursday both teams will be trying to repeat that sort of intensity, and we will certainly see if we can do it again. There's been a long build-up and it's all going to come out at the Gabba – a lot of emotion, a lot of skill."

The English are making no secret of the prize they attach to Ponting's scalp. Since the wounds of the Ashes defeat and much questioning of his leadership once England recovered from the impact of Australian brilliance at Lord's,

Ponting has grown exceedingly strong at the broken places, sweeping back to his position as the world's No 1 batsman and the conqueror in 11 of his past 12 Tests.

That makes him the most successful Australian captain of all time with 22 wins in 30 Tests, seven better than the formidable Ian Chappell, and with a 75 per cent winning record, two per cent ahead of the next best, the brilliantly relentless Steve Waugh. Such legends as Bradman and his successor, Lindsay Hassett, trail in Ponting's wake.

But the 31-year-old Ponting knows that these statistics will not be worth the yellowing paper they are written on if he cannot redeem defeat in England, when he became the first Australian captain to surrender the fabled urn in 20 years.

It means that the man who was once ruled out of the captaincy because he simply wasn't officer material – he once showed up at a press conference with a black eye after an affray in a Kings Cross pub – is simply playing for his place in the charmed corner of the great cricket museum at the Sydney Cricket Club. The England captain, Andrew Flintoff, and his most menacing assistant, Harmison, have noted the pressure on the man who is the cornerstone of the Australian effort and they will attack him from the first delivery he receives. It will no doubt be an assault of the same order as the one that engulfed him at Lord's.

Ponting knows this well enough as he touches the white scar on the right cheek of a face still remarkable boyish when you think of the pace he set in his early life – and the pressure he has absorbed in the past 14 months.

He says: "We've all looked at our own games pretty intensely over the last 14 months to work out the areas we were deficient in last time and, of course, that's what being professional is all about. We've all had the chance to change our games and understand how England are going to attack us. I'm exactly the same as everyone else. I'm not a huge one for looking back and analysing too much but I think I've got a pretty good idea of the way they are going to look to play against us – and how they are going to bowl at me. So it's about executing what you know on the day. I'm looking forward to it."

Ponting curtly deflects suggestions that his place as captain was in jeopardy after the Ashes debacle – and before he led his ageing team back to the No 1 ranking in the world. "No, it's not a worry," he says, "I'm not going to keep everyone happy all the time. Part of the job, any leadership in sport or business, is going to attract some criticism along the way. Some of it may have been fair, some of it may have been a bit unfair, but that doesn't matter now. That series in England has gone and I like to think I'm a better player and captain now. I've lost three Test matches the whole time I've been in charge so things haven't gone too bad."

England thought Ponting was a broken man when he erupted so passionately after being run out at Trent Bridge by one of a small army of substitutes, claiming vehemently a lack of sportsmanship by his opponents. Later, the England coach, Duncan Fletcher, stoked this particular fire when he reflected: "He completely blew his top. I did not think it at the time but looking back that might have been the moment when it became clear that England were going to win the Ashes."

Here this week Ponting's riposte was indirect but not without a little bite. He said Fletcher's choice of Geraint Jones over Chris Read behind the wicket, and the likely choice of Ashley Giles before the more talented Monty Panesar, was "pretty hard to read. You'd think they would be picking their best players. I'm sort of struggling to understand why Jones is playing after Read came in and kept well over a period of time. There's going to be some disappointed players around at changes like that, but it's up to England to decide what to do."

He says it with a shrug. It is, after all, a little routine needling. The real Tasmanian devil's brew, he seems to be saying, can bubble on for another 24 hours.

PONTING SHOW PROVES DAD'S ARMY HAS AMMUNITION TO SPARE

Published: 24 November 2006

For 14 months England's Ashes heroes were eager to draw on the vital difference separating them from the once great Australian team they dragged down from the mountain top. It was, they declared, the difference between youth and age, between fresh, bounding talent and the fatigue that, sooner or later, gets into the bones of even the most brilliant of champions. However, on the first day of the new battle for the fabled urn the old men in the green baggy caps offered another definition.

How about, they asked with often brutal force here, the difference between men and boys? How about the gulf made shockingly apparent by the first delivery of a day so loaded with psychological importance that the smallest phrase of body language was being hungrily analysed by the owners of perhaps as many as a thousand binoculars? Steve Harmison, the man who left the Australia captain, Ricky Ponting, writhing in pain at Lord's in the first dramatic exchanges of the last series, sent it down in a state that was little short of outright petrification. The ball bounced beyond the opener Justin Langer and squirted to a dismayed captain, Andrew Flintoff, at second slip.

For England, it was role reversal of the most devastating kind. Flintoff withdrew Harmison, the strike bowler around whom so much English hope had been built these last few weeks, in humiliating haste.

Only two overs were enough for the captain to see that on this day his prime weapon was capable of firing only duds. And Ponting, padded up and watching with narrowed eyes, suspected that maybe the first part of the battle was over scarcely before it had started.

Just in case there was any serious doubt about this, Ponting proceeded to cut it into small pieces with a sustained and surgical mastery of the batting arts. If you are very lucky, from time to time you get to see great sportsmen at the very height of their powers. You get to see Tiger Woods crossing all known barriers to the most improbable success on a golf course. You get to see Muhammad Ali in a ring or Roger Federer on a tennis court. It was more than a little like that watching Ponting moving relentlessly to his 32nd century, and equalling the Australian record of his predecessor, Steve Waugh. At times almost tauntingly, he split the field by the finest of margins. Fifteen fours flowed seamlessly out of watchful defence and in the fleeting Queensland twilight he stood undefeated on 137 – and vindicated in a way rarely seen even in the demanding culture of his nation's sport.

However England responded on the second day, there was no question that Ponting had thrown down a gauntlet so demanding only the warrior character of a Flintoff could be given the breath of a chance of rallying the shell-shocked troops.

While in 2005 the shrewd leadership of Michael Vaughan was an important element in England's recovery from the thrashing at Lord's, there was no question that it was the force of Flintoff's competitive nature – and the sheer scale of his talent – that made England believe the odds could be upset.

Now, on a slender base of experience, Flintoff must be both leader and warrior and if you were English here and contemplating Australia's first-day stranglehold of 346 for 3, with Michael Hussey not out 63 and proving himself a superb acolyte to his inspired captain, the one small torch of light was that the big Lancastrian had never stopped fighting on his most demanding day as a Test captain.

Having jettisoned Harmison, he knew that there was only one man truly equipped to fight back. It was, of course, himself, and the wickets of Matthew Hayden (21) and Justin Langer (82) represented defiant and possibly redeeming work. This retained Flintoff's fighting aura but it did not, unfortunately, obscure the extent of the statement made by his counterpart, Ponting.

The Tasmanian was gracious about the difficulties faced by English bowlers on a Gabba strip that was far more benign than anything promised by Australian propaganda. He even said that Harmison was a fine bowler who might just recover his nerve. But he was much less persuasive when he suggested he had merely performed another day's work at the office, though indeed it was, astonishingly, his tenth century in 15 Tests – a run of Bradmanesque dimensions, which started with the brave 156 that saved the third Test at Old Trafford.

There was no doubt about the truth that lay at the heart of the Australian offensive. It was that the team sneered at as a Dad's Army by the expert polemicist Ian Botham had come to Brisbane prepared to make something of a last stand. In the case of Ponting, who is still three weeks from his 32nd birthday, this could go on for some years, but for veterans such as Langer, Shane Warne and Glenn McGrath, who was expected to make his first contribution around the time Englishmen at home were first stirring in their beds this morning, the light is surely on the point of fading. First, though, there is this last run at glory and the early evidence was irrefutable. Ponting had spoken for all his men where it mattered most – out on the square.

By comparison, Ashley Giles, who, whatever you think of his claims as a spinner against those of his squad-mate Monty Panesar, had performed manfully in a containing role – and managed to produce enough bounce to dismiss a menacing Damien Martyn – sent out a message almost as dismaying as Harmison's painful disintegration. He said that England were nervous on the drive to The Gabba: "It was a quiet bus. We were all tense." Giles added that this was natural on the first day of an Ashes series.

But natural for whom? Not, plainly, the old boys in the baggy green caps. They will go soon enough but what they seem to be saying here is that it will be in the sweetest of their own time.

FLINTOFF'S FLAMING AMBITION DEFIES AUSTRALIANS' SAVAGE PRESSURE

Published: 25 November 2006

In the circumstances it is not so much, heaven knows, but whatever else English cricket lacked here in the first two days of a Test that might have been devised by the Marquis de Sade it has not been a heroic image.

How could it be? England may be marching to hell in terms of what was conceived as a courageous defence of the Ashes they won so gloriously just 14 months ago but no one has got round to mentioning this to their captain, Andrew Flintoff.

It may also be true that however long he does the job Flintoff will never be mistaken for cricket's answer to Machiavelli. But then if you want something to salvage pride from a battlefield that now seems certain to be the scene of a crushing defeat born of English ineptitudes with both the ball and the bat – for alongside Steve Harmison's haplessly misguided opening salvo we must now place the disastrously weak-minded pull shot of the vice-captain Andrew Strauss – it is the sight of Flintoff bearing down on the brilliant Australian batsman Michael Hussey.

The situation could scarcely have been more desperate. Australia were 407 for 3 and if Hussey's companion, Ricky Ponting, had been described by every morning newspaper as the new Bradman, and was continuing to play to such a wild order, the 31-year-old left-hander who waited so long for the call to glory, and came into this huge match with a Test average of 75.93, was in no mood to be outshone by any cricketer alive. He was playing shots of ravishing composure. If England's misfiring bowlers threw him a scrap, he would turn it into a banquet. His driving was hitting geometric perfection.

He was 86 not out and it seemed that he had only to reach out for another century. But there steaming in was Flintoff, who in the last 24 hours must have felt more than once that in being asked to put out so many fires he was tackling the Blitz with little more than a single water bucket. But however dire his situation on a cricket field – we know now – the recently installed captain of England remains a glorious sight. Perhaps it was that which brought the first cloud of doubt to Hussey. The delivery, anyway, was perfect and the new Australian star's wickets were shattered.

Nothing in England's performance had touched such intensity, and maybe it would not do so again as the Australian attack, led by the perennially cunning Glenn McGrath, cruelly applied pressure to batsmen obliged to contemplate the mountainous scale of the challenge set them by Ponting – 602 for 9 declared. McGrath lured Strauss into his fatal shot, had young Alistair Cook jabbing nervously and terminally into the slips and when Paul Collingwood was outwitted by the stand-in paceman Stuart Clark, England had crashed to 42 for 3.

It meant two things. One was that two young players of bounding reputation, Ian Bell and Kevin Pietersen, had to place alongside their undoubted talent displays of that special character which come not in the flush of glory but when there is the obligation to fight until the last hope is gone. That was vital to the recently soaring name of the English game – so was the need for the ten players who take the field with Flintoff to provide him with fitting company.

This in some ways is no doubt the harshest of assessments. But maybe it is also inevitable in the ferocious climate of a cricket arena where Australia have never been known to take prisoners and where currently their old but magnificently committed team are fighting perhaps as never before to re-establish, perhaps for just one last time, that they are simply the best in the world.

By winning the Ashes so brilliantly in England in the summer of 2005 England elected themselves to judgement only in these terms. They had their parade through London, they had their book launches, and they had their tribute for a job magnificently done.

Now they have to live – or die in terms of reputation – with the consequences of such elevation in the public mind.

In Australia, for 14 months, the failure of Ponting and his men to defend the Ashes successfully has not been a matter for passing reproof. It has been the cause of nothing less than excoriation. The result has plainly caught England by surprise. They have been caught by a ferocity of ambition that was perfectly expressed by McGrath after his latest assault on their already shredded confidence. "We just want to nail home our advantage now," the 36-year-old master paceman said. "We want to remind everyone that we are still the best."

Such force of self-belief, for the moment at least, has left just one

Englishman unfazed. It is, of course, the hero of that summer now dwindling so fast in the public mind. It is Andrew Flintoff still locked in the battle which changed his life. If you look closely at his performance over the first two days here you can only be dazzled by the force of his will. He claimed the wickets of the openers Justin Langer and Matthew Hayden and, after sending back a Hussey committed to new levels of carnage, he also cut short the happily spectacular life of the tail-ender Clark, who twice smote James Anderson for six.

Some have responded better than others to such leadership. Matthew Hoggard, who has known heroics of his own, looked set for a tour of relentless pain on a first day of shocking pressure and failure of impact. But on the second, he fought back, claiming the wickets of the masterful Ponting and an Adam Gilchrist still fighting to find his old blistering touch. Hoggard is the one who has most notably responded to the Flintoff banner.

He earned the praise of his captain despite a challenge so daunting most embattled leaders would have sought the shadows at least until the outcome of their trial. Flintoff said that the fight would be re-engaged with maximum force. He was not disappointed with his troops. He still believed in the strength of their hearts.

Meanwhile, the Australians believed that they were closing for a quick and utterly decisive kill. They have convinced themselves and most independent observers. But not, of course, Flintoff and they are canny enough to know that until they do, not everything can quite be taken for granted. Right now it is the one small but unextinguishable light of English cricket.

FLASHING BLADE DEFIES WIZARD'S DARK ALCHEMY

Published: 27 November 2006

As Kevin Pietersen attempted to close in on the sixth century of his still infant Test career in the small hours of England's wintery morning, his adopted country had reason for a gratitude unbounded by the details of a scoreboard flashing a most improbable Ashes story in the near-tropical heat of Queensland.

Despite producing their first seriously heroic resistance to Australia's unvarnished desire to exact the cruellest possible revenge, England still knew that avoiding defeat, let alone achieving a victory that would be utterly unparalleled in the history of the game, was an ambition that had to be touched by the wildest fantasy.

Yet thanks hugely to Pietersen, and the magnificently obdurate spirit of his yeoman ally Paul Collingwood, they also knew something else. They realised that, amid the psychological debris of what at times over the last four days had threatened to be as much a disembowelling as simply a heavy loss in this first grotesquely unbalanced Test, something precious had been rediscovered.

It was nothing less than the belief fashioned in the glorious summer of 2005, and a first Ashes series win in 18 years, that English cricket might just have enough raw talent and competitive spirit to challenge successfully the team that had so long, and at times so arrogantly, dominated the world game.

This idea, and not without reason, has come under heavy ridicule this last week as the Aussie old guard of captain Ricky Ponting and key, world-beating lieutenants like Glenn McGrath, Justin Langer and, ultimately, Shane Warne, insisted with their deeds more than their words that what happened in that astounding English summer was nothing more or less than an outright aberration.

Ponting made matchwood, it seemed, of England's renewed ambition with his orgy of run-getting, 256 of them for just one dismissal, and then his lordly decision not to enforce the follow-on, despite a first-innings lead of 445.

Ponting said, in so many words, that he could beat England however he pleased. He could wait for the cracks in the wicket to widen while Warne licked his lips. He could rest up the master paceman, Glenn McGrath. He held his former conquerors in the palm of his hand and they were to be crushed at his signal, his whim.

Then the 26-year-old South African-bred Pietersen walked to the wicket and into the middle of his team's latest crisis, 91 for 3 in pursuit of a winning total of 648.

He looked about as intimidated as a crack white hunter adjusting his sights. When he was obliged to call off his mayhem and return to camp, undefeated at 92 and unfazed by the fact that, in rushes of blood, Collingwood, who made 96, and his inspirational captain and friend, Andrew Flintoff, had just thrown away their wickets, it was plainly with the utmost reluctance.

He had simply smashed aside the Australian assumption that victory could come on their terms whenever they chose to exact them – and no one was affected more by this startling intrusion into perceived reality than his erstwhile friend and Hampshire team-mate Warne.

For the moment, at least, and perhaps longer than the term of a contest which was suddenly alive, this celebrity friendship is unquestionably in abeyance. That much was made certain in the flashpoint which came when Warne, the master manipulator of competitive edge, gave way to the frustration created by the rough and commanding treatment he was receiving from Pietersen. He threw the ball in the general direction of the wicket, but it was one the big 26-year-old was guarding and the ball was heading for his head. Pietersen angrily swatted it away and gave Warne the coldest of stares.

At last true battle had been engaged and we can be sure that, however the series develops, there will be no dwindling in this contest of wills.

It is beautifully balanced. At 37, Warne remains a sublime spin bowler of endless creative instinct. By the end of the fourth day, and despite, at times, a terrible buffeting from both Pietersen and Collingwood, he had restocked with scalps the belt that had gone unreplenished in England's pathetic earlier collapse to 157. He had lured Collingwood and Flintoff to their downfall, had invaded again the confidence of Ian Bell, the one English batsman to strike a note of authority in the first innings – and handed him his third duck in his last four Test appearances against Australia – and wiped away the promise of the tall, promising opener Alastair Cook.

That was a decent afternoon's work for even the world's greatest spin bowler, but you could see it meant nothing as long as Pietersen controlled the square so imperiously. There were eruptions of tension each time Pietersen exerted his wonderfully fluent talent, not least when he reached his half-century with a square drive of such withering ease that Warne could not conceal the expression of a scolded schoolboy.

It was as though Pietersen had picked out the heart of the Australian mystique and was attacking it with a single-mindedness built on the conviction that if you destroy Warne's confidence, if you suggest to him that you are untouched by the destructive power of any of his dark alchemy, you are likely to diminish not just the principal tormentor but his entire team.

For the Australian vice-captain Adam Gilchrist, obliged to lead the team in the absence of Ponting, who required treatment on a back injury, it was as severe a test of nerve as that faced by Warne every time he bowled into the maw of the Pietersen cannon. You cannot withdraw even a bloodstained Warne from the action without the heaviest loss of face. You have to trust in his ability to find a way to do damage, and Gilchrist's reward was the sight of Collingwood and Flintoff broken by Warne's cunning.

Pietersen, though, was beyond sorcery. On a day when Flintoff had failed to reproduce his magnificent presence in the field, and at the bowling crease, and when his No 2 Strauss had, for the second time in the match, thrown away his wicket with shocking irresponsibility, Pietersen had given England a weight, a purpose and an aura which might yet rescue a campaign which some feared had died before it could possibly begin.

The ferociously competitive Langer, who had been granted the chance to complete the century that had narrowly eluded him in Australia's first innings, conceded the quality of Pietersen generously enough. He said that he and his team-mates could easily identify with the style of a most powerfully gifted opponent. He was an outstanding talent shot through with the urge to fight every step of the way. In that way, he was an honorary Australian. It was a nice thought but it paled against a warmer reality. England had every reason to embrace the foreigner who had announced himself as committed as any native son.

THE HARDER THEY FALL

Published: 30 November 2006

There is something addictive about watching Australia work in the nets. The rhythm of it reminds you of one of the best pre-fight workouts, when a Roberto Duran or a Sugar Ray Leonard used to reach such a level of intensity that the only proper reaction was awe. One ringsider once said that it was surprising the trainers did not arm themselves with chairs and whips. They weren't working fighters; they were taming lions. It was a little like this at the Adelaide Oval yesterday, even when in mid-afternoon the temperature touched 98 degrees.

Training can create myths, of course. Old pros say that one minute of real action is worth hours of superb practice, and for England here it is a notion to prize – a haymaking delivery from Andrew Flintoff perhaps, or another surge of virtuosity from Kevin Pietersen, and maybe the aura of the resurrected Oz can yet be broken.

But then it is also true that at these nets it is not easy to question the thunderous Australian belief in regained momentum. There is simply no pause, no rumination. The declaration of the captain, Ricky Ponting, that his team has, at least in some of its key components, and perhaps for one last time, found itself again, is supported by a quite seamless flow of effort.

In the shimmering heat, for a little while at least, Australian cricket has been reunited with its past as it attempts to win back the future. For what ghosts of a great past still occupy this place. Sir Don Bradman came here from New South Wales and redoubled his legend. The Chappell brothers, Ian and Greg, made their names at Australia's most beautiful cricket ground. Now it seems that the great tradition is indeed alight again.

It is a powerful suggestion in the expression of players like Justin Langer and Ponting as they go about their work; it is an edge, a restlessness that was once ascribed to the greatest Australian all-rounder of them all, Keith Miller. A Second World War fighter pilot, it was said of Miller that at the peak of competition he carried an expression so alert, so fired, that he might have been scanning the sky for an enemy plane.

For Ponting's team the enemy is the possibility of Australian cricket's hardest fall from grace, another Ashes loss. In the hours before their latest challenge they seem intent on hunting it down.

For the sake of a little English peace of mind, however, it has to be reported that Glenn McGrath, the 36-year-old who claimed seven of their wickets at the Gabba a few days ago, did take an early break from the three-hour work session. His bruised heel was still a little sensitive, a team official said, so the great man merely put the pads on and batted for half an hour. He left with an assurance for a small army of anxious fans that he would be perfectly fine on the dawn of tomorrow's second Test. If he wasn't, young Shaun Tait swiftly announced, Australia would not be without an option of a certain potency. The 23-year-old local hero promptly sent down a barrage of deliveries so quick and so menacing that they created a heat haze of their own.

Still, the net aficionados said, it was a pity that McGrath was in wraps because the last time Australia worked in the Adelaide nets he and his opening partner, Brett Lee, put on a show that was already part of cricket folklore hereabouts. Three stacks of soft-drink cans were placed in line with the wickets at those points which would represent perfectly pitched deliveries. Six balls were delivered, alternately, by McGrath and Lee, working from left to right. Each ball shattered the tins.

However, such a cabaret might not have been injected into yesterday's work even if McGrath had been going full bore. The overwhelming suspicion has to be that this is an Australian team which will be no more subject to distraction and humour than a dedicated firing squad right up to the moment the Ashes yielded in England in the summer of 2005 are regained.

Yesterday in the nets we had the choreography of absolute commitment – a mood that was underlined when the opening batsman Matthew Hayden, one of the veterans who took defeat in England especially hard, dismissed the possibility of any serious menace in England's expected selection of two spinners, Monty Panesar and Ashley Giles. "I don't think," he declared, "this Australian batting line-up has too much threat from either of these players. We are confident because we had to answer some hard questions – like are we still hungry, can we be ruthless again? We think we have answered those questions but we also know we have to keep doing so for four more Test matches.

"At the Gabba we were everything we promised ourselves to be in the 14 months since we lost the Ashes, and I can tell you we remain in that state of mind. After Brisbane, England are now being asked the questions we have had to answer. Are you still hungry? Or are you fragmented? Look, let's be clear, we didn't begrudge the English their celebrations when they beat us, and you know in one way the Australian people have been celebrating the reverse side in that it is true it had been almost monotonous the way their great team had been beating people."

Ponting's current intensity is remarkable even in the tradition of cricket's finest nation of recent years. He says that the seed of recovery was sown as early as the flight home from England.

"In England it seemed as though we couldn't do anything right after taking the first Test at Lord's, but you know I couldn't have been prouder of this bunch of players than when we first arrived home. We were playing the Rest of the World in something called the Super Series, but you know I had the feeling we truly bounced back and applied ourselves and it gave me the feeling that no matter who we happened to be playing, we were bound to win. You could just see it in the guys' eyes.

"We've been able to maintain that for a long period of time now with one eye on the first Ashes Test; now that's gone, we've just got to make sure it carries on the same way. I suppose what we discovered in England was that it is always going to hurt when you lose, and this is something maybe you have to relearn after a lot of success. We came home from England thinking: 'We are better than that'. Now I don't think we have any greater pressure than England . . . in fact, at the Gabba I thought we were able to play pretty much pressure-free. We talked about the situation after the first day's play. I said: 'Look, it's no good having one good day. In our position there is no alternative . . . we just have to keep having good days. What we did today is irrelevant now. It won't mean anything if we don't back it up'. What we have to do is play good, hard Test cricket for five days."

In the nets that resolve has been an intense reality. Hayden says it is engendered by a belief that ground has been regained that can never be surrendered again, not at least in what is left of his own playing days. The Queenslander is 35 and those playing days are no doubt drawing near to their close. But then what better reason to play – and to work – as if there may be only one tomorrow? England, there can be no mistake, are facing no ordinary challenge, no ordinary team. They have to break down a booming state of mind – and a great weight of history.

PANESAR'S ARTISTRY OFFERS ENGLAND A TURNING POINT

Published: 01 December 2006

It was not for any excessive or irrational belief in a young man of splendid heart and charming disposition, but still modest achievement, that made so many yearn for the sight of the bright blue patka of Monty Panesar when England started their attempt to fight back in the second Test which started here today.

Panesar's selection was expected but not guaranteed overnight, a fact which could only increase the sense that a whole dimension of cricket, and maybe its most beautiful one, was still for the English game the most dangerous ground.

England did not believe in Panesar's potential to spin the ball to any real purpose before the first Test in Brisbane that turned into an ordeal of both failed performance and nerve, and here the agony of indecision, crisis of faith – call it what you like – was taken to the ludicrous lengths of an audition in the nets for the 24-year-old left-armer.

At a time when Panesar should have known his fate, and perhaps been steeling himself for the most important challenge of his exuberant life, he was asked, rather like some *X Factor* candidate who had just walked in from the street, to prove himself to the coach, Duncan Fletcher.

This is maybe not the way you usher in a player who might just change your destiny and here, in a land which so quickly scrubbed up the beach boy larrikin Shane Wane and thrust him into the heart of Test cricket, the process has been received with some predictably dark hilarity.

The leading newspaper *The Age* captured prevailing Australian opinion with a front page which asked: "Did you hear the one about the Englishman who walked in to bowl? Panesar to play, but can we take English spin bowling seriously?" More relevantly, can the English? All the evidence suggests not. Ashley Giles, widely derided here for his lack of ambition at the bowling crease, got the nod in Brisbane because of his superior potential as a tail-end batsman. *The Age*, seizing on the fact that in eight Tests against Australia Giles averages just over two wickets per match at a cost of 55 runs each, chose mirthfully to list the names of leading England spinners since the 1970s, starting with the current England selector Geoff Miller and finishing with Giles.

The statistics are not uplifting. In 64 Tests, John Emburey mustered roughly two-and-a-half wickets a match, similar to his Middlesex team-mate Phil Edmonds. Phil Tufnell, perhaps the most talented occupant of the wasteland which spread in the days after Laker and Lock and Underwood and Illingworth, but so often obliged to bowl defensively, got closest to the mountain top of three wickets per match – something that Peter Such did manage, albeit over the shorter haul of 11 Tests.

No one would claim seriously that Panesar has yet made even an infant claim on the tradition of the world's best spin bowler, Shane Warne, who has collected 689 wickets in 141 Tests, but when Warne was conspicuously unsuccessful in his first Test as a 22-year-old, taking 1 for 151 against India, there was no question of standing him down.

Panesar, two years older than Warne at his debut – and five older than Neil Harvey when the teenager made his maiden Test century in Sir Don Bradman's team at Headingley in 1948 – has taken 32 wickets in ten Tests at an average of 32.40. It is also interesting to note that half his wickets serve as a working guide to the aristocracy of modern batsmanship, the scalps of India's past and present captains, Sachin Tendulkar and Rahul Dravid, and the hard core of Pakistani run-getting, Inzamam-ul-Haq, Younis Khan and Mohammad Yousuf.

These were the most brightly lettered of calling cards and yesterday they prompted warm words of encouragement from Stuart MacGill, the fine Australian leg-spinner whose misfortune has been to operate in the age of Warne. This has not prevented MacGill compiling a superb record at the highest level of the game, claiming 198 wickets in 40 Tests at an average of 27.21.

Said MacGill: "I hope Monty plays, and I hope we see someone being himself and not copying Ashley Giles. You should never walk in somebody's else shoes. They don't fit. Monty has an amazing opportunity to dominate England's spin-bowling landscape for years to come. He can make a real mark – if he remembers to be himself and gets the right encouragement."

The argument goes beyond Panesar's ability to help shape this Ashes series. It is partly about how English cricket sees itself. The broad question before the team was announced officially asked if England were finally prepared to break out of the habit of making spin bowling not cricket's ultimately intriguing art but a conservative function of failed nerve.

Panesar's fellow Sikh, Bishan Bedi, once duelled for a large part of a day with England's former captain, Brian Close, before a rapt crowd at Taunton. It was, said enchanted witnesses, the essence of cricket.

Panesar may never be Bedi – with his endlessly beguiling arc of arm and ball – he may never get to the foothills of Warne, but here, now, it is impossible to understate what he has come to represent. It is the difference between defence and attack, doubt and belief, between locking the door – or going out in search of a little beauty and, who knows, something as fundamentally important as a win.

PONTING DONS THE MANTLE OF BRADMAN WITH TOTAL AUTHORITY

Published: 04 December 2006

Here in this graceful cathedral city of Adelaide, whose hauntingly beautiful cricket ground Sir Donald Bradman made his spiritual home, a modern heresy has to be addressed, finally and unequivocally.

It is the one that says that in some vital respects the Australian captain Ricky Ponting may be nothing less than the reincarnation of the greatest batsman the world has ever seen. Long-retired colonels and rear-admirals who, as young men, clapped the Don through the Long Room when he was making his final tour of England in 1948, will no doubt be displeased, and here in his homeland some ancient cricket aficionados are certainly growling at the idea, but on the third day of an increasingly intriguing second Test this mattered a lot less than the evidence of your own eyes.

The conclusion is inescapable. The heretics may just be right.

Different times, different demands, and utterly different men, no doubt, but over the last few days Ponting has linked himself to Bradman in a way that has become unprecedented.

Yesterday he was caught in a paroxysm of rage when he surrendered his wicket for a mere 142 runs.

A week earlier we saw the same scene at the Gabba, when he went for 196, an awesome prelude to the brisk, undefeated 60 he knocked up in the second innings. Staggeringly, this is just a molehill of statistics when you set it amid the torrent of Test runs he has compiled in 2006. He has amassed 1,200 in 11 innings in eight Tests at an average of 109.1. After his latest epic – which stretched over five hours and 53 minutes and was no doubt the main, if not only, reason why Andrew Flintoff's England are not already celebrating a superb comeback victory in a series that seemed already to be over a few days ago – Ponting was emphatic.

"I don't think about statistics, mate, I wasn't worried about that when I was out – I was just thinking that we needed to get through that second new ball. I had been talking to Mike Hussey out there about it most of the day – we had to get back into this game, we had to see off that new ball."

It is no doubt true that, as a strategist, most of Australia wouldn't put Ponting in remotely the same league as such subtle and abrasive warriors as Allan Border, Ian Chappell and Steve Waugh, whose record of 32 centuries for Australia was passed here when the current captain ran a brisk single off his hard-driving rival Flintoff. Ponting is widely blamed for the loss of the Ashes in England and maybe it is this that is driving him to such astonishing levels of personal commitment – and consistency.

But history will not delve into the motivation which turned Ponting, a young man of ferocious habits in both the bars and the betting windows, into someone who at 31 is poised to shatter every record of batsmanship. It will simply record the pace of his assault on the mountain top, one which leaves him just two centuries away from the peak achieved by the Indian maestro Sachin Tendulkar, who leads his legendary compatriot Sunil Gavaskar and West Indies' Brian Lara by one. Many believe that Tendulkar is a burnt-out case, a condition for which Lara has frequently been diagnosed in between bouts of coruscating brilliance. By contrast, Ponting's impact when he goes to the crease is more even – and volcanic.

When he overcame the self-disgust which accompanied the snick off England's hero Matthew Hoggard into the gloves of Geraint Jones, Ponting managed a wry smile and admitted that when he finally puts away his bat he may well linger a little over the great days of run accumulation. "Yes, I suppose I'll look back with a lot of pleasure," he said. "I think that's true of a lot of old players – but not now. That's not my priority for some time. At the moment there is only one. It is winning back the Ashes."

Among his awestruck admirers is the former Australia captain Kim Hughes, who says: "Ponting is a magnificent player and he will end up with more than 50 Test centuries. He already has 33 and he will surely play for another five or six years, scoring three or four centuries a year minimum. He will end up with more runs in centuries than I did in my whole career."

It is against this growing aura of just one of their opponents that you have to weigh the scale of England's achievement over the first three days of this Test match – and the level of the regret that faced Ashley Giles and Paul Collingwood, the double-century hero of Saturday, when they went to their beds knowing they had let slip the greatest single scalp in the game. Giles dropped Ponting when he was on 35 and just 11 runs later the usually deadly Collingwood missed what normally would have been an easy target when the Australian captain scrambled to get home after a suicidal call for a quick single.

When Ponting did fall, even the Barmy Army were momentarily stunned. His impression of permanence had been so brilliantly stated after the reprieves granted by Giles and Collingwood, it was as though a new battle had been called. Ponting's hitherto nerveless lieutenant Mike Hussey, who had unerringly reached 90, was so affected he was almost immediately bowled by Hoggard. In the wake of the quick dismissals of Matthew Hayden and Damien Martyn, which left Australia at a critical 65 for 3, Hussey's balance between defence and attack – he hooked the appreciably restored Steve Harmison for a six of withering power and certainty – had looked utterly impenetrable as England fought impressively to hold on to their advantage.

But then suddenly he was without an anchor, a plight which, for his team's chances of avoiding the follow-on and a devastating blow after the elation which came at the Gabba, was relieved only partly by the partnership of Michael Clarke and Adam Gilchrist which carried Australia to the close.

While Clarke and Gilchrist held off the surging Hoggard, Ponting was haranguing those superior tail-enders Shane Warne and Brett Lee, on his belief that a flat, dry wicket still offered many life-giving runs. They might have said it was easy for him to say – easier, indeed, than any cricketer currently at work, with the possible exception of Pakistan's Mohammad Yousuf, who has hit nine centuries in his last 19 innings at an average of 99.33. Yousuf is not quite at the Ponting mark, but then that has suddenly become the benchmark not just of today but the greatest achievements cricket has ever known.

One ageing Australian, who remembers how it was when the Don carried his great talent into his 40th year, insisted that he saw in Ponting something rather more than an authentic challenge to the deeds of cricket's ultimate hero.

"You know," he said, "the more I look at him bat, the more I'm reminded of Bradman. He has the same, bird-like movement at the crease; he's small and precise and he always seems to know exactly what he is doing."

It is still another daunting aspect of the apparently inexorable rise of a master batsman, this idea that he is taking on the very mannerisms of the man who for so long was believed to have operated in a world of his own. Certainly it will be something to bear in mind if England do build on these last few days of character and high achievement. Refusing to return the Ashes to Ricky Ponting would, no doubt, deserve its own extraordinary place in the history of cricket.

INFANTRYMAN WITH A SECRET WEAPON RISES FROM TRENCHES TO STARS

Published: 05 December 2006

Matthew Hoggard would be a hero in any age of sport because he has the kind of bloody-minded character that takes him to the core of his business, bowling seamers hard and long in any conditions you care to put in front of him.

In the celebrity age, however, his deeds, which periodically sweep beyond those of men with bigger and perhaps less hard-won reputations, and rather more star appeal, seem to carry a special distinction.

From a man so unsung, his highest notes carry the classic resonance of a pure performer. Indeed, sometimes it seems his growth as a cricketer is in direct proportion to the degree of difficulty he faces.

Before this second Test of such huge importance to England's shaky hold on the Ashes, for example, Hoggard's potential to influence events was considered somewhat less than that of his captain, Andrew Flintoff, and even the dismayingly inconsistent Steve Harmison.

But then, as an eruption of Australian virtuosity led by Michael Clarke and the re-emerging Adam Gilchrist threatened to ambush England's retrenchment after the first Test disaster in Brisbane, again it was the 29-year-old Yorkshireman who not only held the line but conjured the possibility, however slight, of victory. While this was happening Flintoff was restricting himself to just four overs, for "precautionary medical reasons," a team official said, and Harmison was being smashed for 11 runs in one over by the suddenly resurgent Gilchrist.

Hoggard just bowled on, adding three more wickets to the four he had claimed on the day when Australia's captain, Ricky Ponting, was marching another step towards the mantle of the legendary Sir Don Bradman.

Ponting smashed his bat into the ground, despite scoring 142 majestic runs, when Hoggard got the better of him with a ball that cut away from his bat and into the hands of wicketkeeper Geraint Jones. It was a typical Hoggard thrust, a mysterious act of bowling brilliance that he swears he does not quite understand. He does it, he says, but do not ask him how. Ponting acknowledged the skill and the competitive nature of his assassin. "Hoggard is a guy who never lets up," he warned his team-mates.

Temperamentally, Hoggard is an infantryman, albeit the kind who might have palled up with Spike Milligan had he also been around to join the fight against Hitler, but when it matters, when he senses that he has an edge, there is suddenly no limit to his swagger.

He doesn't milk the limelight. He turns it into natural energy. Hoggard is an unforced eccentric who, before his latest gut-tearing, brilliant effort here, pulled a series of funny faces as he mocked the industry of cricket analysis, especially that part of it which devotes so much time to explaining the dark art of "swinging" the ball, exploiting the conditions and the seam of the round piece of leather. Sometimes it seems like an aspect of nuclear science, but Hoggard declares: "Don't ask me how weather conditions affect the ball. I just don't know. I do it but I can't explain it. What I do is close my eyes and just bang it down."

No doubt, this is not quite right. Bowlers of any persuasion are notoriously secretive about their technique – and their superstitions – and Hoggard is plainly not the kind of man to shed too much light on either his nature or his art.

Here this week it has been enough, certainly, to value again the force of his instinct to draw from himself every ounce of available talent and effort. In England's first innings this was the supreme achievement of Hoggard's team-mate Paul Collingwood and here from the bowling crease was the perfect balancing performance.

It meant that if England do take worries about their ability to bowl out Australia twice in any one Test match to the next one on another reportedly benign wicket in Perth, Hoggard has defined for all his team-mates the level of commitment that will be required if the job is to be done.

What he has produced here is still more evidence of an extraordinary will that surfaced earlier this year in Nagpur when, amid fears that years of extreme demands on himself had begun to take a toll, he claimed six Indian wickets for 57 runs. Five years ago that kind of potential to dominate a Test was established against South Africa when he took 12 wickets in a match, and career-best figures of 7 for 61.

Here he faced conditions that might have been produced specifically to break the heart of a seam bowler – a reality underlined by the fact that the Australian bowling legend Glenn McGrath is now facing the first serious questions about his ability to stretch his magnificent career any further into his 38th year.

McGrath, who going into England's second innings had failed to claim a wicket, will probably survive a troubling performance and reappear in Perth. But, unquestionably, his selection will be based on an almost mythic reputation for producing something extraordinary when it matters most.

Hoggard has never enjoyed such luxury. He moves from one battlefront to another with a simple obligation. It is to delve into the mystery of his trade and keep coming with something that flies, often at the unlikeliest moments, beyond the professional norm.

In this department of supreme effort Hoggard had only one rival on the pivotal fourth day of this strange and laggardly but utterly absorbing Test match.

It was Michael Clarke, the former infant prodigy of Australian cricket. No one in this tough sports culture sought to disguise the nature of the 25-year-old Clarke's challenge, here and in the first Test in Brisbane. He was fighting for his place in Test cricket. At the Gabba he hit a beautifully composed half-century; on Monday he scored his third century at the highest level, a frequently exquisite piece of work which had started the night before when he was charged with the responsibility of guiding Australia closer to England's first-innings total of 551 after the sudden dismissals of Ponting and Michael Hussey.

Clarke, in his way, met his brief as completely as did Hoggard. He scored 124 and made it virtually impossible for his team to lose the advantage they had gained in Brisbane.

Later, he admitted that there was deep emotion when he finally reached his goal. He thought of several lost years, and the pain he had felt when he fell a few runs short of a century at Lord's in the Ashes series that went wrong, both for his country and for himself. He fought back the tears before he returned to his task – one that ended only when he received a beautifully delivered ball from Matthew Hoggard.

In that moment there was no winner or loser, just two brilliantly motivated cricketers reaching down for the best of themselves. Sport, celebrity-driven or otherwise, had rarely come better than this.

SORCERER SUPREME CASTS HIS MOST MAGICAL SPELL

Published: 06 December 2006

The author of arguably the most stunning victory in the history of Test cricket was asked how deeply he felt the tension when his Australian team-mates Mike Hussey and Michael Clarke drew close to the target that would all but deliver this Ashes series. As he sat padded-up, was he sweating out the possibility that a fall of two quick wickets would take him back into the heart the action? "No, mate," he said, "I wasn't interested in batting. I was drinking pop and eating toasted sandwiches."

Shane Warne is nobody's idea of a super athlete, least of all his own, but at 37 his aura has never blazed so brilliantly. He is the most charismatic performer in the history of cricket and, after systematically reducing England to nothing less than a collective nervous breakdown, he may also be the best, the most influential, the most guaranteed to sow demoralisation into a batsman's heart and mind.

This, certainly, is the regained gravitas he takes to Perth for a third Test next week in which he will once again overshadow team-mates and opponents alike.

He is not so much a cricketer as a maker of spells. Yes, he is portly and has often displayed away from the field an irresponsibility that would be frowned upon in the kind of feckless beach boy he once was.

He is incorrigible, hedonistic and, before his latest epic performance, one former opponent of great distinction was saying that he is probably cricket's answer to Peter Pan – somebody who either cannot, or simply doesn't want to grow up.

Among even his warmest admirers there are fears that he will be a lost soul when he has to face the day when he can no longer go out on the field secure in a world that for a decade and a half now he has dominated in an extraordinary and relentless way.

Yet that day, once again, has been pushed back, assigned to all the other calamities of old age. For the moment Shane Warne is as young as he wants to be. He remains the King of Neverland.

Here today there is no limit to the homage being paid to the man who almost single-handedly won a Test that many hard judges agree was possibly the most remarkable ever played. Australia came to a near standstill as Warne worked his alchemy on a contest which in the morning had seemed to permit only two possibilities – a win for England, 97 runs ahead with nine wickets standing, or a draw. Offices and factories here in Adelaide were emptied as "grieving" workers – and some bosses – had to rush to the scene of family bereavements, by way of the beautiful Oval which Warne had claimed for his own.

Ian Chappell, an Australian captain of ferocious application, said: "There are two reasons why Australia were able to win this match. They have a great team – and the greatest player cricket has ever seen. I have never seen opponents so dominated, so mesmerised. Without Warne, Australia couldn't have won this Test match. You just don't win Test matches after your opponents have put on 551 runs in their first innings. It doesn't happen, it shouldn't happen, but then with Warney we know now anything is possible."

Another former Test captain, England's Mike Gatting, watched Warne with the same stunned countenance he had displayed when he became one of the young bowler's first major victims, the casualty of a leg break so outrageous it shocked the cricket world.

Said Gatting: "I suppose I shouldn't be surprised by anything Warne does, but what happened is going to take a little time to believe."

Maybe it should be said there were at least half a dozen reasons why England's hold on the Ashes urn was loosened to the point of hopelessness when they went 2-0 down in the small hours of Tuesday.

We could start with the cascade of runs pouring from the bat of Australian captain Ricky Ponting, another 49 flowing crucially as his team climbed from beneath the mountain of England's first-innings total of 556 for 6 declared to knock off the 168 runs required with three of the designated 36 overs remaining. That took Ponting's series total to 447 in four innings, one of them undefeated.

Nor can we avoid the fact that England were utterly overwhelmed by the fierce competitive instinct of the Australian game rising so vengefully out of Ashes defeat in England in 2005 and expressed quite superbly by the emerging master batsmen Hussey and Clarke. It is also true that in Brett Lee, Stuart Clark and Glenn McGrath, Australia had a trio of pace bowlers whose ability to bowl a length and a line mocked the efforts of their English rivals, and that included the captain, Andrew Flintoff, the star of that English summer, and first-innings hero Matthew Hoggard.

Yet wherever you turned there was always the sight of Warne, the supreme architect of Australian victory. In the decisive moments of a match which we were so sure England could not lose after the batting performances of Paul Collingwood and Kevin Pietersen, we were confronted again by the same grim picture painted in the first Test in Brisbane – the one of men facing boys.

At the heart of it was Warne endlessly turning his right arm and making psychological mayhem. He bowled for four unbroken hours, until the point when his fingers twitched with weariness and his shoulder ached. "As much as the body was beginning to tire," he said, "the adrenaline kicked in with the knowledge that in 140 Test matches we were about to win the greatest Test match I had ever played in.

"Yes, it was my most satisfying time in cricket. For one thing I had read the rubbish of [coach] Duncan Fletcher that the English batsmen had learned how to play me." Fletcher had been emboldened by Warne's frustration in the first innings, when he claimed just one wicket for 161 runs. This, suggested the England coach, was not the work of a sorcerer but someone whose mystery had dissolved. England had exposed the flight of genius, and what was left? An old, sad routine.

It was a delusion of devastating consequences as Warne laid siege to England's confidence, claiming four wickets and among them the great prize of Pietersen.

Pietersen was Warne's chief tormentor as England apparently insulated themselves against defeat. He forced Warne to bowl around the wicket in an attempt to staunch England's flow of runs and to nag at the patience of the hard-hitting and hugely talented young batsman. That was a little like asking an Old Master to paint the kitchen but then suddenly Warne was working on his own unique canvas once again.

He bowled Pietersen around his legs as he attempted to sweep. It was the moment England's concern at the jittery run-out misadventure of Ian Bell turned into wholesale panic.

Warne seemed to a grow a little more menacing each time he approached the bowling crease. When someone later spluttered out amazement at his ability to meet the relentless demands of his captain, Ponting intervened. "In a situation like that, mate, I'd like to see anyone get the ball off Shane Warne," said the captain. "No one wants the ball more, no one is more willing to bowl forever."

When England's captain faced the world he was still in shock. Flintoff wondered how it was possible to lose a Test match which his team had dominated for all but an hour. It seemed heartless to remind him that anything can happen in Neverland.

BRITTLE ENGLAND
– THE AWFUL TRUTH

Published: 07 December 2006

Even in this land where plain speaking is not an option but a ferocious demand, a terrible charge has been levelled against the cricketers of England.

It is that as holders of the Ashes they are impostors. You wouldn't lightly support such a charge against the team which so gloriously ended 18 years of failure in England in the unforgettable summer of 2005.

You wouldn't want your patriotism questioned. You wouldn't want to overreact to a defeat which is still, 24 hours on, a little difficult to believe. But then if you had watched the disintegration of England on Tuesday, so soon after the terrible beating in Brisbane a few days earlier, you might see in the accusation something rather more than routine Pom-bashing. You might, and it is no easy thing to say, get a glimpse of the truth – an awful, almost unthinkable truth, but a truth all the same.

Here is the verdict of *The Australian*, one of the nation's more balanced newspapers – and the squeamish should look away now: "England's ineptitude was staggering. Its cricket was as uneducated as it was unedifying and its defeat among the most humiliating in the annals of the game. Despite loud claims to the contrary, this England team has neither the personnel nor the mind-set for an Ashes campaign of such intensity. It defies belief it should be in such despair and effectively out of this series after just ten days of cricket . . ." These, believe it or not, are words written with a degree of sadness, and not to accept this would be to miss a crucial factor in the Australian sports psyche.

The fact is that if the nation was cast down when England came through to victory at the Oval 15 months ago, the grief did not last too long. It was swiftly overtaken by the pleasurable anticipation of the fight to get the Ashes back – and the fact that the series had come alive again after nearly two decades of slipping relentlessly down the sports agenda. The Australian captain, Ricky Ponting, confirmed the point on the eve of the English débâcle here. He said that in the first days after his men returned from England you could already see the hunger in their eyes.

We did not see hunger in English eyes these last few days. We saw befuddlement. We saw a team that had neither the spirit nor the nous to exploit the vast advantage of batting first on a lifeless wicket; that, even after the abject collapse of English batsmen on the last day, still had no ambush for the likes of Ponting and his superb lieutenants Mike Hussey and Michael Clarke.

Australian delight was unlimited after the climax of one of the most extraordinary day's play in the history of Test cricket. But unless England stand and fight in Perth in the third Test next week, and the coach, Duncan Fletcher, and captain, Andrew Flintoff, shake themselves into a coherent selection process rather than something that looks uncomfortably like the kind of exclusive old boys' club so recently run by the former England football coach Sven-Goran Eriksson, you can be sure the Australian public will sicken of the slaughter soon enough.

Already there is a crushing sense of anti-climax at the reality of a series which had seemed to promise something rather more than a semblance of a fight.

Ian Chappell, one of the hardest, most driven of Australian captains, has expressed this mood with typical candour. He was appalled by the sight of Flintoff setting a defensive field at the formative stage of Australia's pursuit of 168 winning runs in 36 overs. He said: "Captains set fields for bowlers they can trust to deliver the ball in the right places. If this is the best field he can set for Ashley Giles, there is an inescapable conclusion. This bowler should not be playing Test cricket." It is one of several selection scandals that inevitably is shaping almost every view of the English effort.

Giles, we are told from behind the straight faces of Fletcher and Flintoff, is in the team because of the weight of batting he brings to the position of No 8. Here he scored 27 at the end of England's marathon first innings – and a duck when the pressure was on as Shane Warne, whose meaning to Australia simply mocks Giles's role for England, bowled 32 overs and took four wickets for 49 runs. Not the least staggering aspect of the preference for Giles over the vastly superior attacking potential of Monty Panesar is that he was playing his first top-flight game in a year in Brisbane.

Panesar has played ten Tests and taken 32 wickets, among them some of the great scalps of the international game. He is a player who attacks batsman, undermines them. The Australians were nonplussed when he was excluded from this last Test.

It is the same with the selection of Geraint Jones over Chris Read. Jones is adjudged to be the superior batsman, but here he made one and ten, and where do you begin the calculation of loss if Jones' inferior wicketkeeping technique allows a Ponting or a Hussey to escape England's net? And what do we make of the indulgence of the captain's close friend Steve Harmison? He is a talented bowler trying to remake himself. In the middle of an Ashes series. It is another matter for Australian disbelief.

In the wake of the disaster here Fletcher seemed to be in some kind of denial of logic. He cited Warne's contribution with the bat for Australia, pointing out that, in his century stand with Hussey in the first innings, the master spinner had put pressure on England. It was an astonishing *non sequitur*. Warne plays for Australia not because he is a decent batsman but because of what he does to the minds of his opponents when they walk to the batting crease. To say this is almost like asserting a car's need for petrol. A cricket team needs an attack of variety and threat. Giles is a lower order batsmen of competence but in the league table of spin bowlers he has no place at the highest level. It is why Panesar sat in the dressing room here for five days in a state of scarcely supportable sadness.

In Perth a new drama involves the possible return of Michael Vaughan. It is a mark of English desperation that there is the possibility of another player so long away from the intensity of action at the highest level moving into the front line.

But then the appeal of Vaughan is plain enough, whatever it does to the besieged confidence of the new captain Flintoff, the hero of 2005 but now an almost tragic figure as he struggles for fitness and some glint of light in the huge challenge his leadership now faces.

Sometimes the value of a certain presence in a winning team can only be truly assessed when it has gone absent. This is surely true in the case of Vaughan, but if his sharp – and hard – cricket intelligence has been so sorely missed these last few weeks, the idea of him appearing in the third Test remains bizarre. He cannot hope to do anything more than grope for the kind of batting facility which made him one of the world's top players.

Here, the comparison with Australia's Ponting would become unbearably harsh. Ponting has come into this series aflame with ambition and form. Clearly he will give England no quarter. Defeat in England is more than a wound, it is something that has to be expelled from his thoughts and his system before normal life can resume. The result, already, is threatening to be a historic accumulation of runs.

Against such motivation, and accomplishment, the English position is indeed dire. Whether it constitutes a case of competitive fraud – and their branding as impostors – is, of course, another much more serious charge. But in the current climate it is inevitably in the air.

Here, champions are required at the very least to stand up and show a little fight when it matters most. Thus far, it hasn't happened. It is why Australia have no doubt they will reclaim the Ashes – only the fear that there can be little true glory if England continue to default.

THE ASHES WERE LOST IN ENGLISH HEARTS AND MINDS BEFORE THE DAWN OF BATTLE

Published: 19 December 2006

Let's not waste too much time on the Ashes post-mortem. Forensic science is not required. The explanation of a disaster which was forecast in the sky above the Gabba stadium in Brisbane several weeks ago in the most irrevocable terms required only the most perfunctory analysis.

You cannot beat anybody, let alone the marvellously activated Australian cricket team, if you don't prepare properly, if you pick the wrong players and those who are palpably unfit, and if you have a command structure so incoherent the man allegedly in charge, coach Duncan Fletcher, was pointing out his lack of overall responsibility in the wake of a shocking second defeat.

What happened in Perth early yesterday was as inevitable as a Ponting century or a competitive *tour de force* by his principal lieutenant, Shane Warne.

England were beaten by a team superior at every level and the most important one, unfortunately, flew utterly beyond any of the remedies that were being marshalled with all the usual weight of hindsight in the wake of a defeat that was quite shocking.

The most fundamental reason for failure did not lie in any shortfall of planning or common sense, though heaven knows there was no shortage of any of that. England made a less than nominal defence of the Ashes because they didn't have either the resolve or the spirit to get the job done. The Ashes were lost in English hearts and minds.

A harsh verdict, maybe, but some need not be squeamish about handing it down. Some saw the downfall not as an unpleasant surprise but a screaming *fait accompli*. They also correctly put their fingers on the time when the Ashes series of 2006/07 was lost.

It was not in that ludicrously sketchy build-up to the challenge that was so feebly met in the last few weeks. It was not when England, having embarrassed themselves in the catchpenny Champions Trophy in India, chose to return home for a few days of "relaxation" rather than head off to the scene of the action which would shape whole careers. It was not when Fletcher and his co-selectors decided to break the basic rule that you go with the fit and the hungry rather than gamble on injury and reputation which had plainly lingered too long on the vine.

The Ashes were lost, so soon after their recovery from a near 20-year void, at the point they were grasped at the Oval 16 months ago. They were consumed by the English sporting disease – triumphalism and its incestuous companion, celebrity.

It is this gnawing reality that must create a certain impatience with the flood of reforms being advocated yesterday. Yes, Ian Botham was right to rail against England's terrible lack of preparation, and to say that such third-rate, money-grabbing diversions as the Champions Trophy should never again interfere with a diligent approach to what will remain cricket's greatest challenge as long as the Australians maintain their superb standards of ambition and professional integrity.

Of course the selectorial competence of both Fletcher and captain Andrew Flintoff has to be severely questioned, and used as evidence in support of the need for a new system, after the egregious decisions to prefer Ashley Giles and Geraint Jones to Monty Panesar and Chris Read. Yes, there are many practical things to do. But this should not blind the cricket authorities, any more than those of football and rugby union, into believing that there are any easy solutions.

Recasting the hearts and the minds of an entire sporting culture is a problem, let's face it, that runs a little more deeply.

When Freddie Flintoff emerged from 10 Downing Street as glassy-eyed and as composed as a weekend binge drinker, there was much national hilarity and joy. It was misplaced. Flintoff is a wonderful cricketer on his best days and, unquestionably and legitimately, he joined the front rank of national heroes with his extraordinary deeds in the summer of 2005. But it is a matter of record now that when he was still getting over his celebrations and his commercial exploitation of the Ashes triumph, the Australians were booked into a boot camp which, for mostly ageing cricketers, must have carried all the ambience of a commando crash course.

How willingly did they submit to the strenuous exercise? Says the captain, Ricky Ponting: "You had only to look into their eyes to see how hungry they were. Fighting to regain the Ashes, giving it everything, has been the greatest experience of my cricketing life – just as winning the second Test in Adelaide was the greatest victory."

Some English analysis of that defeat was astonishingly woolly-minded. We were said to have dominated for four days and then, for an hour, let slip the competitive reins. It was an extraordinary conclusion, a little like saying you can separate various elements in a battle and run up a score. You don't do that. You ask which army had the stronger will, the clearest sense of what could be achieved – and then the courage to do it.

Those who rose from their English beds last Saturday morning in time to see Adam Gilchrist hit his extraordinary century may congratulate themselves on witnessing the most pivotal phase of the series. They were right to be pleased with themselves because they certainly did see something to store away with the best of sports memories, but pivotal it was not. The Australians had it won at the Gabba and pushed the issue beyond all doubt at the Adelaide Oval.

They did it there with one of the most amazing acts of will ever seen on a cricket field. Warne achieved some of his ultimate sorcery and then, again, there was Michael Hussey hitting the ball with an assurance which became increasingly marked over the three Tests. It was men and boys at the Gabba and, by the denouement in Perth, comparisons had become pitiful.

What is depressing from the English perspective is the certainty of Australia's reaction to their latest triumph. It is of a satisfaction that means most because it is no isolated grab for glory. It is so demonstrably about the reviving of a tradition that runs back to Sir Donald Bradman and beyond.

Hussey put this into words most persuasively on his own West Australian soil in the moment of triumph. He was asked about his feelings of satisfaction, coming so late to international cricket, with the suggestion that because of his own circumstances his elation must be that much higher than any of his team-mates. No, he said, no one got into the Australian team on the strength of a few flashes of brilliance. It was the long apprenticeship, the gathering of will over the years, so that when you came into the team you knew precisely what was expected.

Against this Australian backcloth, England's handling of their rare triumph at home was made to seem even more inadequate. In the days that followed the climax at the Oval, England's captain Michael Vaughan hammered on the theme that his team had to stay focused, had to stay – it was his word – honest. The significance of his plea is plain enough now. It seems that he sensed what he couldn't bluntly say, that there were currents in his team of heroes which did not augur so well for any seamless maintenance of a winning edge.

The Ashes were lost in English hearts and minds before the dawn of battle

The worry gathered force in the immediate challenge of the Pakistan tour, where home coach Bob Woolmer announced that it would be interesting to see how England reacted to their victory over Australia. Would it put more steel into their game – or would it make them relax? Woolmer was accused of making mischief. No doubt he was. It is what coaches do when they seek to achieve an edge, and they do it with maximum aggression when they have identified a weakness.

Australia read England as though they were an open book before the action started at the Gabba. Time and again Ponting talked about the possibilities of unrest in the England dressing room with the "strange" selections of Giles and Panesar. The captain's hard-nosed team-mate Matthew Hayden worked the theme relentlessly. The Australians latched hard on to the dismaying performance of Steve Harmison at the Gabba; nothing was neglected in the pursuit of an advantage.

They saw a team primed for slaughter and yesterday they completed the job. They not only won an Ashes series. They confirmed a superior way of thinking, of fighting, and sacrificing. And it was here that the real post-mortem had to begin. The rest was relatively minor detail.

WARNE WAS THE HYPNOTIC GENIUS WHO ENHANCED ALL OF OUR LIVES

Published: 21 December 2006

In the sea of tributes now flowing over the *enfant terrible* of cricket who became its ruling genius, transcending all boundaries and all bias, there has to be an ultimate accolade.

It is that Shane Warne has shared with the greatest sportsmen of any age a truth about himself that has always shone like a diamond even when his life has been most chaotic and, let's be honest here, wretched. He has identified the best of himself. It has been to play his game, work his wiles so uniquely, at the bidding of the gods. He once put it with great poignancy. "One thing I know I can be true to," he said, "is the way I love cricket. Sometimes I think proving this is the least I can do."

Through all the personal mayhem, Warne's vocation has been to enhance the lives of all who have followed cricket and felt an undying surge of anticipation whenever he has approached the bowling crease. It is almost to limit his achievement to say Warne has been the greatest spin bowler in all of cricket history. That merely implies excellence of technique and talent. It misses out on the most thrilling ingredient of all: an imagination so fertile, so bottomless, it achieved nothing less than a redefining of the game.

For decades, fast men Dennis Lillee and Michael Holding dominated cricket. Warne said the game could again offer more than artillery fire of the most menacing kind. It could bring beauty and guile back to the trenches.

He has bestowed the gift of endless intrigue, wonderment and a competitive urge that may have been rivalled but never surpassed in any corner of sport.

Warne has let himself down on many occasions. His private life has been a minefield of indiscretion. He has been banned for drug use and punished for consorting with, and receiving money from, the agent of a bookmaker. But if the last of those misjudgements was in one way the worst, somehow it did not compromise the picture of absolute commitment to the idea of winning every game he played.

Warne has been reckless with everything but his God-given gift to make a cricket ball a thing of unchartable magic.

A former captain of England was saying over dinner in Brisbane recently that he trembles for Warne when he has to face the rest of his life after cricket. The day, it seems now, will arrive at the end of the fifth Test match in Sydney in the new year.

The fear is that when Warne can no longer express himself so perfectly, so triumphantly on the field, when the ache in his shoulder is his last tangible contact with the days of glory, his existence will implode as the thrill of the action, the challenge to produce still more improbable deeds, is overtaken by the raw knowledge that the best is over.

Warne will not be alone in facing the dusk. He is likely to be joined by his fellow legend Glenn McGrath after Sydney – and maybe the rest of the old guard, Justin Langer, Matthew Hayden and even Adam Gilchrist, who may decide that he will never reproduce the climactic perfection of his breathtaking century in Perth in the last Test. But Warne, inevitably, seems most at risk. His game has become so central to his life, and it is this that provokes the concern of a man who played against him many times.

Said the ex-England captain: "In all my time in cricket, I have never seen anyone who enjoyed the life, and just everything about it, so completely, who lived in it as though it was some great bubble. You get the feeling that Shane believes he can make everything right on the field in a way that he can't off it. So, yes, you have to ask: 'What will he do when it is over?'"

Immediately, he will take his place among the legion of former Test players who populate the broadcasting booth of Australian television's *Channel Nine*. He will be controversial and amusing and trade on his vast popularity with a public that has learned over a decade and a half to separate the great performer from the former beach boy who in crucial areas of his life simply refused to grow up.

But while Warne treads new ground, his warmest admirers will look anxiously for the trapdoor represented by another lost and reckless night, another ill-advised text message, another raging at the dying of his particular light.

Where Warne is undoubtedly impregnable – as is his likely companion on the last walk from a Test arena, McGrath – is in the strength of his professional reputation. In Warne's case, the aura was created so spectacularly, that all that came later – his world record of 699 Test wickets, so many passages of bowling which left the world's greatest batsmen dry-mouthed with self-doubt and the

Test grounds of the world suddenly alive with expectation – seemed inevitable.

Only the amputation of his right arm could have deadened the belief that as a leg spinner of bewildering creative range, the naturally tubby boy from south Melbourne, who had once dreamed of playing Rules football for his local heroes St Kilda, was capable of ambushing any batsman alive.

The certainty of that belief was written in the sky above Old Trafford 13 years ago. With his first Ashes delivery, Warne not only clean bowled the tough veteran Mike Gatting. He invaded his psyche with a ball that pitched a foot outside leg stump before turning across Gatting's bat and clipping his off bail. The former England captain reflected on that extraordinary impact a few weeks ago as he walked across the parkland to the Adelaide Oval for the final day of a Test match which seemed to permit only two results – an England win or a draw.

Said Gatting: "Logically there can be only one of those two results but when you say that, you know that Warney is going to be bowling probably for two sessions and what that means is that anything can happen. Of all cricketers, I would say that about him, but I have so much company now. You can never be sure quite what he's going to produce."

It is the most compelling aspect of Warne, the sense that he observes no rules of bowling except his own. Only one cricketing nation has challenged seriously his belief that in almost any circumstances he could get the better of a batsman, and significantly it was India, where spin-bowling virtuosity is seen not so much as a gift as a birthright.

Consequently, Warne's ascendancy over all opposition is much less marked against the Indians, who down the years have levied nearly twice as many runs per wicket than his overall average of 26. It is, however, a minor flaw in an otherwise seamless masterpiece. Indeed, Warne's effortless ability to summon the demons which haunt even the greatest batsmen has at times reached mystical levels. The fine South African Daryll Cullinan was said to be so haunted by Warne that he was forced to seek the help of a therapist.

Even for those not enmeshed in his web, Warne's effect has often been close to hypnotic, an endless demonstration of skill and combative spirit. When he claimed his 600th Test wicket at Old Trafford, the place where his Ashes story started so volcanically, there was a sigh . . . and then a great surge of applause. It was more than a recognition of excellence in the enemy. It was the affirmation that appreciation of some sportsmen will never be bounded by the colour of their shirts or their caps.

Warne was the hypnotic genius who enhanced all of our lives

Both Warne and McGrath have played key roles in the current crushing of the English belief that they travelled to Australia with any right to hold on to the Ashes and in doing so, at the ages of 37 and 36 respectively, they have managed to stay true to both their own values and those of a national team who have reasserted their claim to be the greatest force cricket has ever seen.

If you look for the defining moments of both men, it is astonishing that they came at ages when most Test careers are either winding down or have been formally closed.

McGrath confirmed his place in legend after tea at Lord's two years ago. He bowled a line of such divine inspiration it might have been drawn by Leonardo da Vinci. For the essence of Warne, we have only to go back to Adelaide a few weeks ago. There, as Gatting once shook his head, Warne sniffed out the most astonishing victory like some old prospector searching for a glint in the barren hills. Watching him find it was something to place alongside the most brilliant deeds of a Muhammad Ali or a Jack Nicklaus.

The allusion to Nicklaus is not random. When he played his last competitive round at Augusta in 2005 – when Warne was approaching his great but frustrating English summer of 40 Ashes wickets – tough old men had tears in their eyes. They did not cry for the Golden Bear but for themselves; their sense of loss, their feeling that something precious had gone out of their lives.

That was the feeling yesterday when you heard that Shane Warne was preparing to bowl for the last time. Cricket was suddenly diminished, and if you cared about the game to any degree at all, so were you.

ENGLAND ABUSE THE LANGUAGE OF HEROES

Published: 29 December 2006

In Brisbane, Adelaide, Perth, and even in the last gutless minutes of the massacre in Melbourne, it was reasonable to think that it couldn't get any worse.

But each time it has. England are in denial now, and the condition has been growing since the hapless captain, Andrew Flintoff, offered the first set of feeble excuses after the ravaging of his team at the Gabba.

Yesterday Flintoff, besieged by something uncomfortably resembling shell shock, was saying that there was more than enough pride and fight left in the England dressing room to prevent the first whitewash in 86 years. His claim would have been laughable in a dark sort of way had it not been so shot through with pathos.

However, it was the coach, Duncan Fletcher, who drifted furthest from the reality of a truly shameful debacle. He said the essential difference between England and Australia was experience.

It isn't, and if you needed another reason for anger at the pathetic way English cricket has been represented these last few weeks it surely lay in the very need to make the point.

In their 38th and 37th years Shane Warne and Glenn McGrath haven't just learnt how to fight, how to take immense pride and competitive courage out on to the field. They have been doing it all their cricketing lives. They go off into the sunset in Sydney next week with such glory and honour not because they finally discovered the knack of delivering the best of themselves when it truly mattered. It is because it is the only way they know, the only way they have experienced, the only way they have been taught to handle themselves, the only way they have learnt to express the meaning of their careers.

Some might say that the Australian need for total revenge in this Ashes series, their raging intent to settle for nothing less than a 5-0 triumph, speaks of an overweening intensity, an obsessive belief in their own merit. It is one way of looking at it.

Another is that they were so enraged by their own failings when they allowed England, a talented side but one they felt in their bone marrow was not truly in their own league, to claim the Ashes, they simply could not allow the blemish to linger in the annals of the game.

So the whitewash was not something to be merely desired but a psychological necessity. This is the vital difference between the team that staggered themselves – and their nation – by winning the Ashes and the one that couldn't forgive themselves for losing them, not at least until after complete atonement.

This English tour effort is a disaster at every level and the implications, one is bound to say again, run beyond the boundaries of cricket. The pathetic efforts of England's football millionaires in Germany in the summer and the decline of the rugby team since the peak of World Cup victory in 2003 are in one unavoidable sense impossible to separate from what has been happening in Australia.

There are many parallels in all three situations: incoherent preparation; disastrous selection; an unwillingness to tackle the obvious problem of an inadequate coaching set-up. But the greatest link is the failure of the players truly to understand the challenge, and the ongoing requirements, of being the best at what you do.

England's footballers signed their book deals, attended their pre-World Cup party at Beckingham Palace and had their wives and girlfriends installed in the spa town next to their training headquarters.

Similarly, England's cricketers had an orgy of celebration and personal publicity after winning the Ashes and, after a miserable showing in the virtually meaningless Champions Trophy in India, went home to England for "R & R" rather than heading for Australia and vital conditioning. Their wives and girlfriends arrived even as the team were hopelessly failing to gain a foothold.

England played unfit, favoured sons, had their main strike bowler Steve Harmison showing up about as ferociously as a kitten, congratulated themselves at winning the odd session in Test matches that, when it came to the infighting, were never in any doubt, and kept telling us that somewhere, by some magical osmosis, the glory would return.

It wouldn't, and there could be no prizes for intuition for guessing this in the days before the first Test in Brisbane. Australia were perfectly programmed. You had only to be in the same room as the captain, Ricky Ponting, to know how much he ached for the action to begin and when it did all his talk about the hunger in the eyes of his players, even on the flight home from England, could be seen for what it was: not flimflam, not platitude, but the most basic statement of intent.

In the latest English inquest in Melbourne much is being made of the disappointment of the army of English fans, how they have been shockingly short-changed. The point is being made that England's players had a duty to perform for these seriously out-of-pocket holidaymakers – and those at home who have gone sleepless in the hope of seeing a little English fight. Maybe it is true. However, surely the better emphasis is that of *The Independent's* Angus Fraser, a Test bowler of unquenchable spirit whatever the conditions and however unpromising the circumstances. He said that England's players have had one overwhelming duty in Australia. It is to themselves, to their own pride in performance.

That they have failed it, abysmally, is a fact which which will now stand forlornly whatever happens in Sydney.

Defeats, even a stark row of four of them and by such wide margins, are not the worst of it. It is the terrible sense that this is a team which can give only lip service to the principles by which Australian cricket lives so triumphantly, so enduringly.

If you cannot win, at least you can fight, you can hurt, you can raise your fist to the heavens and say: "Yes, you can beat me, but I will not go easily, I will show you something of what I have".

England have consistently failed to do this. It means that someone should take Andrew Flintoff aside and tell him that the time has passed when he and his team-mates had the right to talk of pride and fight. It is, after all, the language of heroes. On the wrong lips, as it was in Melbourne, it is capable of just another insult.

SELF-INDULGENT TRIUMPHALISM EXPOSES THE CENTRAL PROBLEM IN ENGLAND'S CAPITULATION

Published: 06 January 2007

In all the disillusionment of England's truly shocking surrender of the Ashes we are now surely down to one last thin hope.

It is that there is a grown-up reaction to the scale of the humiliation, a proper, decent, professional counterpoint to the sickeningly woolly minded euphoria which enveloped almost everyone connected with the English game when the Ashes were briefly gathered in during the summer of 2005.

Such a response has to embrace more than the basic requirements which have been so abysmally neglected, routine matters – for teams able to justify their own publicity – like preparation and selection based on today's form and not a bunch of gilded memories. It has to include a gut reaction to the problem that crosses all boundaries in English team sport – a willingness to be too easily pleased, to rush into self-congratulation when the job has scarcely started.

What are the chances of such renaissance of thinking and purpose? They are not spellbinding. Indeed, some of the indicators are as dismaying as the scale of the capitulation we have been witnessing for the past six weeks. Unquestionably top of the list is the bland statement of the England and Wales Cricket Board, the authors of the most depressing denouement of a national team since Billy Wright's men suffered near annihilation at the mesmerising feet of Hungary's footballers more than 50 years ago, that to remove coach Duncan Fletcher from his ever-growing ivory tower would be a "knee-jerk" reaction.

Here we have the nub of England's disaster – an absolute failure to distinguish between a "knee-jerk" reaction and the kind of decision-making which is required in the face of the most abject failure in any walk of life.

Round about the time of the third Test in Perth, Fletcher's no doubt previously valuable period of office had effectively ended. His rationale for a series of bizarrely wretched selection decisions had become acutely embarrassing. His team were in tatters. His captain, Andrew Flintoff, the erstwhile hero, was broken in both body and spirit. It was not a question of jerking knees but making contact with an acutely apparent reality.

It was that something more than mere technique and application and match-tuning separated Australia and England.

It was nothing less than a cultural collision that stripped England's illusions quite bare. Yesterday in the tide of inquest analysis there was just, it seemed here, one nugget of a perfectly authentic response. It came from the former England captain Mike Atherton, a man who displayed more fighting character in one innings in Johannesburg than the combined majority of Andrew Flintoff's team had produced in arguably the five most important Test matches of their lives. Atherton declared that the Ashes of 2006/07 were lost in the early autumn of 2005 – in Trafalgar Square.

The point has been made before, here, and no doubt more significantly by Bob Woolmer, the former England Test batsman and an excellent coach of South Africa and Pakistan. He questioned the balance of England's reaction to their unexpected triumph, and every doubt he expressed then was confirmed without respite in Australia.

The sight of England awash on a sea of triumphalism was – we know beyond all doubt now – for the Australian sports psyche both a nauseating example of self-indulgence and perhaps the most demanding call to arms they had ever received in all their years as the world's best cricket team.

Less overwhelming than Atherton's trenchant position, you had to believe, was that of his fellow pundit – and captain of England – Nasser Hussain.

He said that on the last day of the first Ashes whitewash in 86 years he had two flashes of the kind of revelation you might encounter on the road to Damascus rather than the Sydney Cricket Ground. He said that he had finally grasped that Shane Warne loved cricket – and that Glenn McGrath had overcome certain difficulties before establishing himself in the Australia team.

Rightly, if less than luminously, Hussain drew an inevitable comparison with the well-upholstered lives of such under-performing English heroes as Steve Harmison, who on top of all the other dispiriting evidence of a highly talented player utterly unprogrammed for the demands of his sport's highest challenge, said he would await instructions from coach Fletcher as to the course of his next three or four months as a contracted but somewhat under-employed English cricket star.

To be in Australia at any stage of the slaughter was to be invaded by the sense of two teams travelling along entirely different roads and with mind-sets so unrelated it was hard to believe that anything like parity could be achieved.

After England's first-day implosion in Brisbane, Ashley Giles told a stunned audience that England's team bus to the Gabba had been hushed and tense. Naturally, he said, the team were nervous – it was the opening day of an Ashes series. Were these the triumphant campaigners who took their bows in Trafalgar and then lurched out of Downing Street tired and emotional from days of celebration? Those Aussies not aghast were disbelieving.

The extent of Australian disdain mostly lurked behind polite expressions about the quality of England's play in the odd and inevitably indecisive session. But then it surfaced when Paul Collingwood misguidedly engaged Warne in a sledging battle in which the Australian hero's language and sentiments were rough but aimed at the heart of English pretensions. Warne spat out his contempt for "gongs" handed out on the basis of one brief triumph rather than a career of commitment and dazzling achievement.

Here was the heart of the division between winners and losers. Australian mystification at English reaction to the first Ashes win in nearly 20 years was founded on the very bedrock of their nation's claims to be arguably the best pound-for-pound sporting nation in the world. It is that victory is to be expected; it is the norm created by the highest standards of competitive fury. The pain of defeat in England was so acute not because a good young team had risen brilliantly to their challenge but that for once an Australian side had let their standards drift to an unacceptable degree.

"The team came home from England with hunger in their eyes," said their captain, Ricky Ponting, "and I understood why. We had made too many mistakes. We had played sloppy cricket. The mood the team was in persuaded me that we would beat anyone we played. That was our feeling – and it is one that has held ever since that match at the Oval."

When England's grip on the Ashes was formally broken at Perth, Andrew Strauss, almost everybody's idea of the next captain, made what might be described as his team's nearest approach to authentic passion on Australian soil. He reminded everyone of the Australian angst when they lost the Ashes, how determined they were to find redemption. The Aussies had had the most dramatic wake-up call of their careers and the reaction had been ferocious.

Now it would be so in the England camp. The last two Tests in Melbourne and Sydney were far from competitively meaningless farewells for Warne and McGrath and Justin Langer. They were the testing grounds for an England recharged with the ambition that had so thrilled the nation 15 months earlier. But, of course, neither Melbourne nor Sydney was a testing ground for this spineless England. They were just fresh places to run up the white flag.

Strauss, a man of considerable achievement before his largely nightmarish experiences in Australia, had made a call for higher values, for a show of conviction in English cricket that went deeper than a series of optimistic and increasingly valueless soundbites. Sadly he was projecting a world of English cricket which, for the moment, exists only in his own mind.

Maybe as captain he might whip along a sterner approach, but there is only so much one man can do. England's central contract system has created ease and comfort and destroyed, it has to be concluded, the most crucial element of all, the hard edge of ambition which can be achieved only with outstanding effort – and no little sacrifice.

One Australian critic briefly intruded into the English inquest yesterday. It was over the likely future exclusion of England's best wicketkeeper, Chris Read, because he is unable to justify a No 7 placing in the feeblest tail in world cricket. This is despite the fact that in Sydney, particularly, Read's keeping was a rare point of English excellence – and earned the praise of no one less than Australia's doughty Ian Healy. It was the best he had seen from an English gloveman, he said, in 20 years. The Australian solution to England's crisis thus flowed naturally enough. It was to pick your best six batsmen, your best four bowlers, and your best wicketkeeper, and then get them to play.

It was made to seem so simple but if you are Australian of course it is. You play and you fight – or you disappear. For English cricket it had never seemed more like a secret located somewhere on the other side of the moon.

BLAME BELONGS TO FALLEN IDOL FLINTOFF BUT RESPONSIBILITY RESTS WITH GUTLESS HIERARCHY

Published: 20 March 2007

Because Andrew "Freddie" Flintoff will always be associated with one of the most glorious passages of English sport, because he also impressed the nation as an Ashes hero capable of expressing compassion for a beaten foe quite beautifully, his credit was huge enough to seem inexhaustible.

This, however, has not proved true. Flintoff, in terms of any hard-headed assessment of his current role in an England team competing for cricket's alleged top prize, is tapped out.

Stripping him of the vice-captaincy, fining him, and dropping him from the game against Canada has been interpreted in some quarters as strong, even "brave" discipline. It is, of course, nothing of the sort. It is a feeble reaction to outrageously unprofessional behaviour.

If the England team were subject to proper discipline, Flintoff's fate would have been much more severe when he was fished out of the sea near dawn at the end of a drunken spree 36 hours before he was due to play a competitive match. He would have been driven to the airport and ladled into the first plane leaving the Caribbean.

He would also, unless he wanted to stump up some of the fortune accrued as one of the sporting celebrities of his age, have gone in economy class, a mode of travel necessarily used by most of those fans who travel the world in the naïve belief that they are supporting players committed to winning cricket matches. If anyone in the English hierarchy had had the guts to make such an appropriate decision, Flintoff would not have been without companions – he would have been joined by the other good-time boys, Ian Bell, Paul Nixon, Liam Plunkett, James Anderson and Jon Lewis.

"The conduct of the players who have been disciplined was unacceptable," said the England Cricket Board chief executive, David Collier, "and falls below the high standards required."

This is mealy-mouthed to a breathtaking degree. Flintoff's rampage, after a series of warnings about his behaviour during the Ashes series Down Under which broke all records for futility and complacency, didn't fall below high standards. It didn't even brush against a graph measuring responsible behaviour from one to ten. It didn't trouble the scorer.

It was so brainless, so lacking in professional standards, that one reasonable reaction is that Flintoff is out of control and possibly as in need of psychological assistance as his former team-mate Marcus Trescothick, who was unable to meet the demands of the Ashes tour.

Naturally, another great hero, Ian Botham, is only "amused" by the incident and is talking of the hypocrisy of those who so cheerfully tolerated Flintoff's embarrassing fall-about during the Ashes celebrations in London in 2005. Botham's reaction is sound only to a minor degree, in that the hubris which accompanied the England triumph was at the very least disordered, but not everybody saw it as a natural consequence of a famous victory.

The fine cricket man Bob Woolmer, who experienced his own bed of nails leading Pakistan before his tragic death at the weekend, was among the first to see the seeds of England's post-Ashes self-destruction. He wondered how you move from such abandoned celebrations to a competitive mind-set just a few weeks before the challenge of an always difficult tour of Pakistan. Some said he was being mischievous. Others knew that he was putting his finger on incipient disaster.

Botham was a brilliant individual cricketer but as captain of his country he was a self-acknowledged disaster, and if he had any excuse for his excesses it was only that cricket in his day was still patently amateurish.

There were no central contracts – and no sense that star players had been invited to become real professionals. Geoff Boycott was one who accepted the challenge and his reward was mostly ridicule, not least from Botham. Now England cricketers are supposed to be in the mainstream of sport, enjoying the privileges of top performers but with the implication that they also accept the responsibilities. Such a perception makes Botham's latest reaction to the behaviour of his sometime drinking companion Flintoff both pathetic and absurd.

Another former England captain Bob Willis spoke, as he usually does, for the roundheads. But with unimpeachable force. Said Willis: "I think Freddie has been making a fool of himself since the celebrations of the 2005 Ashes. This is not the first time it has happened and I fear it might not be the last. He can't behave like that. Some of the players in the squad are only going to have one opportunity to play in a World Cup and they don't need their talisman behaving like that." Talisman? Flintoff has surely tossed away such status, along with so much else in his failure to maintain anything like the level of effort he set for himself in one glorious summer.

He carries only so much of the blame. The rest can be apportioned on a fairly wide front. The culture of modern English sport is riddled with an unwillingness to pay the price of success at the highest level. The most onerous one for a young, rich athlete is personal discipline, an understanding that getting to the top is a signal for the commitment, and the sacrifice, to intensify rather than decline.

Last summer in Germany we had the appalling self-indulgence of a weeping captain, David Beckham, and the unspeakable circus of the Wags. In the winter we had the sickening chaos and under-achievement of the Ashes series. Now we have an already discredited hero of English cricket as a drunken oaf.

Both sports are in desperate need of real leadership. For cricket, the obligation is to appoint a man plainly in charge of such vital matters as discipline and selection, a man answerable to both the cricket authorities and fans, who, at the moment, must be wondering in quite what they have invested so much time, money and passion.

Duncan Fletcher, we are constantly told, is a good coach. It is not enough. We need a strong hand. We need somebody who would have had sufficient strength to say: "Freddie, I'm sorry, son, but your party is over."

McGRATH DEFIES CRITICS AND SHOWS TRUE GREATNESS BY BOWING OUT AT THE SUMMIT

Published: 28 April 2007

Let's be honest about the World Cup of cricket. It has been too long, too unbalanced, too scarred by the death of Bob Woolmer, too much of a barometer of the shaming inadequacies of, among others, the English sports psyche, too catch-penny, and too ill-equipped to provide the joy and the brilliance on which the game once waxed so lyrically strong in the Caribbean.

It means that when Australia today formally beat Sri Lanka, the only team in the competition fit to share the new Kensington Oval with the perennial champions, one great temptation will be to submit to the purest of relief.

Yet how do you sigh in the presence of Glenn McGrath? How do you remain unriveted when one of the world's great sportsmen shows a whole generation of his peers how to go out precisely as he came in.

This is to say you make your exit when it is still possible for the world to see some of you as you were at the peak of your powers. You measure your resources, you take the flak of critics ushering you towards dotage and, if you are McGrath, you save up for a whole series of reprisals.

He had one in Brisbane a few months ago when many said that he should have slipped away gracefully before the start of the battle to regain the Ashes. After ravaging the English batting, he walked off the field aping the halting strides of a decrepit old man. The Gabba rejoiced.

In Adelaide, in the second Test, the burial detail again reported for duty – and sprang into action when the veteran laboured in the fierce sun. Not only had he struggled against Kevin Pietersen and Paul Collingwood, he was found critically short of speed when Pietersen, the one batsman Australia truly feared, skied the ball beyond mid-on. A younger, quicker man would have sent England back to the pavilion – it was the second last ball of the first day – nursing a gaping wound.

But McGrath didn't have the legs for the chase. He was a yard short and then, with shoulders stooped, he stared at the ball as though it was some mocking skull's head. You could see him aching in his bones and an Englishman might have speculated that here was breaking point. But then

McGrath, when he pulled himself up, would no doubt have said it was the guesswork of a mad dingo.

He was 37 and some reckoned this World Cup was for McGrath several steps too far, that he should have made his exit from international cricket in the imperious and jocular presence of Shane Warne. But that wasn't deemed appropriate by the man who had lived in a caravan in Sydney after leaving his home town of Narromine in the New South Wales bush to make his mark in grade cricket. Warney had his day in the sun and so would he.

In the past few weeks McGrath has been extraordinary in his control and his commitment to finishing properly his life's work as a pace bowler of endless subtlety – and combativeness.

This reached a penultimate point of glory in the ransacking of South Africa in the semi-final. The South Africa captain Graeme Smith denied that his team had choked before the bowling attack led by McGrath, who narrowed his eyes after being slapped for a boundary by Jacques Kallis, then delivered an unplayable ball. "To choke, you have to get close to winning," said Smith with a shrug of absolute resignation.

Too much has gone wrong in this World Cup. It cannot be easily redeemed in today's final and to ask McGrath to do that totally would be a call beyond even his resources. Even the kind of bowling that might remind us that it was in the old version of the Kensington Oval that Michael Holding brought the first chill of humility into the life of Geoffrey Boycott, would probably not be enough to banish the memory of the pratfalls, or worse, of Pakistan and India, the sad pantomime of the great Brian Lara's farewell, and the idiocy of the behaviour of half the England team.

But then McGrath does offer the prospect of some powerful consolation. He promises the last sighting of a player who has always accepted his responsibility to deliver the highest level of performance.

Of all the players in this World Cup, except perhaps the sadly abdicating Lara, the magnetic Muttiah Muralitharan and the Australian bowler's relentless, Bradmanesque captain Ricky Ponting, no one is more entitled than McGrath to leave an over-reaching and ultimately misbegotten tournament with tunes of glory supplied by the steel bands of a people who know cricket, its beauty, its rigours and its capacity to make heroes.

Heroes such as local boy Sir Garfield Sobers, who on this same ground, while still a teenager, duelled brilliantly with McGrath's great predecessors Ray Lindwall and Keith Miller – and men such as Wesley Hall and Charlie Griffith, who brought in the age of West Indian pace domination with blood-chilling force.

McGrath is maybe not the most embraceable of men from the English perspective. When the Poms are on their knees he is about as compassionate as an old hangman. But then it has been his vocation in life. He is an Australian cricketer, right down to his marrow.

He is also a man who has known the kind of crisis beyond the boundary rope that can make the interplay of sport, even at the highest level, seem like the preoccupation of overgrown boys. His nursing of his wife Jane through several bouts of cancer has been devoted in the most steadfast way.

Maybe dealing with such stress, while meeting the need to support a young and besieged family, has given him the perspective that has helped to shape his view of the world and his sport.

It is an unforgiving view, and not least when it is directed at himself. As English cricket contemplates its latest phase of rehabilitation, it could do no better than review McGrath's extraordinary career, and film of its last dramatic expression, and make an educational presentation of it to all present and future members of the Test and one-day teams.

When you think about it a whole embattled game might follow such a lead. Today Glenn McGrath does more than strive for one last trophy. He shows how every game should be played – and how every cricketer should be.

VAUGHAN'S RAPIER TRUTH HURTS THOSE WHO ARE CONTENT TO TOAST ENGLISH MEDIOCRITY

Published: 09 June 2007

Among the charges against the England cricket captain, Michael Vaughan, is that he was either naïve or malicious when he said Freddie Flintoff had holed the team's World Cup effort below the water level while behaving like some addle-brained tourist refugee from the Saturday night lager culture in the company of a pedalo in a Caribbean dawn.

Vaughan, who most regrettably squirmed around more than a little in the wake of the controversy, was being neither malicious nor naïve. He was being honest. Unfortunately, it is not a habit which earns much respect – or understanding – in what passes for the upper level of competition in English sport.

Quite the opposite, in fact. Mention that Flintoff, hero of the Ashes in 2005, but an irresponsible captain who had to be warned on several occasions for his behaviour in Australia last year, was no better than a dolt at a formative stage of the World Cup campaign and you have sneered at the deity. You are the kid pointing out the king has walked from his chamber stone naked.

Apparently, Flintoff's friend Steve Harmison, who no doubt has reasons of his own to blench at any lunge towards plain talking, was particularly upset by the "Fredalo" spat. Too bad – too bad for him, too bad for Flintoff, who in a properly run team would have been packed off home on the first plane.

Surely, "Fredalo" provides a perfect symbol of what is wrong with English sport; why the rugby union World Cup champions came tumbling down the mountain top so quickly; why the footballers get a Himalayan mound of favourable notices for running round against a barely awake Brazil for a draw and then beating one of the worst national teams in the world; and why the cricketers have made that Ashes triumph at the Oval seem like the last word in illusion.

There are, no doubt, at least a dozen technical and motivational reasons why the performance of top-level English teams has been, but for the odd eruption of competence or better, so mediocre for so long. But a refusal to face up to the truth is surely high among them.

Could Flintoff's most fervent supporters really consider for more than a few seconds his antics in the West Indies and not reach the conclusion that he had shown appalling judgement, especially when the team were under such a microscope after their pathetic performance in Australia? In what way was Vaughan wrong to suggest that the inevitable media reaction to Flintoff's excesses put impossible pressure on the rest of the team? Was the reinstated captain, such an impressive guiding influence in the regaining of the Ashes, supposed to brush aside such a breakdown in professionalism when he discussed, at any depth at all, what he considered to be the ethos demanded under the recently appointed coach Peter Moores? Such questions should be an insult to anyone with a grasp on what makes the difference between winners and losers.

Vaughan was being merely consistent. A few days after the euphoria of the Oval in 2005, he sat down with me on a murky afternoon at Headingley and discussed his best hopes after the historic victory. He said he wanted his men to keep their heads, to remember that great teams are not judged on one summer of high achievement; they have to understand, like the great Australians, that one performance is built on another – and that there is only one set of operating principles. It is to play every game as though it is your last. It is to take fresh guard, psychologically, after every 20, 30, or 50. It is to be remorseless like Ricky Ponting, who had been sent home to Australia nursing a thousand wounds. He did not want the tug of triumphalism to eat into what was best about the Ashes success, the constant redoubling of effort and commitment. Most of all, he said, he wanted England to stay honest.

Quickly enough, we saw that Vaughan might have saved his breath. The triumphalism of Trafalgar Square and 10 Downing Street took hold. The late Bob Woolmer, coach of Pakistan, had said it would be interesting to see if England came down from the Ashes high and displayed hard-nosed professionalism. It was a provocative point, but it sailed home like an arrow.

Now we are told that Vaughan and Flintoff earlier this week had a lunch meeting of appeasement. What precisely did that mean? Apparently, Flintoff's hurts were soothed. I just cannot think why. Yes, of course, the big man is a hero with a generous nature, as anyone who was at Edgbaston to see him stoop down and commiserate with the gallantly beaten Brett Lee in the second Test in 2005 can confirm, but that does not mean that he had made some giant stride beyond any reproach. It did not mean that the flaws of a heroic past have to be airbrushed away. That is the way of entrenched failure, not of a Ponting, who at times early in his career could make the drinking sprees of Flintoff seem like someone getting slightly out of hand at a church social.

Ponting and his team flew home ablaze with determination to avenge their loss. The captain said he could see it in the eyes of his team-mates. This was at a time when the eyes of Flintoff, understandably enough, did not speak of steely resolve but a swimming pool filled with champagne and beer.

Understandably, that is, in the first thrill of triumph. No self-respecting captain or professional could extend that tolerance at the early stages of a tournament in which his team had a desperate need for redemption.

Michael Vaughan, however off-guardedly, spoke the truth. He should be celebrated, not vilified, for doing something that is sadly rare but will always be precious.

BOTHAM DESERVES TO BE A KNIGHT – EVEN IF HE DID SAY I SHOULD GET A THUMPING

Published: 16 June 2007

When Sir Vivivan Richards, the emperor of Antigua, very publicly told me that if I did not start behaving myself I would be leaving his island under something other than my own locomotion, the then Mr Ian Botham was asked for his reaction to a controversy which, no doubt because it was a silly season for news, had briefly occupied a prominent place on certain front pages and the television news.

"Beefy", apparently assuming his most statesmanlike pose, gave the question a few moments' thought before announcing: "I just wish Viv had finished the job there and then." Typical Botham. At the time – Good Friday 1990 – the leaders of the United States and the Soviet Union were meeting in an attempt to pull the world back from nuclear oblivion (the *Daily Express* front page noted this with a small headline "Gorby tells Bush Back Off", beneath the splash "King Viv Blows His Top") but here was one of the nation's greatest sportsmen advocating personal violence of the most vengeful kind.

So why is it that the expected announcement that Her Majesty the Queen will shortly be saying "Arise, Sir Ian" is something to provoke uncomplicated pleasure. It is because in an age of sickenly inflated celebrity, when the honours system has been polluted so thoroughly in so many different ways, there is still, it seems, a capacity to recognise genuine achievement and character – and a man who walked the walk, literally, so many times on behalf of young victims of leukaemia.

He raised more than £10m, travelled the length of the land from John O'Groats to Land's End and across the Alps, because one day he walked into a children's ward, was given some bleak statistics, and was touched to his heart. Botham contributed in a most meaningful way to a vast improvement in those desperate odds and he did not do it in any tax-deductible distribution of career rewards that most reasonably balanced people would deem obscene. No, he hit the road, and he stayed on it when the oxygen of publicity for a good cause had been exhausted.

That he still has the tendency to utter opinions hard to distinguish from buffoonery, including his recent suggestion that Freddie Flintoff's only crime on a binge during the World Cup in the West Indies was to be caught, is beside the point. Botham lifted the spirit of the nation as a stupendous cricketer and when his career – and a deluge of lifestyle and political incorrectness – was over, he continued to be an uplifting, if somewhat unprogrammed, presence.

This holds true today, however erratically he sometimes offers his views on the game he enhanced so brilliantly for so long.

Younger readers may not be overwhelmed if they look up the Botham Test statistics, formidable though they are in an all-rounder who for most of his career retained the ability to change a match in the course of a couple of superb outswingers or a few mighty blows to the boundary ropes. He scored 5,200 runs, took five wickets in an innings 27 times, compiled 14 centuries and had a top score of 208.

Those of us privileged to see him in action, however, can cut an easy route through the numbers and see a huge and self-confident figure whose place in legend, if it had ever been in doubt, was confirmed at Headingley in 1981. Anyone interested in cricket knows the details; for those who do not, they can be covered quickly enough.

England were heading for defeat so clearly, bookies ranked their chances of winning at 500-1. At 135 for 7, Botham launched a massive counter-attack, carrying his bat for 149 runs. He then claimed the first Australian wicket before Bob Willis led the charge to victory.

On the 20th anniversary of what has been ranked the fourth-best innings in the history of Test cricket, Botham reflected cheerfully: "The Aussies could have been a little more gracious. They said it was a slog. They were right, of course. But they should have got it right. It was a magnificent slog."

Beefy's knighthood is remarkable in some ways. He was scarcely a paragon of family life, despite the warmth of his nature. He was known to smoke an illegal substance. In the prime of his athletic life he undoubtedly drank too much. But then, Sir Walter Raleigh was also a bit of a lad.

Sir Ian Botham sounds right because what he did, ultimately, was to make the nation feel better about itself. If he was laddish at times to an unfortunate degree, he was plainly also a man. If he was a toker, albeit briefly, he was also a supreme fighter.

There was never anything wet about him; misguided, impetuous, ill-mannered perhaps, from time to time, but there was a thread of courage and competitive zeal.

Most impressive of all, Ian Botham showed that he was aware of his good fortune and the kind of life he had been able to lead. He proved that in the long – 11 in all – walks he made for the children whose lives he undoubtedly helped to save. His knighthood, above all, is about great deeds – and a huge spirit. It is the affirmation, in this age of cheaply manufactured fame, of a real and generous life.

ECHOES OF GRACE RESOUND AS TENDULKAR AND COMPANY EXPOSE ENGLISH FRAILTIES

Published: 30 July 2007

If Sachin Tendulkar was not such an unassuming cricket legend, the umpire who is generally rated the best in the world might just have heard something close to the growling breath of the great W G Grace.

The good doctor's famous declaration, after suffering what he considered a wrong and impertinent dismissal, was that the great crowd had come to watch him bat rather than some wretched umpire get it wrong. Support for such a sentiment, even among some of England's staunchest followers at Trent Bridge, surely reached into every corner of this historic ground yesterday when the Australian Simon Taufel ruled that a delivery from Paul Collingwood would have hit Tendulkar's off stump had it not first collided with the Little Master's pad.

This was plainly wrong – and particularly unfortunate for two reasons. One, and most important, was that Tendulkar had batted with beautiful certainty to get within nine runs of still another record, his 38th Test century.

The other was that Collingwood, for all his virtues of professional zeal, would normally wake up and apologise if he even dreamt that he might just beat a Tendulkar who had played himself to the point of draining the life out of an England team which had supposedly healed the wounds inflicted so deeply in Australia last winter and the World Cup in the spring.

In fact, long before the Tendulkar breakthrough – India were 342 for 3 at the time, 144 ahead on first innings – the new, and so far winning, England coach Peter Moores must have been experiencing his own private moment of truth.

It was that while England were able to mop up the sadly diminished West Indians easily enough, any assumption that they are now back in rude competitive health has to be considered premature.

As they now fight a hugely uphill battle against going 1-0 down to a team three places below them in the world rankings – and their first home series defeat since they were eviscerated by Steve Waugh's Australians six years ago – Moores has to be concerned about what can only be described as a parody of emotional equilibrium.

This, after all, is the team who for two days now have been generating the kind of sledging, body-language aggression that any self-respecting Aussie would probably suggest might be most appropriately dressed in a girl's blouse.

There wasn't much of even this pale version of battling commitment when Tendulkar, Sourav Ganguly (79) and V V S Laxman (54) stretched the Indian lead to 283 before England faced 16 overs in the evening sunshine. But then it erupted, on schedule, when the Indian tail-enders began to appear, Kevin Pietersen provoking both umpires into a complaint to the temporary captain Andrew Strauss when he greeted the first-innings bowling hero Zaheer Khan at the crease with an abusive volley.

England's defence is that they are still smarting over their failure to nail down victory before darkness came to Lord's in a first Test they believed they had done more than enough to win.

They also feel that the flying start to the Indian first innings provided by Dinesh Karthik and Wasim Jaffer was substantially helped by the kind of umpire error which sent back both Tendulkar and Ganguly yesterday. Result: an unconvincing bowling performance yesterday that was redeemed mainly by the aggressive instincts of Ryan Sidebottom. The hirsute hustler is never likely to win any style awards, but when he isn't giving a poor man's version of paceman histrionics he bowls with great spirit and application, and when he removed one of the Indian batting heroes of Lord's, Mahendra Singh Dhoni, it was fair reward for a serious and good-hearted body of work. But then Sidebottom is unlikely to survive the return to fitness of Steve Harmison and, above all, Andrew Flintoff.

In some quarters such relief is being painted as something close to the arrival of the Seventh Cavalry, but the reality here yesterday seemed to be suggesting that England's priority is not to rely on old glory – which is stretching back two years now to the Ashes summer – but taking a step closer to the kind of consistency of performance which was shown yesterday by opponents who were supposed to have long ago entered the ranks of the under-achievers.

That was exposed as somewhat ludicrous analysis when you considered the frailties of England's first-innings batting performance and the extraordinary contrast provided yesterday by three of India's four great contemporary batsmen, captain Rahul Dravid having disappeared in Saturday night's dusk while in the foothills of what promised to be another knock of daunting facility and nerve.

All of Tendulkar, Ganguly and Laxman produced moments of withering authority as they accumulated between them a total of 224 runs which, you have to believe, would have been significantly augmented if first Tendulkar, then Ganguly had not gone through official error. Tendulkar is usually close to a pinnacle of philosophical maturity when the umpires conspire against him, but this time he was not quite the paragon of forbearance.

He lingered for five seconds, reflecting on what television evidence would confirm in the split second that followed his decision to pad up against a ball that he knew was going to pass his off stump. How did he know? Because he is Sachin Tendulkar. Because it is a sense you acquire when, like Brian Lara, his only other rival as the greatest batsman of his age, you pass a total of 11,000 runs. While amassing such a total, you know when to play, and when to leave it and that is why he dragged his way from the field and out of the sunshine.

Nor was Ganguly thrilled, whatever the report of a "snickometer", when he was sent on his way.

His, in fact, was the innings of the day. Unlike Tendulkar, who was willing to graft with ultimate concentration after the sickening, faceguard-popping bouncer he received from James Anderson on Saturday, and Laxman, who appeared to have entered a coma towards the end of his innings, Ganguly was always intent on writing the day's agenda. In the early part of his innings he stroked some beautiful boundaries through the offside. Always a scrapper, and often an *agent provocateur*, here was a former captain pushing hard behind the gut feeling that England were on the run.

At the finish, Andrew Strauss and Alastair Cook were showing a degree of defiance. They were disputing the possibility that the new England were inevitably going to be set back by the old and subtle force of the best of one generation of Indian talent.

Today, and maybe tomorrow, we will no doubt get a deeper guide to the strength and the resolve of a team which fell so far, so quickly, from those days when they thought that by winning an Ashes series they had conquered a cricket world that would stay beaten for some time. Yesterday the story was rather different, and it required new depths of effort.

England's response, it had to be said, was a little too erratic to inspire too much confidence. They could only be grateful for that thunderous echo of W G Grace.

ENGLAND MUST PASS ON THE JELLY BEANS IF THEY WANT TO RECOVER GLORIES OF 2005

Published: 04 August 2007

King Football may be about to return to its vulgar, diamond-encrusted throne and Frank Lampard's big toe to join his contract negotiations as a matter of most compelling public interest, but then is it not just possible a few courtiers will defect to the Oval next weekend?

Of far more immediate interest here, certainly, is whether it has dawned on the cricketers of England that they have an overwhelming duty to prove that they recognise finally the need to grow up. On another level, as a finely balanced contest, England v India surely outstrips anything on offer in the first rush of economically unbalanced Premiership fare.

Even with England's juvenile infusion of jelly beans, and India's failure to retain a certain aloof Oriental mysticism and disdain, the second Test at Trent Bridge managed to pile ridicule on the decision to split the summer between the hauntingly diminished and Lara-less West Indians and an Indian team brimming with old quality and new promise.

India's recovery from indifferent form and a fortuitous draw at Lord's was magnificent and if the current series had started earlier, and stretched to five Tests, we have every reason to believe that at least some of the competitive buoyancy that made the 2005 Ashes series one of the nation's greatest sports experiences would have been re-established much earlier in the summer. As it is, England's attempt to square the duel – and avoid their first home defeat since Steve Waugh's Aussies picked them apart limb by limb in 2001 – surely carries some of the promise that came with the showdown against Ricky Ponting's team two years ago.

This is because it is not just a matter of cricket talent and form. It is also a question of manliness, of an understanding that fame – and its rewards – in sport should carry with it a little extra baggage. Chief among this should be behaviour which doesn't send all those involved, players, coaches, and spectators, back to the schoolyard.

It is true there was a certain amount of backlash to the childishness which gripped the Trent Bridge Test and was, let's be perfectly objective about this, initiated mostly by the English team. The small army of former England Test captains and players who inhabit the broadcasting booth were broadly critical, to be fair, but there was also much wishy-washy talk about how lines had not been crossed.

Tossing jelly beans on the wicket may have been more than anything evidence of an adolescent mindset but it did cross a line; the one that separates those who are prepared to compete, as hard and as ruthlessly as you like, and the others who are emotionally and intellectually challenged when ideas of their own superiority are seriously challenged.

Among those splendidly unprepared to pussyfoot were David Lloyd, a TV analyst of increasingly sound and amusing touch, and my colleague Angus Fraser.

Both were helped by the valuable perspective granted to them by Test action in which they were required to perform gallantly against formidable odds and unpromising physical prospects. No doubt it helped them distinguish between resolute competitiveness and infantile posturing. Fraser, whom one recalls bowling brilliantly at Sydney Cricket Ground despite back pain requiring a steady diet of painkillers, was uncompromising in his criticism of the antics at Trent Bridge. They didn't pass his litmus test for proper, mature endeavour.

For a little added perspective on why Lloyd should be so forthright, I'm grateful to another colleague, Brian Viner, who in his excellent, wry book – *Ali, Pelé, Lillee and Me* (now in paperback) – recalls some insights on the competitive side of cricket provided by the Lancastrian on a wet afternoon at Old Trafford.

For obvious reasons, these centred most vividly on the occasion in Perth when the ferocious Jeff Thomson landed a direct hit on Lloyd's private parts, an event which, as Viner noted, the player dined out on from the moment he got his voice back. Lloyd reported: "I was wearing a pink *Litesome*, one of them flimsy pink cricket boxes that looked a bit like soap holders. They had these holes around the edge and when Tommo hit me the force inverted the damn thing and pushed one of me knackers through the holes. From time to time you hear people asking: 'Is there a doctor in the ground?' That day they had to send for a welder."

Maybe Lloyd's disgust at the boyish gamemanship of Trent Bridge, which he described as "puerile rubbish", had its anguished origins in the WACA.

The facts that Sachin Tendulkar took a hit on his visor only marginally less dislocating, at least for the moment, at Trent Bridge from James Anderson before batting beautifully for a century denied only by umpire error, that Michael Vaughan then reminded us of his outstanding quality with a superb 100, and that the bowling of such as Zaheer Khan and Chris Tremlett bristled with, respectively, cunning and raw menace, made the schoolboy lapses all the more regrettable.

At the Oval demands on individuals are surely cranked up accordingly. Kevin Pietersen earned his share of disdain for his complaint of "tiredness" and if Andrew Strauss produced a reminder of the assurance he was displaying so regularly before the meltdown in Australia last winter, there is new pressure on Alastair Cook and Ian Bell.

The brilliant Indian mid-order axis of Rahul Dravid, Tendulkar, Sourav Ganguly and VVS Laxman produced batsmanship of wonderful grace and touch but, in the important cases of Tendulkar and Ganguly, it was confounded by the errant judgement of the normally impressive umpire Simon Taufel. It is another reason to see the Oval as the place where an intriguing but unfortunately brief story can reach out for a little more depth and fulfilment.

No one will wish for this more than the England coach, Peter Moores, who after the relatively formal task of demolishing the ill-formed West Indians is involved in his first serious challenge as the man to rebuild among the ruins of the Ashes triumph of 2005. Ruins? Yes, if there is great promise in Moores' tough style that the self-indulgent idiocies which followed victory over Ponting's team will be rooted out and dismissed, if Vaughan's century has given him back some of his old, desperately needed authority, there is no doubt that at Trent Bridge England were still in some vital respects a parody of the team which regained, so briefly, the Ashes.

That was a team, Vaughan said in the aftermath of the parade in Trafalgar Square and the lurch through Number 10, which had to stay honest. Two years on, there is another, even more pressing requirement. Ludicrously, it is to pass on the jelly beans.

DRAVID SETS OUT TO BUILD MONUMENT TO INDIA'S THREE GRACES

Published: 13 August 2007

When India's captain Rahul Dravid finally allowed England a glimpse at the mountain peak target of 500 runs he had fashioned for them with considerable Oriental subtlety, if not befuddling obscurity, the crowd remembered they were in a cricket ground of some significance. The Mexican wave stopped promptly. Ironic cheers for Indian runs ceased.

Though it is true that scoring 12 runs in 140 minutes was not exactly a major contribution to the Twenty20 culture, Dravid, known affectionately in his own land as "The Wall", no doubt had reason enough to see himself as something other than a Sunday afternoon entertainer.

Like his brilliant contemporaries Sachin Tendulkar and Sourav Ganguly, Dravid was not playing for fun here at The Oval – no more than he was at Trent Bridge two weeks ago when he and his team gave England a systematic re-education in the realities of grown-up Test cricket.

Dravid, fidgeting at the crease, squinting into the middle distance, was making a pact with history that he was intent on making unbreakable. The odds are that the great trio of Indian batsmen will never pass this way again on competitive business and Dravid, making it clear with every defensive prod, was utterly committed to maintaining his team's 1-0 edge for their first series win in England for 21 years.

Perhaps he had the wild idea that Friday's fusillade of fours and sixes from such as Anil Kumble and Mahendra Singh Dhoni had provided the kind of high-calibre spectacle that might have held off the need for a Mexican wave for at least 48 hours, if not forever, and thus left Dravid and Tendulkar, both 34, and Ganguly, 35, free to leave something more of a mark than some dazzling statistics and an aching sense of how much more there might have been.

That ache, Dravid resolved, would be soothed whatever the Kennington lust for tearaway cricket. Of course, that particular mood was not exactly vibrant here two years ago when England secured the Ashes triumph that sent them rushing off to Trafalgar Square and 10 Downing Street. Then Ricky

Ponting's Aussies donned sunglasses in the gloom as England, leading 2-1 in the series that meant something quite fundamental to their self-respect, snatched at the offer of bad light.

Dravid had no such option yesterday. He merely refused to enforce the follow on, out of fear that somehow crisis might spring at his throat late today if the home side managed to come back after trailing by 319 runs on the first innings. Dravid simply was not interested in such a possibility. Time was for him the immediate enemy, and if not a dire threat, certainly a shadow over a campaign which had been marked by a gathering determination to assert talent that too often in the past had been easily patronised as brilliant but, ultimately, just a little too frail.

There was nothing fragile about Tendulkar in the first innings here and if his face was wreathed in pain yesterday when he played on to James Anderson with just one run against his name, there was no shortage of comfort in a series of performances that most of all spoke of an old champion's refusal to let the years, and a fading touch, take away the old knack of fighting successfully at the highest level of the game.

It is cricket's worst kept secret that the Little Master is no longer the greatest batsman artist on earth. But if he cannot any longer make a mockery of the striving of lesser men, he can still exert a competitive streak that seems to have grown ever broader with the dwindling of the days.

On Saturday, he deprived England's Kevin Pietersen, some critics' idea of the new heir apparent to the title of the world's most naturally gifted batsman, of his wicket and in his eyes you might have sensed that he had been given the deeds to his native Mumbai. In the dusk last night Dravid called him to the bowling crease again in the hope that his leg spin might conjure another breakthrough as Andrew Strauss and Alastair Cook moved in the smallest foothills of England's massive challenge.

Tendulkar scored 82 on the first day of India's final push on Thursday, and in some ways it was like watching a man negotiate a fog. But that is what he did. He negotiated the most unpromising circumstances. He moved warily, and if he did not find the bright light of his youth, he was a huge contributor to India's stranglehold on a Test match that the old guard, the three of them, had declared could not be lost.

In some ways Ganguly, the third member of the captain's circle, carries most distinction from one of the last tests of his will and his talent. In the league table of centurions, Ganguly has not covered a third of Tendulkar's extraordinary march to 37 Test hundreds, but in some ways his talent has aged more easily, and more gracefully.

Yesterday, as Dravid brought the old ground close to coma, Ganguly played beautifully through the offside. It is his classic strength as a batsman; as a man, he has plainly developed into a point of philosophical maturity, something that has glowed through his ability to survive some potentially crushing injustice this summer. At Trent Bridge, he was deprived of a century when in the most beautiful groove and here he suffered a similar outrage, losing an lbw decision in the first innings which might in the old days have conjured a rush of anger.

Not here. He smiled a wounded smile and retreated to the dressing room. Yesterday, he was back in the middle of the challenge facing India's great generation of cricketers, who want so keenly to leave as winners rather than men who have too often failed to deliver the hard results that their sublime ability has sometimes demanded without satisfaction.

Dravid, Tendulkar and Ganguly now have to negotiate a last day of that old yearning on English soil. They will do it, no doubt, with a developed understanding of their huge advantage in the odds.

It is one of the fascinations of their game that extraordinary things can happen but here last night, when the Mexican waves in the crowd had disappeared like noisy, inappropriate gatecrashers at a gathering of more reflective quality, the old guard moved with a bright and optimistic stride.

Tendulkar tried his hand with the leg spin, Ganguly fielded on the balls of his feet and Dravid had the expression of a man who knew, whatever the passing frustrations, that his time as a cricketer and a leader had almost certainly arrived.

His resolve not to leave anything to chance, and his relentless refusal to take anything like a risk at the crease, had perhaps left the old ground in less than a party mood. But there was no shortage of music, you had to believe in the spirit of the old warriors who had come to England to fight as they had rarely done before. This was a day, for them, which had a point and a challenge which had nothing to do with pleasing the terraces. Indeed, the Mexican waves might have been happening on another planet.

TWENTY20 SLOGGING MAY GIVE US A VISION OF THE FUTURE, BUT IT CERTAINLY ISN'T CRICKET

Published: 18 September 2007

If ever you get into a debate about the sheer soul-numbing degradation of cricket that is currently being enacted under the pyjama-clad guise of World Twenty20, you might care to submit Exhibit A.

It is a paragraph composed with splendid economy by a wire reporter in his account of Sri Lanka's massacre of Kenya in Johannesburg.

Having described the ravaging of Kenya's bowlers by such as Mahela Jayawardene and Sanath Jayasuriya, he wrote: "They were outdone by Jehan Mubarak, who hit five sixes and three fours to reach 46 from a dozen balls. One more boundary would have broken Mohammad Ashraful's record for the fastest half-century, but he missed the final delivery of the innings completely."

Here, I believe, we have an impeccably accurate record of facts made utterly banal by their context.

Twenty20 is not cricket. It does not have growth, that sublime building of skill and concentration and timing which makes the Test game so ultimately intriguing – nor much of the declining, but sometimes still visible, fundamental qualities of the game which are offered down the food chain until, as in the crudest making of an omelette, the eggs are smashed in the version which is now having imposed upon it, in another money-grubbing lunge, the dignity of a world title.

In the process, cricket uses up its prime talent with the profligacy of a doomed punter chasing from one casino to another.

Sure, cricket is picking up a new audience with its catch-penny offerings, but maybe it should reflect on the fact that you can squeeze the cantaloupe only until the pips start squeaking. Novelties are fine, but then that's what they are: short-lived and best found not in a sport which has a great tradition, and no doubt a challenge to compete in the modern cornucopia of televised sport, but in some trinket shop at the end of a pier.

The point about the pummelling performance of Mubarak is that it ended in a stroke which would have brought sniggers on the average village green – and posed the question: how many times can you roar and gasp before subsiding into a shrug? I was once chastised on a TV show by Britain's top boxing promoter, Frank Warren, for a failure of enthusiasm for the way Prince Naseem Hamed was being promoted. Dry ice, jiggling entrances and dances over the prone figures of grossly inadequate opponents, might not gladden the hearts of the old fight crowd, but we all had to remember that boxing was looking for a new audience.

Yet we know that if boxing tomorrow produced a fight of genuine competition by two outstanding masters of their trade the world would be instantly fascinated. It remains as the great Muhammad Ali once said: "The whole world wants to know – who's gonna win, who's gonna win?"

The dry ice and the stagey entrances didn't do Hamed, or boxing, much good, when he was finally ordered into the ring – by his American TV paymasters – against an opponent who was equipped to administer some of the old game's verities. Marco Antonio Barrera proved that the best of any sport doesn't have to be sold, but merely presented.

The latest drama from Twenty20 is that England's Kevin Pietersen and South Africa's Shaun Pollock were involved in a sensational run-out controversy.

Sensational? What is really sensational in a game built on the allure of a blacksmith's slog?

Certainly, it is not the kind of slow-building drama that made cricket the compulsion of most sports lovers in this country deep into the start of a new Premiership season two years ago, when the Ashes were finally, and so tragically briefly, won back. Or the thunderous glory of the Ian Botham slog that emerged from within the disciplined limits of an unforgettable Ashes Test match at Headingley. Or the sublime Garfield Sobers smiting Malcolm Nash for six sixes in an over. That last feat was a diamond which, when we saw it, we knew would glitter forever. In Twenty20 it would probably have brought on not much more than a bout of flatulence.

Streamline cricket by all means. Emphasise its allure. But do not destroy its fundamental quality. Do not heap upon us this trashy version which would have made Don Bradman and Denis Compton squirm, which insults all that is best about the game which we know can still, in its highest form, bring whole nations to the edges of their seats.

Where Twenty20 brings us is to that novelty shop with the funny masks – and the stink bombs.

NASTINESS AND INTIMIDATION ORDERS OF THE DAY AS SLEDGING DRAGS CRICKET DOWNHILL

Published: 08 January 2008

Mike Procter, a fine South African cricketer and a charming man who has spent much of his life negotiating the treacherous ground of racism in sport, had no option in banning India's guileful spinner Harbhajan Singh for three Tests. Not after concluding he had called Australia's Andrew Symonds a monkey. Though Procter was in a terrible corner, he could tell himself he didn't make it. Cricket, by neglect, did.

Procter was no doubt fully aware that a potentially glorious series between two brilliant teams would immediately come under threat. But if the decision of the match referee was a dismal no-brainer, it is now dwarfed by another problem. It is the game's inability to draw a line between sledging, which in the past has been greeted, especially in laddish circles, as an entertaining enrichment of the game, and something far more sinister.

The question can be isolated easily enough: when does a natural, verbal outcrop of hard competition slip into something quite different, something that in recent years appears to have become part of a winning team's tactics almost as fundamental as field placings, the balance of pace and spin, and the selection of an extra batsman?

Lest any of us should believe that this is a controversy on the other side of the world, with no relevance to our own preparations for the tour of New Zealand, it perhaps needs to be pointed out that one of the reasons offered by former England coach, Duncan Fletcher, for his extreme reluctance to play Chris Read, far and away the best wicketkeeper at his disposal, was that he wouldn't have made his mark as a sledger even in Salvation Army circles.

Read was far too passive, suggested Fletcher, while approving the decision of the regime that followed him to elevate the now discarded Matt Prior above the Nottinghamshire man. The latter's failure was that he was not so good at "putting pressure on a batsman". Translation: he didn't have a natural aptitude for hurling abuse.

No matter that Read, unlike Prior, didn't need an outsized fish net to catch anything that came down his right side. No, if Prior was at least theoretically a better batsman, there was no question about his ability – or willingness – to harangue an incoming batsman.

In one respect, at least, he had a touch of the great Australian sledger Rod Marsh, who is alleged to have once greeted Sir Ian Botham with the cheery enquiry: "How's your wife – and my kids?" Botham is credited with the quickfire response: "The wife's fine but the kids are retarded." Maybe it wouldn't have survived a script meeting of *Men Behaving Badly*, or *Top Gear*, but for such hard-nut characters as Marsh and Botham that kind of exchange was part of their remit to wage war on opponents they loved to hate.

What may be developing now is something more sinister, a trend which is not about the natural collision of aggressive performers but the equivalent of psychological carpet bombing, a wall of hostility which has to be manufactured if it doesn't spring naturally from the collision of highly competitive and able cricketers.

The Aussies, of course, are generally credited with inventing and significantly developing the art of sledging and certainly it appears possible, if not likely, that their proficiency in the murky business was a key factor in their record-equalling achievement of winning a 16th successive Test match in Sydney.

True, vicious tongues would not amount to much that was decisive if they didn't happen to be accompanied by matchless professionalism and a competitive streak that at moments of pressure can stretch as wide as the Tasman Sea. However, the question that lingers in the mind is whether cricket has even begun to assess the potential damage when different cultures, with sharply varying views on the depth of an insult, compete for the highest prizes and the most lucrative rewards.

Some thought the Indians may have reacted excessively when, last summer, England played the childish prank of littering the pitch with sweeties. But then one man's playful jibe is another's insult to the bone – a fact underlined many years ago in Pamplona at the running of the bulls, when an American tourist spotted a young Spaniard sleeping off an excess of red wine at a café table. The American placed coins on the boy's eyes. He was lucky to escape with his life.

Sledging will never be eliminated, and nor is there a pressing reason when it carries an edge of humour. But this is not the same as tolerating systematically applied malign spirit. When sledging is acceptable it is about wit and psychological enterprise, not dull bullying or gang aggression.

Some of the best of it pre-dates the Australian mastery of the art, with one of the finest examples coming from a frustrated seam bowler named Charles Kortright. Five times he was denied when he appealed for the wicket of WG Grace; five times the decisions of the umpires were greeted with disbelief not only by Kortright but the entire ground.

Finally, Kortright uprooted two of Grace's stumps. The great man lingered at the crease for a moment or two, then reluctantly departed for the pavilion. But not before Kortright exclaimed cheerfully: "Surely you're not going, Doctor, there's still one stump standing." What would cricket have given for such a touch of irony in the Sydney Cricket Ground this week? Unfortunately for Mike Procter, and all of cricket, it was on another planet and in another age.

SAD CAPITULATION TO MISTRUST AND GREED

Published: 09 January 2008

If the International Cricket Council had placed Steve Bucknor's head on a silver platter, put an apple in his mouth, and made a formal presentation to the chief mogul of rupee-laden Indian cricket, Sharad Pawar, they would have only been underlining a dispiriting point.

It is that, however strenuously principle still attempts to walk in cricket, it is money that talks, relentlessly and without shame.

Some might say that the ICC has simply reacted to the reality of Bucknor's nightmare performance in the second Test at Sydney, that to keep him for the next match in Perth would have been to court another disaster in which the collapse of respect between the Australians and the Indians would tumble to a new low.

The problem is that this says more about the lack of trust in the captains and players of two wonderfully gifted Test teams than the dwindling competence of an official who has recently been shedding much of the distinction accumulated in 120 Tests. It says that what promised to be a superb exploration of some of the game's most exhilarating talent is now confirmed as an ordeal of resentment, even hate.

When Pawar first cast doubt about the Indian board's willingness to continue with the tour after the decision to ban Harbhajan Singh for three Tests for calling Andrew Symonds a monkey, the ICC faced a simple test of its powers of leadership. It had to say that, despite Bucknor's poor performance, he was an elite umpire who, while subject to error, could not be swept aside on the protests of one injured party. Where would that leave cricket, where would it place any umpire operating in the pressure of an age when technology provides an eye that, while virtually all-seeing, is of only marginal assistance at critical moments? It would leave both the game and the official at the mercy of the good faith of those who play the game and exert power over it.

When Malcolm Speed, the ICC chief executive, yesterday announced that Bucknor would be stood down, we knew the quality of that mercy . . . and the judgement which sends the Indians to Perth knowing that pressure works, that money doesn't so much talk but bellow.

Of course it is complicated. Of course the Indians could point to the shameless confession of Symonds that he was utterly aware that he was out in the early stages of his match-winning century in Sydney, but these things worked themselves out and did anyone really want him to recall all the occasions decisions had gone against him?

This was in the light of a pre-match captains' agreement that an honour system would operate, one which even the Australian media – not always a beacon of objectivity – are suggesting that the home team violated most overtly. Astonishingly, there is apparently a public backlash against the hard-nosed attitudes of an all-conquering team, even suggestions that the ultimately competitive captain, Ricky Ponting, may have cause to review his position.

Perhaps there is some hope if a public which has gorged itself on success for so long is making the point that sometimes victory can come at too high a price; but then, if there are stirrings of conscience, how effectively can they be expressed when one aggrieved team threatens to walk away – and immediately gets its way?

Pawar and his Indian colleagues were certainly doing little to conceal their delight. Said the president: "Definitely, I'm happy. We had appealed to the ICC to review the performances of the umpires in the last two matches and take appropriate action. I'm grateful the ICC has taken the decision to remove him. The Indian board is quite happy about that." It will be even happier if Harbhajan, who will be allowed to play in Perth pending an appeal, is cleared of a charge which was made to the satisfaction of the knowing old pro, match referee Mike Procter.

In the meantime, the ICC is calling in its chief referee, Ranjan Madugalle of Sri Lanka, to mediate between the teams. Speed explained: "Ranjan is a very respected figure within the game and we are bringing him in as a facilitator in an effort to prevent any ill feeling that may have been present at the Sydney Test rolling over to Perth."

Cricket doesn't need a facilitator. It needs a leader. It needs someone to look beyond the ledgers and the profits and see that there is something more important than turning a dollar or a pound in Zimbabwe or maintaining the profits of India's current tour Down Under. It needs an understanding that somewhere down the road there could be a point of revulsion which goes beyond any yearnings to see a winning team.

What can we expect of Perth? A transforming miracle worked by the facilitator? A sudden flowering of old values? Hardly, because there has been no attempt to attack the problem, no appeals to conscience, no official condemnation of behaviour which makes a fossilised joke of cricket's old claims on fair play. There has been only the now familiar routine of one compromise placed upon another; only the gratification of those incapable of seeing beyond their own and immediate interest.

The rulers of cricket had still another chance to stand their ground and say it was time for players of good heart to step forward – and for others to face up to their responsibilities. Predictably, we didn't get that. We got another greasing of the wheels.

AN AFTERWORD

12 May 2008

When five New Zealand tourists, including the captain, announced they would be delaying their arrival in the English spring, the reaction was not of shock but resignation. It was once a pinnacle of a Kiwi cricketer's career, the Old Country and a walk through the Lord's Long Room. Now it is not a glory to embrace but an accommodation to be made.

It was hard, though, for anyone who has a mortgage to pay to dispute the decision of the New Zealanders to join in the bonanza of the Indian Premier League's short Twenty20 season when they should have been acclimatising in England.

Even the piece-rate terms offered by such teams as the Kolkata Knight Riders and the Chennai Super Kings dwarfed the earnings of a Test player and this reality had to be fed into any optimism created by the decision of Kevin Pietersen to reject, at the first time of asking, the invitation to be one of the highest earning stars of a form of cricket for which he might have been born.

The trouble is for the deepest lovers of the ancient game of willow and leather, we are not really talking about a form of cricket. We are discussing a mutation that is already suggesting it is beyond the control of anyone who asserts that it is at best an amusement, a diversion, the cricket equivalent of a football session of "keepy-uppy". Worst of all, the fear is that it will devour its audiences, sate them with spectacle upon spectacle, and then leave them empty, by which time the disciplines and the rhythms and the beautiful eruptions of vital play that have for so long provided the appeal of Test cricket will be beyond recall.

Twenty20 is the plunderer of cricket at two levels. It is seductive, for some, in the excitement of its raw material, heaving shots, often cross-batted, creating a deluge of sixes and breakneck running. It is also insidious because it works away at a different set of values, creating an appetite that can only be satisfied by that which has become so easy and familiar and so instantly gratifying. It is fast food as sport – and those who provide it become not so much master chefs as short-order cooks.

The Indians dismiss such reservations. They point to a vast and instant marketplace – and huge audiences for the eight competing teams. Like the

Australian money-man Kerry Packer three decades ago, they say that cricket must change or die, and that the classic careers of such men as Sachin Tendulkar and Sourav Ganguly were not the inspirations of a new generation but the last evidence of a vanishing civilisation.

No, you cannot criticise England captain Michael Vaughan if he hints at interest in the personal benefit of a superannuation scheme hatched in financial heaven, no more than you can be comforted by the claim of England coach Peter Moores that county cricket will always provide the foundation for English Test cricket.

Testing that theory is a chore already accomplished by all those sports-minded insomniacs who surf the television channels. There is the tumultuous action and the adoring crowds of Rajasthan and Bangalore, there is Adam Gilchrist or Matthew Hayden smiting a six – and there is the action from the Rose Bowl or Old Trafford, a group of players celebrating the fall of a wicket for the benefit of terraces empty but for the odd retired civil servant, a dog and a few sparrows. Or so it seems in the wee small hours.

You cannot remake the past. You cannot check the whims of fashion.

All you can do is hope that the best of the past is not submerged and lost completely by the impulses of the day.

Certainly you can mourn for the old battles of cricket in its purest form. You can remember the timeless thrill of a duel between, say, the artistry and guile of a Bishan Bedi and the obduracy of a Brian Close. You can remember Michael Atherton resisting so long and so successfully in Johannesburg. You can remember what the old stonewaller Trevor Bailey represented when he came to the wicket.

What was it precisely? It was the laying down of a standard. It was the rejection of cheap victories. It was a register of greatness – not a McDonald's menu.

ACKNOWLEDGEMENTS

Of all the privileges of the sports writing life, few compare with that of covering Test cricket in such places as the Caribbean, Australia, the Indian subcontinent, South Africa, and New Zealand; and, of course, when the weather holds, at such classic venues as Lord's and Old Trafford, the Oval and Trent Bridge.

One certainty is the quality of the company both in the press box and the watering holes.

Of all the reminders of this, few came more enjoyably than on a stroll across beautiful parkland to the Adelaide Oval a few years ago. It was, by chance, with former England captain Mike Gatting. We discussed the prospect of another absorbing day of cricket involving men like Shane Warne and Ricky Ponting and – another subject of mutual fascination – where supper might best be taken. The recommendations of "Gatters" were, as always, brilliantly detailed.

Such indebtedness, as I come to acknowledge all the help and the support and companionship received down the years, is maybe impossible to cover in its entirety in the allotted space here, but all of it is treasured.

Most thanks are due *The Independent*, who for the last eight years have allowed me to include Test cricket in my working itinerary, and before that the *Daily Express*. At *The Indy*, the editor, Simon Kelner, and two sports editors, first Paul Newman and now Matt Tench, have provided unfailing support, and at the *Express* sports editors David Emery, Alex Butler and Mike Allen provided the encouragement. The current *Express* sports editor, Bill Bradshaw, kindly gave permission to re-visit his newspaper's files on my controversial, but happily concluded, collision with Sir Vivian Richards.

Among those who have always been generous with their friendship and their knowledge in the field are Mike Atherton, who kindly wrote the introduction to this collection of articles, my *Independent* colleague Angus Fraser and, before him, Derek Pringle; and cradle journalistic team-mates like Stephen Brenkley and Stephen Fay, and, at the *Express*, Colin Bateman. Imperishable, also, are the memories of discussing the prospects of the day, and the racing programme, at the old Fleet Street offices of the *Express* with the Sunday paper's cricket writer, a certain Denis Compton.

The good times are countless, but many of them, I can recall with reasonable clarity, have been spent in the company of such colleagues as the late Ian Wooldridge, Simon Barnes, Roy Collins, Michael Henderson, Matthew Engel, Jim Holden, Peter Hayter, David Norrie, Simon Wilde, Graham Otway and Ted Corbett.

Particular thanks are due to the editor of this collection, my friend Ivan Ponting, and the publisher, Dewi Lewis, who, by happy chance, gave me his business card when we first met, casually, in the coffee shop of Frankfurt airport.

Another friend, the great artist Harold Riley, gave me the inestimable honour of sitting in a place once occupied by Pope John Paul the Second and Maria Callas when he sketched the likeness which appears, with my deepest thanks, in this book.

James Lawton, June 2008

For a full list of our sports titles please visit our website

www.dewilewismedia.com

JAMES LAWTON
ON FOOTBALL

introduced by John Giles

£9.99 softback,
256 pages
ISBN: 978-1-905928-02-6

All human emotion is there. James's words educate, inspire and seduce. He is a master craftsman.' – James Nesbitt, actor

On Football brings together a selection of the best from the columns of James Lawton. His writing gives a powerful commentary on the state of football over the last decade. Lawton never pulls his punches, writing with both intelligence and wit, and with an enviable knowledge and understanding of the game.

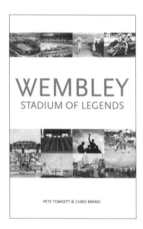

WEMBLEY
STADIUM OF LEGENDS

Pete Tomsett & Chris Brand

£12.99 hardback
160 pages
ISBN: 978-0-954684-39-6

Wembley: Stadium Of Legends combines remarkable archive images with fascinating information: tales of enigmatic entrepreneurs and entertainers, courageous athletes and odds-defying sportsmen. Through unique photographs, the later chapters tell of the transition from old to new, from the faded grandeur of the old stadium, through its demolition, especially the heartbreaking destruction of the twin towers, to the construction of the new building and its dramatic arch.

RAFA BENÍTEZ

the authorised biography
by Paco Lloret

£12.99 softback
224 pages
ISBN: 978-0-954684-37-2

In this authorised biography, Paco Lloret gives a real insight into what motivates Rafa Benítez, his attention to detail, his man-mangement skills, his sharp football mind and his constant quest to develop the skills of himself and his players. We also discover the steely determination with which he faced his early setbacks, his personal trauma at the tragic death of his brother-in-law, his public anger after the Madrid bombings, and the complex intrigue at Valencia which led to his move to Liverpool.

JOSÉ MOURINHO
MADE IN PORTUGAL

the authorised biography
by Luís Lourenço

£12.99 softback
224 pages
ISBN: 978-0-954684-33-4

When José Mourinho arrived in London in 2004 he had a powerful and frequently controversial, impact on English football. This fascinating book charts his rise from relatively humble beginnings as assistant coach to Sir Bobby Robson, to become the most sought-after club manager in Europe. Long-term family friend, Portuguese journalist Luís Lourenço guides us through the formative years in Mourinho's coaching career, as he returns to Portugal from Barcelona at the turn of the millennium to embark on the remarkable journey which led him to Chelsea.

www.dewilewismedia.com

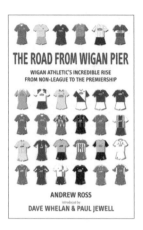

THE ROAD FROM WIGAN PIER

Wigan Athletic's extraordinary rise
from non-league to The Premiership

by Andrew Ross
foreword Dave Whelan & Paul Jewell

£9.99 softback, 224 pages
ISBN: 978-1-905928-01-9

In ten short years Wigan Athletic have gone from skid row, at the bottom of the Football League and on the verge of bankruptcy, to millionaires' row, proudly sitting alongside the Chelseas and Manchester Uniteds of this world. How they got there is extraordinary. This is not just a story of a small town football club struggling for years before being rescued by a local multimillionaire. It is a story of dreams and disasters, of faltering attempts to establish a foothold for the game in the town – to finally emerge triumphant at the pinnacle of English football.

ALAIN BAXTER
UNFINISHED BUSINESS

the authorised biography
by Andrew Ross

£12.99 softback, 224 pages
ISBN: 978-0-954684-35-8

Nicknamed 'The Highlander', Baxter first skied at the age of 2. By his teens his dream was to challenge for top honours in the sport. He began a ten year slog, driving around Europe, living on overdraft, sleeping in hostels and cheap hotels or in his car. In 2002 Alain Baxter caused the biggest Winter Olympic upset by clinching Britain's first ever skiing medal. Agonisingly, the ecstasy was short-lived. After a hero's welcome home he learned that he had failed a drugs test and would be stripped of his medal. Stunned and mystified Baxter began the challenge which would eventually clear his name.